The Final Prophet

Proof of the **Prophethood of**

MUHAMMAD

Mohammad Elshinawy

KUBE

The Final Prophet: Proof of the Prophethood of Muhammad ﷺ

First published in England by
Kube Publishing Ltd.

Markfield Conference Centre
Ratby Lane Markfield
Leicestershire, LE67 9SY
United Kingdom

Tel: +44 (0) 1530 249230

Website: www.kubepublishing.com
Email: info@kubepublishing.com

Cataloguing in-Publication Data is available from the British Library

ISBN Paperback: 978-1-84774-207-0
ISBN Ebook: 978-1-84774-208-7

Cover Design: Rola El Ayoubi
Creative Direction: Nida Khan
Illustrations: Rola El Ayoubi & Hafiizh Hamid
Editor: Justin Parrott
Reviewed by: Sh. Ismail Kamdar, et al.
Typesetting: LiteBook Prepress Services

Printed by: Books Factory

Contents

Foreword

All praise be to Allah. Noticing firsthand the passion that Shaykh Mohammad Elshinawy had for the subject of this book, I knew its intellectual vigour would be mixed with the author's passion to produce a masterpiece.

There is no subject I can think of that needs our attention and dedication more than the proof of prophethood. In an age of uncertainty, scepticism and cynicism, there is nothing more important than helping people build certainty in a most salient truth: the prophethood of Muhammad ﷺ. It is that certainty that will open wide for them the gates to inner peace and happiness in this life and the one to come.

The book covers a wide array of proof from the historical necessity of the Prophet's dispatchment to the greatest of his miracles—the inimitable Qur'an—without neglecting his character, accomplishments, message, prophecies, and physical miracles. It has the necessary academic integrity without its emotional austerity. It is detailed, yet not superfluous.

Whether you place more importance on the evidentialist or naturalist approach to faith in God, the proof of prophethood should be an integral part of faith in Islam. A probabilistic approach using inductive reasoning does not preclude the attainment of certainty through it. If the arguments are strong and plentiful, then certainty can still be achieved. It can then be further grounded by spiritual experience and enlightenment.

In addition to the importance of the subject, I also find great pleasure in writing a foreword for this book because of its author, of whom I have great expectations, and I hope that Allah will use him in serving the cause of Islam in this land and around the globe.

May God's blessings and peace be on the one He sent as a mercy for all creatures, the seal of prophets and greatest of messengers, Muhammad ﷺ.

Hatem al-Haj[1], MD, PhD
Dean of Mishkah University
Resident Fatwa Committee, AMJA

1 It was originally a presentation delivered by Dr Hatem al-Haj in Edison, New Jersey, USA, that inspired this book. Four years of gathering and writing later, this journey culminated with the meticulous, perfectionist critique of a world class historiographer who insisted upon anonymity and improved it beyond measure. My debt to these two scholars can never be repaid, while also acknowledging the gracious contributions of my other colleagues from the Yaqeen Institute and elsewhere.

Preface

Quenching a Parched World

It was too beautiful a day to go inside our building just yet, so my mother and I sat together on the brick ledge surrounding our neighbour's blooming garden. We lived in Borough Park, Brooklyn, in New York City, where over 90 per cent of the neighborhood is comprised of Hasidic Jews, who seemed as committed to their Judaism as we were to our Islam. That must have contributed to the concerns that crowded my thoughts back then, along with the popular sentiment I encountered everywhere that offered another take on religion: that it is irrelevant. It has been over twenty years since that moment, but I have yet to forget my sense of anxiousness as I sat there, gathering the courage to confront my mother with the audacious question. But my thirst for an answer, and my confidence in the ocean of affection that sat beside me, catapulted the words from my mouth: 'Mama, how do we know Islam is right?'

She smiled and locked eyes with me. I proceeded to say: 'Think about it. Every parent tells their child, "This is the true religion," so what makes us so sure that we are the ones who are *actually* right?' What she said next was something along the lines of 'just have faith'. It was the very thing I was afraid to hear, especially as an inquisitive thirteen-year-old in the postmodern world, let alone a Muslim in New York City who would soon experience Islamophobic sentiments being ramped up by the 9/11 attacks that would occur only a few miles away. But in hindsight, it was exactly what I needed to embark on my own faith journey and endure that coming wave of animosity towards Islam and Muslims. Ultimately, it generated this very book you hold, a resource I wish was available when I first explored the world's major religions, assuming that they were all, without exception, taken on blind faith, irreconcilable with a critically thinking mind, and subsequently unworthy of being held on to when socially inconvenient.

I pray this addition to the English library can mitigate the wildfires that are ablaze in many of our hearts and homes today. May it heal some of modernity's wounds with the coolness of conviction, and quench some of the uncertainty that leaves our lives parched for security, fulfillment and balanced direction. God knows that for a myriad of reasons, authorship is uncomfortable territory for me, but how can a person sit idle when the virtuous hallmarks of humanity are increasingly trampled beneath the feet of nonreligion, and when the cravings of our caged spirits continue to scorch us at every turn? I pray this book offers some assistance to those who struggle with their own faith or that of their loved ones, those of whom I meet almost daily in my community work or online, and the many more I hear about but cannot reach individually. It is in this vein that I felt called to brave the unfamiliar seas of authorship, and I ask Allah to forgive where I may have erred en route.

This book seeks to highlight humanity's undying need for prophethood, and the many compelling justifications for the prophethood of Muhammad ﷺ in particular. By doing so, it subsequently aims to offer a coherent proposition on the true purpose of life that leads to an impregnable inner peace which is only possible through beholding the sunrise of certitude firsthand.

Independent works written on the topic of the proof of prophethood (*dalā'il al-nubuwwah*) have always been part of the

Muslim intellectual tradition, from as early as the eighth or ninth century. That this literature has been a mainstay of Islamic scholarship is a powerful testament to its commitment to rigorously establishing the bases of its truth claims. Abū Manṣūr al-Baghdādī (d. 1037) reports that Imam al-Shāfiʿī (d. 820) was the first to compile a book on the proof establishing the prophethood of Muhammad ﷺ, as the Brahmins had rejected the possibility of prophecy or divine revelation.[1] There are over ninety works from this canon whose titles are known until today, the most famous of them being *Dalā'il al-Nubuwwah* by Imam al-Bayhaqī (d. 1066). The aim of these authors was to increase the believers in their conviction, dispel doubts regarding Muhammad's ﷺ authenticity, and consolidate this evidence in a readily accessible location for anyone inquiring about the truth of his prophethood.

The Proof Within Us

The primary proof of prophethood is God Himself, for it is He who guides us to intuitively seek Him out, and subsequently investigate the claimants to prophethood for an opportunity to better connect with Him. All people are instinctually driven to believe in the existence of God and have an innate impulse to discover this higher power which they sense so strongly. While not every human civilization was driven to develop craftsmanship or formal education, each one committed itself to some form of religious practice. People have done this throughout recorded history, and thus anthropologists have yet to find an indigenous society of atheists; some scientists today argue that belief in God or a higher power is hardwired into our genes.[2] Even communists who disavowed religion still deified Lenin by putting his statue

1 Fakhr al-Dīn al-Rāzī, *Manāqib al-Imām al-Shāfiʿī, al-Kitāb al-Musammā Irshād al-Ṭālibīn ilā al-Manhaj al-Qawīm* (Beirut: Dār al-Kutub al-ʿIlmīyah, 2015), 85.

2 Dean H. Hamer, *The God Gene: How Faith Is Hardwired into Our Genes*. (New York: Doubleday, 2004), 6.

everywhere and reciting his works as if they were scripture. Similarly, modern atheists exhibit a consistent pattern of quasi-religious behavior and are often found seeking alternate forms of spirituality. For instance, only about one million US adults identify as pagan or Wiccan, yet a staggering 60 per cent of Americans ascribe to at least one 'New Age' belief such as belief in astrology and/or psychics, or the belief that objects like crystals contain spiritual energy.[3] Ultimately, this metaphysical yearning we all experience is a powerful, universal force, created within us by God, that drives us to seek out the prophets He elected to guide us to Him. Their message regarding God, His greatness, His guidance, and the reality of this life and the next resonates so deeply within us that we find ourselves compelled towards faith.

We are not just 'driven to God' by an inner surety about Him and the impetus to connect with Him, but also by a fascinating 'trust' in our ability to find Him. People may not appreciate that while reason may argue for God existing, being wise, and being purposeful, it cannot explain why our minds are reliable instruments of reason in the first place. When the rationalist René Descartes embarked on his intellectual journey, he realized that unbridled scepticism would drown him in uncertainty. Descartes then sought a safeguard that would ensure that our existence is real, as are our senses that perceive, as are our minds that process. How can we dismiss the possibility that we are merely a figment of an extraterrestrial creature's imagination, and what guarantee is there that our thinking is not manipulated by evil demons? Descartes was forced to conclude that 'trust' was a fundamental necessity here, without which every mode of thought, investigation, and analysis would be pointless. His 'I think therefore I am' proposition was adrift without this anchor, and nothing qualified to ground it but God Himself. In Descartes's framing, we must accept that God cannot be a de-

---

3 Claire Gecewicz, 'New Age' Beliefs Common Among Both Religious and Nonreligious Americans,' *Pew Research Center*, October 1, 2018.

ceiver because deception is an imperfection, and since He has equipped us with the faculties to arrive at certain truths, then we should pursue truth. He writes,

> [T]hat the sun is of such and such a figure, etc., or which are less clearly and distinctly conceived, such as light, sound, pain and the like, it is certain that although they are very dubious and uncertain, yet on the sole ground that God is not a deceiver, and that consequently, He has not permitted any falsity to exist in my opinion which He has not likewise given me the faculty of correcting, I may assuredly hope to conclude that I have within me the means of arriving at the truth even here.[4]

While being given the ability to correct 'any falsity' is an overestimation of the human intellect, Descartes was correct in realizing that without first conceding that God is responsible for our capacity to think straight, no rational arguments can follow. When skeptics seek an explanation for God, when God is the explanation for us, circular reasoning becomes inescapable. This is why one of God's Divine names in the Qur'an is al-Ḥaqq: the Ultimate Reality, the One without whom no truth or reality is possible.[5] Critical thinkers will recognize this as their indispensable philosophical stronghold, a refuge against dogmatism, and the bedrock upon which all empirical and rational proof must stand. It is their only guarantee that polemical acrobatics and fancy language will never become a Trojan horse that breaches their defenses, corrupts their worldview and renders them powerless prey before the fangs of radical skepticism.[6]

---

4 René Descartes, Elizabeth S. Haldane, and G R. T. Ross. *Philosophical Works: Rendered into English* (Cambridge: University Press, 1911), 191-192.

5 (*al-Furqān* 24: 25)

6 See: Nazir Khan, 'Atheism and Radical Skepticism: Ibn Taymiyyah's Epistemic Critique,' *Yaqeen Institute for Islamic Research*, July 7, 2020.

Hence, it is ultimately God who created within us knowledge of Him, an insatiable appetite to connect with Him, and a confidence in our ability to investigate the proof offered by anyone who claims to speak in His name.

THE MULTIPLE FORMS OF PROOF

It is from God's mercy that He sent with each prophet and messenger signs that were relevant to his context, and He surrounded Muhammad 🕮 with a plethora of proof, for he was God's 'mercy to the worlds', and hence had to be relevant not only to all at his time but also for all time to come. The variety of forms of proof are what make them relatable to every era, culture, and mindset. During the Prophet Muhammad's 🕮 lifetime, some accepted his ministry after one glance at his face. 'Abdullāh ibn Salām 🕮 said, 'I immediately knew that this was not the face of a liar.'[7] Another was brought to firm conviction after hearing a few short statements espousing the values of Islam. Ṭufayl ibn 'Amr 🕮 said, 'I have never heard anything superior or more balanced than this.'[8] Others confirmed his prophethood based on his reputation for being truthful. The leadership of Quraysh said, after living forty years with him, 'We have experienced nothing but honesty from you.'[9] Others believed after witnessing miracles, understanding that nothing ordinary could have explained these astonishing occurrences. By this variety, a nomadic shepherd in the Himalayas can follow any number of pathways to certainty, as can the ivory tower philosopher, as can the buzzing hordes under the skyscrapers of New York City, as can the banana workers in Ecuador.

---

[7]   Muhammad ibn 'Īsā al-Tirmidhī, *Sunan al-Tirmidhī* (Beirut: Dār al-Gharb al-Islāmī, 1998), 4:233 #2485; authenticated by al-Tirmidhī in the comments.

[8]   'Abdul-Malik ibn Hishām, *Al-Sīrah al-Nabawiyyah* (Cairo: Maktabat wa Maṭba'at Muṣṭafā al-Bābī al-Ḥalabī, 1955), 1:323.

[9]   Muhammad ibn Ismā'īl al-Bukhārī, *Ṣaḥīḥ al-Bukhārī* (Beirut: Dār Ṭawq al-Najāh, 2002), 6:111 #4770.

God also made the proof that verifies Muhammad's ﷺ prophethood crystal clear, so that any honest seeker can recognize them. As for those who obsess over the material world, or those who give precedence to their social relationships over their supreme Creator, or those whose self-conceit has blinded them to the flaws of their arguments, they will only find clouded judgment. In many of these cases, their flawed justifications may go unnoticed even by themselves, for people have always been able to lock themselves in echo chambers, surrender to groupthink, and effectively silence their consciences and the guilt of denying the undeniable. As Allah says, *'And [even] if We opened to them a gate from the heaven and they continued therein to ascend, they would say, "Our eyes have only been dazzled. Rather, we are a people affected by magic."'*[1]

In Islam, believing in all the prophets and messengers of God is a fundamental requirement of valid faith, and Muhammad ﷺ is certainly no exception to that rule. Allah says, *'Muhammad is not the father of [any] one of your men, but [he is] the Messenger of Allah and the last of the prophets. And ever is Allah, of all things, Knowing.'*[2]

Given this verse, whoever believes in Allah's words must accept that Muhammad ﷺ was His Final Prophet and messenger, and, conversely, whoever rejects Muhammad ﷺ has disbelieved in the One who sent him. But in case a person is still investigating the Qur'an, we will first begin with why prophethood in general is necessary, why Muhammad ﷺ in particular was most certainly a prophet of God, and then conclude by establishing the divine origins of the Qur'an.

---

1 (*al-Ḥijr* 15: 14–15)

2 (*al-Aḥzāb* 33: 40)

1

Humanity's Need for Prophethood

1. The Spiritual Necessity of Prophethood

Within us all is a restless craving for spiritual fulfillment. When ignored, the spirit experiences intense thirsts which send it chasing one mirage after another, each offering it momentary hope of an oasis before yet another letdown. This is the tragedy of the human condition whenever it seeks inner peace from the outer world, or seeks to self-actualize through carnal pursuits, when it was created to transcend all that for a higher purpose: sincere devotion to God. Allah says in the Qur'an, *'And I did not create the jinn and mankind except to worship Me.'*[1]

Servitude to God, not just the inborn recognition of His existence, is therefore not only a duty but also a fundamental human need. It is necessary to nourish our spirit just as food and oxygen are necessary to nourish our body. It attunes us to our reality as spiritual beings in physical bodies, not physical beings that happen to enjoy a spiritual dimension. Of course, none of

1 (*al-Dhāriyāt* 51: 56)

that is possible without the Creator communicating to us through prophets on how to have a meaningful relationship with Him. Without this communication, we would be unable to know and love Him on deeper levels, and it is only through living for Him that we experience what it truly means to be alive. As the Prophet Muhammad ﷺ once said, 'The similitude of someone who is mindful of Allah and someone not mindful of Allah is that of the living and the dead.'[2]

When Abraham Maslow amended his famous hierarchy of needs, he set the desire for self-transcendence as the greatest motivator of them all, above self-actualization.[3]

2 al-Bukhārī, *Ṣaḥīḥ al-Bukhārī*, 8:86 #6407; Muslim ibn al-Ḥajjāj al-Qushayrī, *Ṣaḥīḥ Muslim* (Beirut: Dār Iḥyā' al-Kutub al-'Arabīyah, 1955), 1:539 #779.

3 Lloyd Greene and George Burke, "Beyond Self-Actualization," *Journal of Health and Human Services Administration* (2007): 116-128.

However, without the prophets and divine revelation, even that insight remains somewhat uninstructive. It allows for notions such as monism (being one with the universe) or altruism (being selfless) to be misperceived as equally fulfilling as devotion to God. Altruistic people often report higher life satisfaction, and that is expected since being selfless is, by definition, a more transcendent purpose than being self-centered. But the essential need to self-transcend will never be fully satisfied by just any involvement in ends greater than oneself (such as serving the human collective). There is a unique tranquillity that hinges squarely on one's devotion to the absolute greatest: the Almighty. Serving others can be part of that, but can never replace it, as Allah says, *'Unquestionably, it is only by the remembrance of Allah that hearts are assured.'*[4]

Ibn Qayyim (d. 1350), a renowned Muslim theologian, writes,

> In the heart, there exists an anxiousness that nothing can calm but drawing nearer to God. And a loneliness overcasts it that nothing can remove but enjoying His company in private. And a sadness dwells within it that nothing can alleviate but the joy of knowing Him and genuinely devoting oneself to Him. And a worry unsettles it that nothing can reassure but focusing on Him and fleeing from Him to Him. And the flames of regret continue to flare inside it, and nothing can extinguish them but becoming content with His commands, prohibitions, and destiny, and patiently holding onto all that until the time one meets Him. And in it exists a pressing demand; it will not stop until He alone becomes its pursuit. And in it is a dire need; nothing will satisfy it except loving Him, constantly remembering Him, and being sincerely devout to Him. And if a person were given this entire world and all it contains, it would never fulfill that need.[5]

---

4 (*al-Ra'd* 13: 28)

5 Ibn Qayyim al-Jawziyyah, *Madārij al-Sālikīn Bayna Manāzil Iyyāka Na'budu wa Iyyāka Nasta'īn* (Beirut: Dār al-Kutub al-'Arabī, 1996), 3:156.

Hence, to avert this psychospiritual tragedy, and to live for Almighty God, prophethood is an existential necessity. The same, most compassionate God who afforded us all we need on this planet for life and what sustains it, has ensured for us through prophethood what we need most: guidance to Him and His pleasure in this life and the next.

2. The Moral Necessity of Prophethood

With the notion of moral autonomy being widespread in our era, people often demand a rational explanation for why someone cannot 'just be a good person' without faith and scriptural morality. Certainly, humanistic virtues such as compassion and justice are independently praiseworthy, partially inborn, and can invite God's blessings in this life. However, in the grander scheme of salvific eligibility in the hereafter, accepting God's message—upon discovering it—is necessary for validating one's goodness before God. Being good is contingent upon one's existence, good intentions, and the various faculties and resources (such as strength and wealth, among others) by which a person enacts these intentions. Since all these qualities and characteristics are endowed by God, rejecting God would render this good unrewardable in the afterlife, for it would then be, in essence, a plagiarized goodness. We as people rightfully view the most impressive research with awe and admiration, but that sentiment quickly transforms into disgust upon realizing it was actually the work of another whose contribution this fraudulent person deliberately hid. People do not just see plagiarism as disgraceful, but rather as condemnable. Another reason why believing in the messengers is inseparable from being a good person is that only the messengers can thoroughly define good, through the inspiration they receive from God. Moral philosophers, for instance, have never been able to agree on how to apply the widely accepted principle of 'do no harm' because of the complexity of varying contexts. Even with the 'golden rule' of treating others as you would like to be treated, though it is accepted by nearly everyone in theory, striking the perfect balance between competing virtues is not always easy in practice. Aristotle famously discussed this challenging need to find the 'golden mean' between two poles of excess in moral behavior. History also attests that people—even those with good intentions and advanced education—often live their lives with principles that are destructive and, like cancer, the damage caused can sometimes remain hidden until it is irreparable. Such people may have genuinely sought 'being good,' and 'not hurting anyone,' while oblivious to the evil and hardship their ideas inflicted against themselves and society. In a word, the 'do no harm' rule always risks being sacrificed at the altar of subjective morality. For this reason, God sent His final messenger ﷺ to fully define goodness, protecting humanity against shortsightedness, the desensitization we all experience from social conditioning, and the perversions of our perceptions that often follow. Allah says,

> *And know that among you is the Messenger of Allah. If he were to obey you in much of the matter, you would be in difficulty, but Allah has endeared to you the faith and has made it pleasing in your hearts and has made hateful to you disbelief, defiance, and disobedience. Those are the [rightly] guided.*[6]

Pure monotheism (*tawḥīd*), which is to single God out in everything unique to Him, is the ultimate supreme good, and this would also be impossible without the messengers. Humanity cannot know God, nor know His beauty and grandeur, nor know the path to His pleasure, nor know His promises and threats, nor embody His prescriptive will which He lovingly ordained for the betterment of His creation, without the prophets and messengers. Consider the dismal state of the world before God sent Noah (Nuh ﷺ) or the darkness that smothered humanity after Jesus Christ (Isa ﷺ)

---

6 (*al-Ḥujurāt* 49: 7)

and shortly before the advent of Prophet Muhammad ﷺ, to understand humanity's moral need for prophethood at every junction of human history.

3. The Historical Necessity of Prophethood

The Prophet Muhammad ﷺ once said,

> Indeed, Allah looked towards the people of the world and resented the Arabs and non-Arabs alike, except for some remnants from the People of the Book. And He said, 'I have sent you [O Muhammad] to test you and test [others] through you. And I sent down to you a Book that cannot be washed away with water.[7]

Many experts believe that the sixth century was the worst in which to live. It was not 1346–1353, when the Black Death killed half of Europe, nor 1520, when smallpox killed 60–90 per cent of the indigenous people of the Americas, nor 1918, when the Spanish Flu led to the deaths of over fifty million people. As Harvard University's Michael McCormick[8] posits, it was actually the year 536 and the misery it spawned which could be the worst period of all known human history.[9] While his books and research focus on ecology, the moral regression of the world followed in parallel. Wherever a person turned, darkness prevailed. In Roman coliseums, crowds would cheer a lion as it mauled a screaming prisoner. In Persia, even the imperial family practiced incest, as by the late Sasanian period, next-of-kin marriages had become normative

7 Muslim, *Ṣaḥīḥ Muslim*, 4:2197 #2865.

8 Michael McCormick is the Francis Goelet Professor of Medieval History, and chair of the Initiative for the Science of the Human Past at Harvard University. He is an award-winning author, and a pioneer in bridging the worlds of archeology and climate science.

9 Ann Gibbons, 'Why 536 was "The Worst Year to be Alive",' *Science Journal*, November 15, 2018.

in Zoroastrian law.[10] Uniformity of worship was only achieved by the Sasanians through violent persecution of unorthodox practices, even against co-religionists within a common Zoroastrian framework.[11] In India, those at the bottom of the caste system were equivalent, if not inferior to, rodents and vermin—since such animals were sometimes considered holy temple dwellers. In Arabia, finding a stone heart that could stomach burying his infant daughter alive was no challenge. In Christianity, mystery triumphed regarding the identity of Jesus Christ, many claiming he was God incarnate, while other faith groups alleged that he was an imposter preacher born out of wedlock. Further East, people worshipped fire, water, weapons, and genitalia instead of the Creator. In many societies, a woman was seen as having no soul, or as having been created only to serve man, and at times that could even mean pawning her over a recreational gamble with his friends or being burned alive at his funeral. Many infants did not survive childbirth, and even fewer reached adulthood. Those born into slavery were generally unable to change their status, and in some major civilizations of that historical period, this sector of society exceeded 75 per cent of the population.[12]

With this being the condition of the world, how could God not offer a glimpse of hope for the people of this planet? It is unfathomable that a supremely compassionate, all-capable God would not intervene. Indeed, the Most Merciful did not abandon His creation, but reached out to them yet again, '*so that those who perished [through disbelief] would perish upon evidence and those who lived [in faith] would live upon evidence.*'[13] By sending the Final Prophet, Muhammad ﷺ,

---

10 Michael Stausberg and Yuhan S.-D. Vevaina, *The Wiley Blackwell Companion to Zoroastrianism* (Chichester, West Sussex, UK: Wiley, 2015), 292.

11 Robert C. Solomon and Kathleen M. Higgins, *From Africa to Zen: An Invitation to World Philosophy* (Lanham, Md: Rowman & Littlefield Publishing, 2003), 175.

12 Niall McKeown, *The Invention of Ancient Slavery?* (London: Bristol Classical Press, 2011), 115.

13 (*al-Anfāl* 8: 42)

God did not fail them, even if some choose thereafter to fail themselves by deciding after the clarification to decline his message.

4. The Biblical Necessity of Prophethood

In this grim sixth century, it was not only the condition of the world and its atrocities that necessitated relief from a most compassionate God. Alongside this, many of those versed in biblical scripture were awaiting a final prophesied messenger, of whom there was a crystal-clear description in their literature. Hence, Allah says about the Qur'an and subsequently its bearer, '*And has it not been a sign to them that it is recognized by the scholars of the Children of Israel?*'[14]

Though some contemporaries of the Final Prophet ﷺ rejected him out of animosity and prejudice, and others simply had not yet been guided, some of the biblically versed—such as 'Abdullāh ibn Salām ؓ—quickly accepted Islam, and that was one of the proofs Allah cited against the idolators of Arabia, since most Arabs were illiterate, did not ascribe to any scripture, and held that the Jews were superior to them for being People of the Book.

Despite adulteration, strong indicators of the prophethood of Muhammad ﷺ remain even today in the Judeo-Christian texts, of which we will showcase the following:

i. A Gentile Prophet Like Moses

> I will raise up for them a Prophet like you from among their brethren, and will put My words in His mouth, and He shall speak to them all that I command Him.[15]

---

14 (*al-Shu'arā'* 26: 197)

15 Deuteronomy 18:18, New King James Version.

In this passage, God reveals to Moses (Musa ﷺ) that He will send another prophet to the Israelites, and that he will emerge from among their brethren. The New International Version of the Bible chose an exclusivist translation of this, qualifying it as 'from among their fellow Israelites', but the Bible itself also refers to non-Israelites as their brothers. For instance, in Deuteronomy 2:4, God says that 'You are about to pass through the territory of your brethren,' referring to the lands of the Edomites. This led some biblical exegetes to suggest that a Gentile (non-Israelite) prophet could in fact be intended here;[16] a prophet hailing from some 'brethren' of the Israelites such as the Ishmaelites or Edomites (Arabs or Nabateans). Also, restricting this prophecy to the Israelites would mean it has never been fulfilled, since according to Deuteronomy 34:10, 'But since then there has not arisen in Israel a prophet like Moses.'

Deuteronomy 18:18 also establishes that the awaited prophet would have a striking resemblance to Moses. Both Moses and Muhammad ﷺ were prophets born of two parents, both married and had children, both came with a new comprehensive code of law, both faced persecution causing them to leave their homelands, both returned to defeat their oppressors, and both experienced natural death and burial. No other two prophets, especially in the Abrahamic tradition, come close to this degree of similarity.

Deuteronomy 18:18 also describes this awaited prophet as someone who will serve as a faithful mouthpiece for God, only conveying from Him that which He commands. The Prophet Muhammad ﷺ was tireless in teaching his followers this very fact: that not a single word of the Qur'an should be credited to him: *'By the star when it descends, your companion (Muhammad) has not strayed, nor has he erred, nor does he speak from [his own] inclination. It is but a revelation revealed.'*[17]

---

16 Marc B. Shapiro, *The Limits of Orthodox Theology: Maimonides' Thirteen Principles Reappraised* (Oxford: Littman Library of Jewish Civilization, 2004), 89.

17 (*al-Najm* 53: 1–4)

ii. John the Baptist and the Awaited Prophet

> Now this is the testimony of John, when the Jews sent priests and Levites from Jerusalem to ask him, 'Who are you?' He confessed, and did not deny, but confessed, 'I am not the Christ.' And they asked him, 'What then? Are you Elijah?' 'Are you the Prophet?' And he answered, 'No.'[18]

Here, we find John the Baptist being questioned about the nature of his ministry and whether he was claiming to be '*the* prophet'. This proves that some Jews were still awaiting the fulfillment of this divine promise in Deuteronomy 18:18, that of the Mosaic antitype, up until the time of Jesus Christ and even thereafter.[19] It also begs the question: who is this luminary who is neither Christ nor Elijah? Who is being referred to here as '*the* prophet' and not just 'a prophet', as if his name does not even require stating, and his coming was eagerly anticipated? Indeed, they were awaiting the greatest prophet of all, the Final Prophet who would illuminate for humanity the path to God one last time, and whose identity could not be mistaken. It is for this reason that Allah said, '*Those to whom We gave the Scripture know him as they know their own sons. But indeed, a party of them conceal the truth while they know [it].*'[20]

iii. God's Servant Where Kedar Lives

> Behold! My Servant whom I uphold; My chosen one in whom My soul delights. I have put My Spirit upon him; he will bring forth justice to the nations. He will not cry out nor raise his voice, nor make his voice heard in the

---

18 John 1:19-21, New King James Version.

19 See: David K. Rensberger and Harold W. Attridge, 'The Gospel According to John', in *The HarperCollins Study Bible: Fully Revised & Updated* (New York, NY: HarperCollins, 2006).

20 (*al-Baqarah* 2: 146)

> street. A bent reed he will not break off and a dimly burning wick he will not extinguish; he will faithfully bring forth justice. He will not be disheartened or crushed until he has established justice on the earth; And the coastlands will wait expectantly for his law.[21] ... Sing to the LORD a new song, Sing His praise from the ends of the earth! You who go down to the sea, and all that is in it; You islands, and those who live on them. Let the wilderness and its cities raise their voices, The settlements which Kedar inhabits. Let the inhabitants of Sela sing aloud, let them shout for joy from the tops of the mountains.[22]

This description of the 'servant' in Isaiah 42 seems to position the Prophet Muhammad ﷺ as its worthiest candidate. His primary title throughout the Qur'an is *'Our servant.'*[23] His homeland being Arabia matches that of the Kedarites; the Bible identifies Kedar as the direct son of Ishmael (Ismail ﷺ).[24] It was under the leadership

---

21 Isaiah 42:1-4, New American Standard Bible.
'Amr ibn al-'Āṣ—a Companion of the Prophet Muhammad ﷺ—said that among what was foretold in the Torah about the Prophet ﷺ was, 'You are My slave and My messenger; your name is al-Mutawakkil (the Reliant upon God). He is neither harsh nor aggressive, and he does not yell in the marketplace. He does not repay evil with evil, but rather overlooks and forgives. Allah will not take him (in death) until He has straightened a crooked nation through him, having them say there is no god but Allah, and [not before] he has opened hard hearts, deaf ears, and blind eyes.' (*Ṣaḥīḥ al-Bukhārī*, 3:66, #2125)

22 Isaiah 42:10-11, New American Standard Bible.

23 '*[All] praise is [due] to Allah, who has sent down upon His Servant [Muhammad] the Book and has not made therein any deviance.*' (*al-Kahf* 18: 1); '*Blessed is He who sent down the Criterion upon His Servant that he may be to the worlds a warner.*" (*al-Furqān* 25: 1)

24 'And these are the names of the sons of Ishmael, by their names, according to their generations: the firstborn of Ishmael, Nebaioth; and Kedar, and Adbeel, and Mibsam.' Genesis: 25:13, King James Version. See also: 1 Chronicles 1:29.
The rabbis understood Kedar to be a reference to the Arabs, would refer to all Arabians as Kedarites, and to Arabic as *layshon Kaydar*, meaning the

of Muhammad ﷺ that the Ishmaelites (Arabs) finally became a 'nation' as God had promised Abraham (Ibrahim ﷺ) they would,[25] after being scattered feudal tribes for around two millennia. And only after being unified did they amass enough power to successfully establish 'God's justice' in the region as Isaiah 42:4 foretells. It is problematic to assume the servant in Isaiah was Jesus Christ because Christianity and Islam agree that he rose without bringing justice to the nations; his handful of disciples did not possess the political strength to enforce God's law in their society. This servant also cannot be Moses for the same reason; after forty years of wandering the desert, he died outside the Promised Land on Mount Nebo according to the Bible, without having 'established justice on the earth'. He also never abolished idolatry among the Kedarites, as Isaiah 42:17 explicitly says 'the prophet' would, while the Prophet Muhammad ﷺ most definitely did.

iv. Jesus and the Comforter

> Nevertheless, I tell you the truth. It is to your advantage that I go away; for if I do not go away, the Helper will not come to you; but if I depart, I will send him to you …[26] I still have many things to say to you, but you cannot bear them now. However, when he, the Spirit of truth, has come, he will guide you into all truth; for he will not speak on his own authority, but whatever he hears he will speak; and he will tell you things to come.[27]

Jesus could not be implying the Holy Spirit here, calling him the Comforter that cannot arrive until Jesus departs, since the Holy

tongue (*lisān* in Arabic) of Kedar. See: Wilhelm Gesenius, 'Qêdār', in *Gesenius' Hebrew and Chaldee Lexicon to the Old Testament Scriptures*, translated by Samuel Prideaux Tregelles (Piscataway: Gorgias Press), 2019.

25 'And also of the son of the bondwoman will I make a nation, because he is thy seed.' Genesis 21:13, King James Version.

26 John 16:7, New King James Version.

27 Ibid., 16:12-13.

Spirit was always with Jesus. Jesus could not be implying Paul or the papacy, since they did away with laws instead of perfecting them, and did not present proof that they communicated with the heavens. It was only the Prophet Muhammad ﷺ who revived the honour of Jesus without burying his legacy of worshipping the Creator alone. In this respect, the Prophet Muhammad ﷺ said, 'I enjoy the closest proximity to Jesus, the Son of Mary, in this life and the hereafter.' His Companions asked, 'How is that, O Messenger of God?' He said, 'The prophets are all paternal brothers, with different mothers, but they have one religion. Also, there was no other prophet between us (myself and Jesus Christ).'[28] Furthermore, Muhammad ﷺ would accurately foretell future events (see Chapter 5), and brought definitive guidance on all truths, perfecting the divine code of law for humanity until the end times (see Chapter 4).

In conjunction with this, Jesus Christ also supplied the famous Vineyard Parable in Mark 12 amidst his final sermon, wherein he prophesied that the allegorical 'vineyard' would be pulled from the corrupt murderous tenants 'and given to others'. Ultimately, the Jews were enraged upon realizing that this parable was about them, their hostilities towards God's prophets, and God's covenant and prophecy leaving them as a result. This further elucidates that the awaited Comforter, the Spirit of Truth, must be a non-Israelite prophet who also came from the Abrahamic line.

v. Zamzam and the Flourishing City

> Then God opened her [Hagar's] eyes, and she saw a well of water. And she went and filled the skin with water and gave the lad a drink. So God was with the lad; and he grew and dwelt in the wilderness, and became an archer. He dwelt in the Wilderness of Paran; and his mother took a wife for him from the land of Egypt.[29]

28 Muslim, *Ṣaḥīḥ Muslim*, 4:1837 #2365.

29 Genesis 21:19-21, New King James Version.

Within Arabia's city of Makkah, the historical epicenter of Islam and birthplace of Muhammad ﷺ, there exists the well of Zamzam—what may be the oldest active spring of water the world has ever known. Put the two millennia before the Prophet Muhammad ﷺ aside, and merely consider the millions of pilgrims visiting for hajj and *ʿumrah* over the past 1,500 years, who each return home with gallons of Zamzam water. In addition, a round-the-clock supply of this water is transported to Qubā' and the Prophetic Mosque in Madinah, while residents of Makkah have tanks installed in their homes for regular Zamzam delivery. This was clearly a blessed well which Hagar (Hājar ﵂) and Ishmael received, and the first brick set by God for this sacred city to flourish.

In addition to Zamzam, consider the construction of the Kaaba. Even the idolatrous Arabs recognized Abraham as the ultimate patriarch, and due to their esteem for him, all paid homage to him by visiting the House he built for God's worship in Makkah. Even though they were idolaters, these polytheists affirmed that Makkah was a special sanctuary venerated by God. They saw themselves as the heirs of that heritage, and thus they felt compelled to honour this Kaaba that Abraham had erected. Why else would God command Abraham to just leave Hagar and his firstborn infant in a particular place, and a barren wilderness at that? It is difficult to conceive that Allah sent Abraham to construct the Kaaba, established the blessed well of Zamzam beneath it, gave rise to a great nation because of it, and protected it from invasions—just so it would be surrounded by idols and become a venue for depravity. It is no surprise, then, why many people at that time believed that something was about to happen, something momentous that would change the entire scene in that part of the world and far beyond it.

Some may wonder how the present author may invoke the Bible as evidence for the prophethood of Muhammad ﷺ, when the

Qur'an asserts that parts of the previously revealed texts have been distorted. As quoted earlier, the Qur'an also calls our attention to biblical experts affirming these descriptions in their scriptures. To reconcile, we recognize that the original message of Jesus Christ has been at least partially lost, as is exemplified—for instance—in the non-traceability of the Bible's revisions and source manuscripts. However, this does not prevent us from being critical readers of history who infer from an inductive scan of these texts a preponderance of evidence in favour of the prophethood of Muhammad ﷺ. Put simply, while no single passage in the Bible today squarely says 'Muhammad', they collectively point to him more than anyone else. In defining those who will win God's grace and salvation, Allah said,

> *Those who follow the Messenger, the unlettered prophet, whom they find written [i.e., described] in what they have of the Torah and the Gospel, who enjoins upon them what is right and prohibits them from what is wrong, and makes lawful for them what is good and forbids them from what is evil, and relieves them of their burden and the shackles which were upon them. So they who have believed in him, honoured him, supported him, and followed the light which was sent down with him—it is those who will be the successful. Say, [O Muhammad], 'O mankind, indeed I am the Messenger of Allah to you all, [from Him] to whom belongs the dominion of the heavens and the earth. There is no deity except Him; He gives life and causes death.' So believe in Allah and His Messenger, the unlettered prophet, who believes in Allah and His words, and follow him that you may be guided.*[30]

---

30 (*al-Aʿrāf* 7: 157)

2

The Prophet's Character

The Bible reports that Jesus Christ offered the following logical criteria for distinguishing true prophets from false ones:

> Beware of false prophets, who come to you in sheep's clothing, but inwardly they are ravenous wolves. You will know them by their fruits. Do men gather grapes from thornbushes or figs from thistles? Even so, every good tree bears good fruit, but a bad tree bears bad fruit. A good tree cannot bear bad fruit, nor can a bad tree bear good fruit. Every tree that does not bear good fruit is cut down and thrown into the fire. Therefore, by their fruits you will know them.[1]

The Prophet Jesus may have intended by these 'fruits' that actions speak louder than words about a person's character, and therefore the personal conduct of a true prophet must be good. He may have also intended that the positive impact of his teachings on others will be good, or that the message itself must be a clear

---

1 Matthew 7:15-20, New King James Version.

call to purity and goodness. The beauty of analyzing the ministry of Muhammad ﷺ is that all three interpretations would stand true for him. The following three chapters will illustrate how his character, his accomplishments, and his message all make a powerful case for his prophethood—beginning with the analysis of his character in this chapter.

God combined in Muhammad ﷺ the most illustrious qualities, as evidence that he was in fact authorized by the Divine. His character sparkled from every angle, and this was noticed both by those who experienced him firsthand and those who later read his biography. They all found in Muhammad ﷺ a lifestyle of extraordinary sincerity, conviction, and virtue that posed a formidable challenge to any doubter in his prophethood. As Ibn Taymiyyah (d. 1328), an eminent Muslim theologian, said,

> It is known that someone who claims to be a prophet is either one of the best and noblest of the creation, or the worst and most wicked of them … so how could there ever be any confusion between the best and noblest and between the worst and most wicked? … There has never been any liar who claimed prophethood except that his ignorance, dishonesty, wickedness, and devilish ways became clear to anyone who possessed the smallest degree of discernment.[2]

A person may wonder about the historical reliability of the reports in the following pages, and why trust that these are anything more than pious exaggerations by Muhammad's admirers on the greatness of his character. This concern will be revisited in greater detail amidst the discussion on miracles, but let us cite here the testimony of two non-Muslim historiographers who specialized in the traceability of Islam's prophetic traditions. David S. Margoliouth (d. 1940), the famous English Orientalist,

---

2 Taqī al-Dīn Aḥmad ibn Taymiyyah, *Sharḥ al-'Aqīdah al-Asfahāniyyah* (Riyadh: Maktabat al-Rushd, 2001), 156-157.

said regarding the isnād system in Islamic scholarship, which requires that reports only be transmitted through a rigorously scrutinized chain of narrators,

> [I]ts value in making for accuracy cannot be questioned, and the Muslims are justified in taking pride in their science of tradition. In other ancient records, we have to take what is told on the author's assertion: it is rare that a Greek or Roman historian tell us the source of his information.[3]

Even a staunch Orientalist like Bernard Lewis (d. 2018), who was a sharp critic of Islam and Muslims in modern times, acknowledged the strength of the Hadith tradition. The British-American historiographer wrote:

> But their careful scrutiny of the chains of transmission and their meticulous collection and preservation of variants in the transmitted narratives give to medieval Arabic historiography a professionalism and sophistication without precedent in antiquity and without parallel in the contemporary medieval West. By comparison, the historiography of Latin Christendom seems poor and meagre, and even the more advanced and complex historiography of Greek Christendom still falls short of the historical literature of Islam in volume, variety and analytical depth.[4]

The following pages will demonstrate how even a brief overview of Muhammad's character not only refutes the oft-recycled charges leveled against him—being an imposter prophet or a ruthless warlord—but also establishes the truth of his claim that he was God's Final Prophet to the world.

---

3 David S. Margoliouth, *Lectures on Arabic Historians: Delivered before the University of Calcutta 1929* (Kolkata, India: University of Calcutta, 1930), 20.

4 Bernard Lewis, *Islam in History: Ideas, People, and Events in the Middle East* (Illinois: Open Court Publishing, 2001), 105.

1. His Honesty and Integrity

The Prophet ﷺ was a person whose honesty was common knowledge to those around him. In fact, his clansmen had officially titled him the Trustworthy (al-Amīn).[5] Even when they persecuted him and rejected his message, they still trusted him with their most precious possessions. ʿĀ'ishah ﵂ said:

> He instructed ʿAlī ﵁ to stay behind in Makkah, to return all the property the Messenger of Allah ﷺ had held in trust for people. There was nobody in Makkah (even his enemies) who had valuables that he feared for except that he kept them with the Messenger of Allah ﷺ, due to the honesty and trustworthiness that was known [to all] about him. ʿAlī ﵁ stayed back for three days and three nights to deliver everything entrusted by the people to the Messenger of Allah ﷺ, and then caught up with him after completing that task.[6]

His honesty was so evident that even people from different eras, backgrounds, and religions recognize it. It is indeed difficult to imagine a fair person reading his life and arriving at a different conclusion. Although the Scottish philosopher and historian Thomas Carlyle (d. 1881) had his reservations about Islam, his fascination with the Final Prophet's sincerity at times seemed to veer between scepticism and apparent conviction. For instance:

> It goes greatly against the impostor-theory, the fact that he lived in this entirely unexceptionable, entirely quiet and commonplace way, till the heat of his years

[5] Ibn Hishām, *Al-Sīrah al-Nabawiyyah*, 1:183, 197.

[6] Aḥmad ibn al-Ḥusayn al-Bayhaqī, *Al-Sunan al-Kubrā* (Beirut: Dār al-Kutub al-ʿIlmīyah, 2003), 6:472 #12696; See also: Ismāʿīl ibn Kathīr, *Al-Bidāyah wal-Nihāyah* (Cairo: Dār Hajar, 1997), 4:445.

> was done. He was forty before he talked of any mission from Heaven. All his irregularities, real and supposed, date from after his fiftieth year, when the good Kadijah died. All his 'ambition,' seemingly, had been, hitherto, to live an honest life; his 'fame,' the mere good-opinion of neighbours that knew him, had been sufficient hitherto. Not till he was already getting old … and peace growing to be the chief thing this world could give him, did he start on the 'career of ambition;' and, belying all his past character and existence, set up [by others] as a wretched empty charlatan to acquire what he could now no longer enjoy! For my share, I have no faith whatever in that [impostor-theory].[7]

In the same book, Carlyle says, 'The lies (Western slander) which well-meaning zeal has heaped round this man (Muhammad) are disgraceful to ourselves only.'[8]

Historical figures who dismissed the imposter theory as preposterous slander existed well before Carlyle. When Prophet Muhammad ﷺ first corresponded with Heraclius (d. 641), the Byzantine emperor, calling him to embrace Islam, Heraclius immediately dispatched a brigade to find anyone who could verify this man's claims to prophethood. The leading adversary of Muhammad ﷺ at that time, Abū Sufyān ibn Ḥarb, was among those apprehended and interrogated in the presence of the Byzantine dignitaries. Heraclius—a military commander versed in Judeo-Christian scriptures—asked Abū Sufyān a series of key questions, and then cross-checked his answers with his fellow clansmen. Upon completing his investigation, the following is some of what Heraclius said to Abū Sufyān:

---

7 Thomas Carlyle, David R. Sorensen (ed.), and Brent E. Kinser (ed.), *On Heroes, Hero-Worship, and the Heroic in History* (New Haven: Yale University Press, 2013), 59.

8 Ibid., 52.

> I asked you whether you ever accused him of lying before he stated what he stated [about prophethood]. You replied in the negative, and I know that he would not refrain from lying about others and then lie about God … And I asked you whether he ever betrayed [anyone]. You replied in the negative, and likewise the messengers never betray… If what you are saying is true, he will conquer the place of these two feet of mine. And I knew [from scripture] that he would soon emerge, but I never assumed that he would be from among you. And if I knew that I could reach him [safely], I would have been bent on meeting him. And if I were in his presence, I would personally wash his feet.[9]

In the history of humanity, many imposters have claimed prophethood, but it was always a matter of time before they were discovered to either be psychologically disturbed individuals or unethical opportunists. The first category has never had any influence on the world stage, let alone produced a complete system of beliefs and laws that would earn the respect of thousands of sages, historians, philosophers, and other men and women of wisdom. The second category is eventually exposed with the passage of time as sinister and manipulative, with the notorious Joseph Smith (d. 1844) being an iconic example of this in recent history. These are endemic qualities that permeate this second category, and should be expected to, because just as lying about your friends is worse than lying about a random person, and just as lying about your parents is worse than lying about your friends, there is nothing uglier than a person lying about God. So, when a man who had the unique impact on the world that Muhammad ﷺ did (see Chapter 3) was also known for his impeccable honesty, despite his public and private life being documented with

---

9 al-Bukhārī, *Ṣaḥīḥ al-Bukhārī*, 1:8 #7.

granular detail, then his claim of being God's prophet should not be disregarded.

Another powerful testament to his integrity was his adamant refusal to allow anyone to aggrandize him. Jābir ibn ʿAbdillāh ﷺ narrates that there was a solar eclipse on the day that Ibrāhīm, the son of Allah's Messenger ﷺ, had died. When the people began to say that the eclipse was due to the death of this young child, Allah's Messenger ﷺ rose at once and said, 'The sun and the moon are not eclipsed because of the death or birth of anyone. Rather, they are two of God's signs, by which He instills fear in His slaves. When you see an eclipse, pray and invoke God.'[10] Had the Prophet ﷺ been a narcissistic imposter, this would have been the perfect opportunity to capitalize on such a convenient credibility booster. These coinciding events represented an immense opportunity for any personal agenda, and yet the Prophet ﷺ would not allow others to interpret this as the skies being saddened for Ibrāhīm. Though hurting from the tragic loss, he still ascended the pulpit, dismissed the false interpretation, and established that eclipses follow nothing but the cosmic order set by God in the created universe.

On another occasion, Ḥudhayfah ibn al-Yamān ﷺ came to the Prophet ﷺ prior to the Battle of Badr with an ethical dilemma. The pagans of Quraysh had just released Ḥudhayfah ﷺ and his father on the condition that he would not join Muhammad's ranks and fight Quraysh alongside him. Despite the Muslim army being disadvantaged and about to face a military force three times its size, the Prophet ﷺ still said, 'Then proceed on [to Madinah]. We will keep our promise to them, and we will seek aid from Allah against them.'[11] His prophetic morals did not allow him, even in an extremely vulnerable position, to compromise the principles of honesty and uprightness.

---

10 al-Bukhārī, *Ṣaḥīḥ al-Bukhārī*, 2:39 #1060; Muslim, *Ṣaḥīḥ Muslim*, 2:630 #915.

11 Muslim, *Ṣaḥīḥ Muslim*, 3:1414 #1787.

2. His Simplicity and Humility

The simple, austere lifestyle of the Prophet ﷺ is a major indication that his mission could not have been self-serving, especially when contrasted with the decadent, extravagant lifestyles of so many false prophets in world history. After all, this was a man who controlled all of Arabia by the end of his life. Even before that, he had thousands of followers in Madinah, followers who obsessed over him and would have done anything in the world for him. Yet, we see no signs of luxury in any sphere of his life.

3D Rendering by Yaqeen Institute. Inspired by Amany Saqqāf, 2009, Jeddah, Saudi Arabia Exhibition.

His living quarters were so tight that when he wished to pray, he would tap ʿĀ'ishah ﵂ to bend her legs to make room for him to prostrate. To drink or bathe, he would reach for the small leather water skin that hung in his room. For months on end, no fire would be kindled for cooking in his home, and his family was content with dates and water unless someone gifted them some milk.[12]

'Umar ibn al-Khaṭṭāb ﵁ reports that he once entered the room of the Messenger of Allah ﷺ to find him lying down and noticed that the coarseness of the straw mat under him had left marks on his side. Upon noticing that, and the meager rations of barley and leaves, and the leather bag hanging in the corner, his eyes welled with tears. The Prophet ﷺ said, 'What makes you weep, O son of al-Khaṭṭāb?' He said, 'O Prophet of Allah, how can I not cry after seeing how the mat has left these marks on your side, and how little you have in your food cupboard? Caesar and Chosroes live surrounded by fruits and springs of water, while you are the Messenger of God and His chosen one, and yet this is your condition.' The Prophet ﷺ said, 'O son of al-Khaṭṭāb, does it not please you that these [luxuries] are for us in the Hereafter and for them in this world?' He said, 'Of course.'[13] In another narration, the Prophet ﷺ began his response with, 'Are you in doubt, O son of al-Khaṭṭāb? These are a people whose pleasures have been expedited in the life of this world.'[14]

Edward Gibbon (d. 1794), a historian and member of England's Parliament, wrote:

> The good sense of Muhammad despised the pomp of royalty. The Apostle of God submitted to the menial offices of the family; he kindled the fire; swept the floor; milked the ewes; and mended with his own hands his shoes and garments. Disdaining the penance and merit of a hermit, he observed without effort or vanity the abstemious diet of an Arab.[15]

---

12 al-Bukhārī, *Ṣaḥīḥ al-Bukhārī*, 8:97 #6459.

13 Muslim, *Ṣaḥīḥ Muslim*, 2:1105 #1479.

14 al-Bukhārī, Ṣaḥīḥ al-Bukhārī, 3:133 #2468.

15 Edward Gibbon, *Decline and Fall of the Roman Empire: Volume the Fifth* (London: Electric Book Co, 2001), chapter L, 252.

In other words, he not only endured the coarseness of an austere life, but it came naturally to him. He was not trying to encourage monkship or stoicism, nor was he faking this minimalism to earn praise. Gibbon continues,

> On solemn occasions, he feasted his companions with rustic and hospitable plenty. But, in his domestic life, many weeks would pass without a fire being kindled on the hearth of the Prophet.[16]

According to Washington Irving (d. 1859), an American biographer and diplomat,

> He was sober and abstemious in his diet and a rigorous observer of fasts. He indulged in no magnificence of apparel, the ostentation of a petty mind; neither was his simplicity in dress affected but a result of real disregard for distinction from so trivial a source.[17]

Irving also wrote:

> His military triumphs awakened no pride nor vainglory, as they would have done had they been effected for selfish purposes. In the time of his greatest power, he maintained the same simplicity of manners and appearance as in the days of his adversity. So far from affecting a regal state, he was displeased if, on entering a room, any unusual testimonials of respect were shown to him.[18]

Regarding these 'unusual testimonials of respect,' Anas ibn Mālik ﷺ said, 'Nobody was more beloved to them (the Companions) than the Messenger of Allah ﷺ. Despite that, when they would see

---

16 Ibid., 251-252.

17 Washington Irving and Bertram R. Davis, *The Life of Mahomet* (London: G. Routledge & Co, 1850), 186-187.

18 Ibid., 203.

him, they would not stand for him, knowing how much he disliked that.'[19] Bosworth Smith (d. 1908), a reverend and author, writes,

> Head of the State as well as the Church; he was Caesar and Pope in one; but he was Pope without the Pope's pretensions, and Caesar without the legions of Caesar, without a standing army, without a bodyguard, without a police force, without a fixed revenue. If ever a man ruled by a right divine, it was Muhammad, for he had all the powers without their supports. He cared not for the dressings of power. The simplicity of his private life was in keeping with his public life.[20]

Until this very day, the canons of literature on Islamic ethics, and the weekly sermons of Muslim preachers, are replete with examples of the Prophet ﷺ as the paragon of humility. He was the educator who was never ashamed to say 'I don't know,'[21] the general who would allow others to share his riding animal,[22] the busiest statesman who would allow the weakest members of society to take him by the hand for their needs,[23] the elder who would compete with the youth to carry the bricks of the first mosque,[24] and the considerate husband who noticed subtle signs of his wife being upset with him.[25] Finally, he was the greatest messenger of God who would reiterate throughout his life:

> My similitude compared to the prophets before me is that of a person who built a beautiful, brilliant structure—

---

19 al-Tirmidhī, *Sunan al-Tirmidhī*, 5:90 #2754; authenticated by al-Tirmidhī in the comments.

20 Bosworth Smith, *Mohammed and Mohammedanism* (London: Smith, Elder, and Co., 1874), 235.

21 Muslim, *Ṣaḥīḥ Muslim*, 1:1 #8.

22 al-Bukhārī, *Ṣaḥīḥ al-Bukhārī*, 8:74 #6228.

23 Abū Dāwūd, *Sunan Abī Dāwūd* (Sidon: al-Maktabah al-ʿAṣrīyah, 1980), 43:46 #4818.

24 al-Bukhārī, *Ṣaḥīḥ al-Bukhārī*, 5:58 #3906.

25 al-Bukhārī, *Ṣaḥīḥ al-Bukhārī*, 7:62 #5228.

> completing its construction save for a single brick in one of its corners. People began to walk around it, admiring its construction, but saying, 'If only that final brick were set in place, it would have been perfect.' I am that brick, and I am the seal of the prophets.[26]

In another hadith, he humbly cautioned, 'Do not aggrandize me as the Christians exaggerated in praising the son of Mary. I am but a slave, so call me the slave of God and His messenger.'[27]

3. His Mercy and Compassion

The Prophet's 'character was the Qur'an',[28] as described by his wife, 'Ā'ishah ﷺ. He practised everything that he preached, and since the Qur'anic message preached mercy above all, this quality was more pronounced in his practice than anything else. The Prophet's call to mercy was therefore not mere words, but rather teachings that he held to be sacred and felt he must embody better than any other adherent of Islam. In the clearest terms and on various occasions, he would announce to the people, 'The merciful will be shown mercy by the Most Merciful. Be merciful to those on the earth, and the One on the heavens will have mercy upon you.'[29]

Even while observing the ritual prayer, a pillar of Islam and its most important physical act, the Prophet ﷺ remained cognizant of people's suffering. Abū Qatādah ﷺ narrates that the Prophet ﷺ once said, 'I sometimes stand in prayer then hear a child crying, so I make my prayer brief due to not wanting to cause hardship for his mother.'[30] In another hadith, he cautioned, 'When one of you leads the people in prayer, he should be light, for among them

---

26 Muslim, *Ṣaḥīḥ Muslim*, 43:22 #2286.

27 al-Bukhārī, *Ṣaḥīḥ al-Bukhārī*, 4:55 #3445.

28 Muslim, *Ṣaḥīḥ Muslim*, 1:512 #746.

29 al-Tirmidhī, *Sunan al-Tirmidhī*, 3:388 #1924.

30 al-Bukhārī, *Ṣaḥīḥ al-Bukhārī*, 1:143 #710.

are the weak, and the ill, and the elderly. And when one of you is praying alone, then let him elongate it as he pleases.'[31]

The authentic narrations on the Prophet's exemplary mercy with children, and his counseling of mercy towards them, would fill dozens of pages. In one telling exchange, al-Aqraʿ ibn Ḥābis ☙ became perplexed at Muhammad's elaborate display of affection, upon seeing the Prophet ☙ kiss his grandchild. This Companion's rugged Bedouin upbringing made him feel that this was contrary to masculinity, and so he said in pride, 'You kiss your boys? I have ten sons and have never kissed any one of them.' The Prophet ☙ responded, 'And what do I possess [to help you] if Allah has plucked mercy from your heart?'[32]

While parents naturally love their children, many overlook the child's emotional need for expressions of that love, but the Prophet of Mercy ☙ never did. In fact, it was not just his own children that he treated this way. Anas ibn Mālik ☙ narrates that the Prophet ☙ once entered to find a son of Abū Ṭalḥah ☙ in a sad state, and quickly noticed that his pet nughayr (sparrow) was no longer around, so he lightheartedly said to him in consolation, 'O Abū ʿUmayr, what happened to the nughayr?'[33] He inquired about the creature because it meant so much to the young child, and called him the father of ʿUmayr despite him not yet being a parent, to rhyme with the word nughayr and playfully uplift his spirits with the thoughts of his future manhood.

The Prophet Muhammad's heart even empathized with the pain of animals. He would tell his followers about sinners of the past who were forgiven by God for climbing down into a well to retrieve water for a parched dog,[34] and stated on another occasion, 'In every living creature is an opportunity for charity.'[35]

---

[31]   al-Bukhārī, *Ṣaḥīḥ al-Bukhārī*, 1:142 #702; Muslim, *Ṣaḥīḥ Muslim*, 1:340 #466.

[32]   al-Bukhārī, *Ṣaḥīḥ al-Bukhārī*, 8:7 #5998.

[33]   Abū Dāwūd, *Sunan Abī Dāwūd*, 4:293 #4969.

[34]   al-Bukhārī, *Ṣaḥīḥ al-Bukhārī*, 4:130 #3321.

[35]   al-Bukhārī, *Ṣaḥīḥ al-Bukhārī*, 8:9 #6009.

He taught that sharpening one's blade is a necessary part of the kindness due to a sacrificial animal,[36] and forbade that a harmless animal be killed for sport or for anything other than consumption. He would reprimand his followers for overworking their camels in the fields, and for not relieving their riding mounts of the loads they carried promptly after reaching their destination; he once warned them of a woman who was bound for Hellfire due to trapping a cat without food.[37] In one beautiful hadith, 'Abdullāh ibn Masʿūd ﵁ narrates that as they once travelled on a journey with the Messenger of Allah ﷺ, he stepped away to relieve himself. The Companions then saw a nest of young birds and captured them. The mother then came, frantically flapping its wings in panic. When the Messenger of Allah ﷺ saw this, he said, 'Who caused this bird to grieve over its young chicks? Return its young ones to it!'[38] Such a kindhearted disposition even towards animals is not unexpected, especially when Allah (the Most High) affirmed in the Qur'an, *'And We have not sent you [O Muhammad] except as a mercy to all the worlds.'*[39]

Finally, his profound and universal mercy was above all reflected in his concern for people's salvation. The Qur'an would often address his deep grief over people's resistance to guidance, in verses such as, *'Then perhaps you would kill yourself through grief over them, [O Muhammad], if they do not believe in this message, [and] out of sorrow.'*[40] The Prophet ﷺ would weep passionately during his night prayers, pleading to God to spare his nation of the torment that many former nations had faced, until Allah ultimately instructed the archangel, 'O Gabriel, go to Muhammad and tell him that We will please him regarding his nation, and We will not disappoint him.'[41] In another hadith, 'Ā'ishah ﵂ reports that

[36] Muslim, *Ṣaḥīḥ Muslim*, 3:1548 #1955.
[37] al-Bukhārī, *Ṣaḥīḥ al-Bukhārī*, 4:176 #3482.
[38] Abū Dāwūd, *Sunan Abī Dāwūd*, 4:367 #5268.
[39] (*al-Anbiyā'* 21: 107)
[40] (*al-Kahf* 18: 6)
[41] Muslim, *Ṣaḥīḥ Muslim*, 1:191 #202.

upon seeing the Prophet's facing beaming cheerfully one day, she said, 'O Messenger of Allah, supplicate to Allah for me.' He said, 'O Allah, forgive 'Āʾishah for her past and future sins, those in secret and those in public.' Ecstatic at the fortune she just secured, 'Āʾishah 🌸 laughed so hard that her head fell from his lap. The Prophet 🌸 then added, 'Did my supplication make you happy?' She said, 'How could your supplication not make me happy?' He said, 'By Allah, this is my supplication for my nation in every single prayer.'[42]

4. His Clemency and Forgiveness

When the Prophet Muhammad 🌸 began to call to Islam openly, his initial followers discovered that merely professing faith meant facing ruthless torture and even execution. Some were beaten to near death in the streets, and others were dragged out to the desert to scream for hours under the inferno of its midday sun. Hefty, sizzling hot stones were situated atop their chests to crush them, scorching suits of chainmail armor were fastened to roast their bodies, and some like Khabbāb ibn al-Aratt 🌸 were hurled directly upon ignited coals which caused them to smell their own flesh cooking.[43] Many of these atrocities only escalated as this tragic decade progressed, and the Prophet 🌸 himself suffered brutal abuse from the idolaters of Quraysh. They spared no opportunity to demonize him, they divorced his daughters and they starved his entire clan for three years, which led to the death of his wife and his most supportive uncle.

In terms of physical assault, 'Uqbah ibn Abī Muʿayṭ would strangle him from behind when he prayed in public, Abū Jahl ordered bloody camel intestines to be dumped over him while he prostrated, 'Utaybah ibn Abī Lahab spat at him, and others beat

[42] Muḥammad ibn Ḥibbān, *Ṣaḥīḥ Ibn Ḥibbān* (Beirut: Muʾassasat al-Risālah, 1993), 16:47 #7111.
[43] Abū Nuʿaym, *Ḥilyat al-Awliyāʾ wa Ṭabaqāt al-Aṣfiyāʾ* (Egypt: Maṭbaʿat al-Saʿādah, 1974), 1:143.

him unconscious. These examples are a drop from the ocean of cruelty and persecution faced by the Prophet ﷺ and the earliest Muslims. And yet, this ocean was never able to drown the mercy, goodwill, and protective concern the Prophet's heart had for friends and foes alike. The following are a few brief depictions of his magnanimous character, even at the height of his power, in the face of enmity and insult.

Abū Jahl was one of his earliest and staunchest adversaries; the pharaoh of his nation. Despite all the physical and emotional wounds he inflicted on the Prophet ﷺ, and despite breaking his Companions' bones and later leading the first army against them, the guidance and salvation of Abū Jahl was still on the Prophet's mind. He used to say while still in Makkah, 'O Allah, strengthen Islam with Abū Jahl ibn Hishām or 'Umar ibn al-Khaṭṭāb.' A short time thereafter, 'Umar ibn al-Khaṭṭāb ؓ embraced Islam.[44] Abū Jahl being a heartless murderer did not prevent the Prophet ﷺ from praying for him, nor from appreciating his promising leadership qualities that could potentially be used for good.

Upon wielding the power of a statesman, the Prophet ﷺ never enacted a policy of vengeance or intolerance. Instead, he implemented a system of mercy that was in direct opposition to the cruelty he and his followers had been subjected to in Makkah. On one occasion, a group of Jews from Madinah entered upon the Prophet ﷺ and mockingly said, 'Al-sāmu 'alaykum (death be upon you),' in place of the customary Islamic greeting of 'Al-salāmu 'alaykum (peace be upon you).' His wife, 'Ā'ishah ؓ, appalled by their brazen disrespect, repeated the curse back to them, but the Prophet ﷺ said, 'O 'Ā'ishah, begentle! Allah is Gentle and loves gentleness in all matters, so beware of harshness and vulgarity.'[45] His authority in that phase still did not tempt him to retaliate, or respond in kind, or to even let his wife respond harshly to those who had insulted him.

---

44 al-Tirmidhī, *Sunan al-Tirmidhī*, 6:58 #3681.

45 al-Bukhārī, *Ṣaḥīḥ al-Bukhārī*, 8:85 #6401 and 9:16 #6927.

During the Battle of Uḥud, Quraysh's army—3,000 strong against the Muslims' 700—managed to ambush the Prophet ﷺ. His front tooth was broken, his body was battered, and blood flowed from where his helmet had pierced his face. Somehow, after bleeding at their hands yet again, the Messenger of Allah ﷺ still had the resilience of character to say as he wiped the blood from his face, 'O Allah, forgive my people, for they do not know.'[46] In other narrations, he first said, 'How can a people succeed after they have wounded their Prophet and caused him to bleed as he calls them to Allah?' Then, he fell silent for a moment, before appealing to Allah with the prayer for forgiveness. His Companions came to him and said as the dust cleared, 'Invoke a curse against the polytheists.' He said, 'I have not been sent as a curser. Rather, I was sent as a mercy.'[47] Though the Qur'an mentions that the wicked among the Israelites were cursed on the tongue of their prophets,[48] and though the Prophet ﷺ cursed certain practices like usury, and initially asked Allah to curse the leading persecutors, his normative demeanor was to seek forgiveness for those who wronged him and his followers.

Years later, as the Muslims traveled home from Dhāt al-Riqāʿ, the Prophet ﷺ and his Companions dismounted and sought shade from the midday sun. He rested under a leafy tree and hung his sword on it. The army slept for a while, but then heard the Messenger of Allah ﷺ calling for them. Jābir ibn ʿAbdillāh ؓ reports that upon their arrival, they found sitting with him a Bedouin man named al-Ghawrath ibn al-Ḥārith. The Messenger of Allah ﷺ said, 'This person drew my sword as I slept, and I awoke to find an unsheathed blade in his hand.' He said to me, "Are you afraid of me?" I said, "No." He said, "Who will protect you from me?" I said, "Allah," thrice, and so he returned the sword to its

46   Ibn Ḥibbān, Ṣaḥīḥ Ibn Ḥibbān, 3:254 #973.
47   Muslim, Ṣaḥīḥ Muslim, 3:1417 #1791.
48   See: (al-Māʾidah 5: 78)

scabbard. And thus, here he is, sitting.'[49] Jābir ﷺ added, 'And the Messenger of Allah ﷺ did not punish him thereafter.'[50]

In another narration, the sword fell from his hand, so the Prophet ﷺ took it and said, 'Who will protect you? … Be the better victor.' And, 'Will you still not testify that none is worthy of worship except Allah?' The Bedouin man said, 'I will promise to never fight you, nor be with a people that fight you.' The Prophet ﷺ let him go, and so the man returned to his tribe and said, 'I have come to you from the best of people.'[51] Just like that, the Prophet ﷺ forgave him unconditionally and released him despite the man's refusal to convert to Islam.

Hind bint ʿUtbah was the wife of Abū Sufyān and the daughter of ʿUtbah ibn Rabīʿah, two nobles from Quraysh who were both belligerent enemies of the Prophet Muhammad ﷺ. Hind was a woman who boiled with venomous hate against Muhammad ﷺ, and personally campaigned against Islam and the Muslims. She was among those who recruited Waḥshī to kill Ḥamzah ibn ʿAbdil-Muṭṭalib ﷺ, the paternal uncle of the Prophet ﷺ, promising him great rewards for avenging her father who was slain at Badr. Early chroniclers report that she had Ḥamzah's ears and nose cut off and used for a necklace, and some report that she gouged out his liver and attempted to eat it. When the Prophet ﷺ located his uncle's mutilated body after Uḥud, he was devastated as he bade farewell to his beloved uncle, saying, 'May Allah have mercy on you, my uncle. Indeed, you used to maintain the ties of kinship, and always rushed to do good.' ʿAbdullāh ibn Masʿūd ﷺ says, 'Never did we see the Messenger of Allah ﷺ weep as intensely as he wept for Ḥamzah.'[52]

---

49 Muslim, *Ṣaḥīḥ Muslim*, 4:2006 #2599.

50 al-Bukhārī, *Ṣaḥīḥ al-Bukhārī*, 4:39 #2910.

51 Aḥmad ibn Ḥanbal, *Musnad al-Imām Aḥmad ibn Ḥanbal* (Beirut: Mu'assasat al-Risālah, 2001), 23:369 #15190.

52 Ṣafī al-Raḥmān al-Mubārakfūrī, *Al-Raḥīq al-Makhtūm* (Cairo: Dār al-Wafā', 1987), 1:255.

Five years later, Hind stood at the Conquest of Makkah, chastising Quraysh for surrendering to the Muslims. But she soon realized that resisting was futile, and that the heavens really did seem to support Muhammad ﷺ, and so she went to him among a group of women and gave her pledge of allegiance as a Muslim. Upon learning who she was, the Prophet ﷺ kindly replied, 'Welcome, O Hind.' Touched by the unexpected magnanimity of the Messenger ﷺ, she proclaimed, 'By Allah, there was no household that I wished to destroy more than yours, but now there is no household that I wish to honour more than yours.'[53] As for Waḥshī, the Ethiopian slave-assassin who earned his freedom by killing Ḥamzah, he fled the city at the conquest of Makkah, certain that killing a ruler's family member warranted his death. However, the Prophet ﷺ was unlike any ruler. Waḥshī ؓ later said, 'I heard that no matter how grave a person's crime against him, the Prophet Muhammad ﷺ always chose forgiveness.' This encouraged him to eventually return to Makkah, embrace Islam, and experience firsthand the forgiveness of the Messenger of Allah ﷺ.[54] Waḥshī could hardly believe he lived long enough to redeem himself. He would often recall it and say, 'Allah honoured Ḥamzah ibn ʿAbd al-Muṭṭalib and al-Ṭufayl ibn al-Nuʿmān [with martyrdom] at my hands, and did not humiliate me [by being slain while a disbeliever] at their hands.'[55]

5. His Bravery and Valour

The consistent and matchless bravery of Muhammad ﷺ indicated that he was not only truthful, but certain of his truthfulness, which serves as yet another endorsement of his prophethood. The Prophet ﷺ never fled in battle. Rather, he at times fought fearlessly on the front lines. It would have been perfectly

---

53 al-Bukhārī, *Ṣaḥīḥ al-Bukhārī*, 9:66 #7161.
54 al-Bukhārī, *Ṣaḥīḥ al-Bukhārī*, 5:100 #4072.
55 Muḥammad ibn Sa'd, *Al-Ṭabaqāt al-Kubrā* (Beirut: Dār Ṣādir, 1968), 3:573.

understandable for the Prophet ﷺ to shield himself behind the army, for his early death would have meant the end of the message. Yet, 'Alī ibn Abī Ṭālib ﷺ, the celebrated warrior, would say, 'I myself witnessed on the Day of Badr how we used to stay close to the Prophet for cover, and he was the closest of us to the enemy, and he was the fiercest warrior on that day.'[56]

A man once said to al-Barā' ibn 'Āzib ﷺ:

'Did you flee on the Day of Ḥunayn, O Abū 'Umārah?' He replied, 'I can testify that the Prophet of Allah ﷺ did not retreat. There were some hasty young men who met—without adequate arms—a group from Hawāzin and Banū al-Naḍīr. They happened to be excellent archers, and they shot at them a volley of arrows that exposed their ranks. The people turned [for help] to the Messenger of Allah ﷺ, whose mule was being led by Abū Sufyān ibn al-Ḥārith. He dismounted, prayed, and invoked God's help. What he said was, "I am the Prophet; this is no untruth! I am the son of 'Abd al-Muṭṭalib! O Allah, send Your help!" By Allah, when the battle grew fierce, we would seek protection behind him, and only the bravest among us could stand by his side in battle.'[57]

When Allah revealed, *'O Messenger, convey that which has been revealed to you … and Allah will protect you from the people,'*[58] the Prophet ﷺ forbade his Companions from continuing to stand guard at night by his door.[59] One night, the Muslims—who remained anxious that the Romans would attack Madinah at any time—awoke startled by a loud crash. Rushing to the scene, they found the Prophet ﷺ already returning bareback on a horse belonging to Abū Ṭalḥah ﷺ, his sword hanging around his neck, reassuring

56 Ibn Ḥanbal, *Musnad Aḥmad*, 2:81 #653; authenticated by al-Arnā'ūṭ in the comments.

57 al-Bukhārī, *Ṣaḥīḥ al-Bukhārī*, 4:30 #2864; Muslim, *Ṣaḥīḥ Muslim*, 3:1401 #1776b.

58 (*al-Mā'idah* 5: 67)

59 al-Tirmidhī, *Sunan al-Tirmidhī*, 5:101 #3046.

them that it was a false alarm.[60] It takes exemplary courage, to race out alone to face potential danger like that, courage that even the bravest souls would admire.

6. His Generosity

Everyone who interacted with Muhammad ﷺ recognized him as the most generous of people, and it was well known that he never consumed any of the charity he collected. He would even share the wealth he acquired with his enemies to help them overcome their prejudices.

Zayd ibn Suʿnah ؓ was one of the leading rabbis of Madinah. Shortly before deciding to become Muslim, Zayd thought of testing the Prophet ﷺ by lending him eighty mithqāl (350 grams of gold) for a fixed period. A few days before repayment was due, Zayd grabbed the Messenger of Allah ﷺ angrily by his cloak, in front of all the senior Companions, and said:

> 'O Muhammad, why are you not paying what is due? By Allah, I know your family well! You are all known for deferring your debts!' The Prophet ﷺ said to the infuriated ʿUmar ؓ who threatened to kill Zayd for his insolence, 'O ʿUmar, we do not need this ... Go with him, pay off his loan, and give him twenty additional ṣāʿ (32 kilograms) of dates because you frightened him.' It was that response that convinced Zayd ibn Suʿnah to embrace Islam. He explained to ʿUmar, 'There was not a single sign of prophethood except that I recognized it upon looking at Muhammad's face—except for two that I had not yet seen from him: that his tolerance overcomes his anger, and that intense abuse only increases him in forbearance. I have now verified these, so know, O ʿUmar, that I accept Allah as my Lord, Islam as my

60 al-Bukhārī, *Ṣaḥīḥ al-Bukhārī*, 4:66 #3040.

> religion, Muhammad as my Prophet, and that half my wealth—for I have much wealth—is a donation for the nation of Muhammad ﷺ.'[61]

On another occasion, Anas ؓ reports, 'I was walking with the Messenger of Allah ﷺ, and he was wearing a Najrāni cloak with a rough collar. A Bedouin man caught up with him, then violently pulled him by his cloak, causing the cloak to tear, and leaving its collar hanging on the neck of Allah's Messenger ﷺ. I looked at the Messenger of Allah's neck, and the cloak's collar had left marks from how roughly he had snatched it. Then, he said, "O Muhammad, instruct them to give me from Allah's wealth that you hold!" The Messenger of Allah ﷺ turned to him, smiled, and then ordered that he be given something.'[62]

ʿUqbah ibn al-Ḥārith ؓ reports that he once offered the afternoon prayer with the Prophet ﷺ, after which he quickly stood and entered his apartment. Then, he reemerged and noticed some wonderment on people's faces due to his haste. To clarify, he said, 'I remembered while I was praying that we had some gold remaining, and I disliked that our evening pass while we still have it, so I instructed that it be distributed.'[63]

In a similar incident, ʿĀ'ishah ؓ narrates that the Messenger of Allah ﷺ had entrusted her with seven or nine gold coins around the time of his final illness. She says that despite the severe agony he was experiencing, he kept asking her to confirm that it had been given away in charity, and each time she would explain that she could not due to being preoccupied with caring for him. Finally, he insisted, 'Give it to me,' and upon receiving the gold in his hands, he said, 'What should Muhammad expect if he were to dare meet Allah while still holding onto these?'[64]

61 Ibn Ḥibbān, *Ṣaḥīḥ Ibn Ḥibbān*, 1:521 #288.
62 al-Bukhārī, *Ṣaḥīḥ al-Bukhārī*, 8:24 #6088.
63 al-Bukhārī, *Ṣaḥīḥ al-Bukhārī*, 2:67 #1221.
64 Ibn Ḥibbān, *Ṣaḥīḥ Ibn Ḥibbān*, 2:491 #715.

7. His Perseverance and Trust in God

The Prophet Muhammad ﷺ showed exemplary endurance and consistency throughout his life. Consider a man who never knew his father, lost his mother at a young age, then lost his grandfather, and then his uncle and wife simultaneously. Consider a man who lived to witness five of his six children die, and who was treated like a menace and fugitive after decades of building a flawless reputation among his people. Consider a man who experienced physical abuse until he would faint, was starved for years by his own people, and faced countless campaigns of character assassination. Consider a man who was driven out of his home, sent fleeing to Madinah for shelter, only to find hypocrites there awaiting every opportunity to betray him. Consider a man watching assassination attempts against his life unfold regularly, as well as the murder and mutilation of his relatives and Companions, and then the slander of his cherished wife, 'Ā'ishah ﵂, the daughter of his most loyal comrade. Somehow, he still persevered with hope and persisted in matchless ethics.

The Prophet ﷺ rose from that abyss of negativity and not only survived but became a fountain of mercy and empathy for people, animals, and plants alike. Should we not consider this miraculous? Does it not suggest that he must have been granted unique aid from the heavens? Only God brings the dead out of the living, and produces a spring from a rock, and nourishes a rose in the desert. Only God could have kept him smiling throughout, playing with his grandchildren, maintaining his principles, and lifting the spirits of those who had suffered so much less than him. Only God could have empowered him to have compassion for the heartless, forgiveness for his enemies, and concern for the arrogant. Only God could have kept his heart grateful at times when others could not even be patient, and his heart merciful at times when others could not even be just.

Though the incidents reflecting his perseverance are innumerable, it suffices the honest person to simply familiarize himself with the boycott in the ravine of Abū Ṭālib. For an utterly brutal three years, the Prophet ﷺ watched the lips of his Companions turn green from eating leaves and gnawing at animal hides, out of desperation for any nourishment. In fact, he watched his dearest family members slowly deteriorate in front of his eyes. Khadījah ؓ and Abū Ṭālib were so debilitated by the embargo that they never recovered from it; they both died soon thereafter. And with the protection of Abū Ṭālib gone, the Prophet ﷺ received in that year the most humiliating treatment of his life.

ʿĀ'ishah ؓ reported that she once asked the Prophet ﷺ, 'Have you ever encountered a more difficult day than the Battle of Uḥud?' The Prophet ﷺ said:

> Your tribe [Quraysh] has troubled me a great deal, but nothing was worse than the day of ʿAqabah when I presented myself to [the chief of Ta'if] ʿAbd Yālayl ibn ʿAbd Kulāl, and he did not respond as I had hoped. I eventually departed, overwhelmed with grief, and did not return to my senses until I found myself at a tree where I lifted my head towards the sky to see a cloud shading me. I looked up and saw Gabriel. He called out to me, saying, 'Allah has heard your people's statements to you and how they have replied, and Allah has sent the Angel of the Mountains so that you may order him to do whatever you wish to these people.' The Angel of the Mountains greeted me and said, 'O Muhammad, order what you wish, and if you like, I will let the two mountains fall upon them.' I said, 'No, rather I hope that Allah will bring from their descendants people who will worship Allah alone without associating partners with Him.'[65]

In other reports, he spent ten days in Ta'if after speaking to its leadership and calling its people to Islam, before the mobs

---

65 al-Bukhārī, *Ṣaḥīḥ al-Bukhārī,* 4:115 #3231; Muslim, *Ṣaḥīḥ Muslim,* 3:1420 #1795.

gathered to drive him out. They then made two rows and forced him to walk through them, while they hurled obscenities and pelted stones until blood ran down his blessed legs. The head of Zayd ibn Ḥārithah ﷺ, his adopted son, was also gashed in that assault as he attempted to shield him.[66] But even in that darkest hour, all this compounded anguish still did not break the Prophet's perseverance.

It is equally remarkable how the Prophet Muhammad ﷺ never lost hope in the support and victory of Allah, regardless of how hopeless his situation would sometimes appear.[67] This optimism tells of a heart filled with supreme faith. Upon leaving Makkah for the migration, the Prophet ﷺ and Abū Bakr al-Ṣiddīq ﷺ were tracked to a cave. Mercenaries stood at the mouth of the cave, and simply had to bend over to look inside, and nothing would have prevented them from noticing and capturing the Prophet ﷺ. In that unnerving moment, when despair would penetrate even the firmest of souls, the Prophet ﷺ calmly said to his Companion, 'O Abū Bakr, what do you think of two when Allah is their third?'[68] The Qur'an later referenced this incident by saying,

> *If you do not aid the Prophet, Allah has already aided him when those who disbelieved had driven him out [of Makkah] as one of*

---

66 Ibn Sa'd, *Al-Ṭabaqāt al-Kubrā*, 1: 212

67 A narration exists from al-Zuhrī about the Prophet ﷺ experiencing suicidal ideation when the Revelation paused for a short period. This report has a *muʿallaq* (incomplete) chain of transmission, as Hadith specialists such as Shuʿayb al-Arnā'ūṭ showed in his critique on *Musnad Aḥmad* (43:114). Even if it were traceable, it simply portrays the suffering, turmoil, and sadness that he endured. After all, he never surrendered to these passing thoughts but instead quieted them. Therefore, this incident proves—if anything—that his optimism overrode his pains, and that nothing about his life and humanness was ever hidden. Ultimately, this hiatus in revelation served to increase Muhammad's longing for the angelic visits, and to ensure he would never take these Divine communications for granted.

68 al-Bukhārī, *Ṣaḥīḥ al-Bukhārī*, 5:4 #3653; Muslim, *Ṣaḥīḥ Muslim*, 4:1854 #2381.

> *two, when they were in the cave and he said to his Companion, 'Do not grieve; indeed, Allah is with us.' And Allah sent down His tranquillity upon him and supported him with angels you did not see and made the word of those who disbelieved the lowest, while the word of Allah that is the highest. And Allah is Exalted in Might and Wise.*[69]

A skeptic may wonder how we know that Muhammad ﷺ did not fabricate this verse after the event, to portray a false image of his unwavering conviction in God? Such a suspicion not only ignores the established trustworthiness of Muhammad ﷺ, but also overlooks that Abū Bakr ؓ personally witnessed how calm and collected the Messenger of Allah ﷺ was in those terrifying moments and attested to it for years thereafter.

Thus was the conviction the Prophet Muhammad ﷺ had in his faith, whereby the promise of Allah that his heart saw overrode the hopelessness his eyes saw. This is identical to what occurred to Moses at the shore: *'And when the two companies [the Israelites and Pharaoh's legions] saw one another, the companions of Moses said, "Indeed, we are to be overtaken!" He [Moses] said, "No! Indeed, with me is my Lord; He will guide me."'*[70] This degree of certitude was unique to the Prophets and Messengers; even if the world lost hope, they would never unravel.

The preceding provides a glimpse of the incredible personality of the Prophet Muhammad ﷺ. His truly great moral character was evident to those centuries and seas apart from his lifetime. In the words of Stanley Lane-Pool (d. 1931), a British Orientalist,

69 (*al-Tawbah* 9: 40)
70 (*al-Shuʿarā'* 26: 61–62)

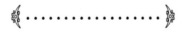

> He was the most faithful protector of those he protected, the sweetest and most agreeable in conversation. Those who saw him were suddenly filled with reverence; those who came near him loved him; they who described him would say, 'I have never seen his like either before or after.' He was of great taciturnity, but when he spoke it was with emphasis and deliberation, and no one could forget what he said.[71]

While the Prophet Muhammad ﷺ is the single most followed individual in human history (see Chapter 3), his greatest followers were undoubtedly his Companions, and this is what distinguishes their testimony for his character and the truth of his message. When evaluating the integrity of Muhammad's character, one must not overlook how profoundly admired and emulated he was by his Companions, even in the most private and nuanced particularities of his demeanor. William Montgomery Watt (d. 2006), a Scottish historian and Emeritus Professor in Arabic and Islamic Studies, wrote,

> His readiness to undergo persecution for his beliefs, the high moral character of the men who believed in him and looked up to him as a leader, and the greatness of his ultimate achievement—all argue his fundamental integrity. To suppose Muhammad an imposter raises more problems than it solves. Moreover, none of the great figures of history is so poorly appreciated in the West as Muhammad ... Thus, not merely must we credit Muhammad with essential honesty and integrity of purpose, if we are to understand him at all; if we are to correct the errors we have inherited from the past, we must in every particular case hold firmly to the belief in his

---

71 Stanley Lane-Poole, *The Speeches and Table-Talk of the Prophet Mohammad* (Macmillan & Co: London, 1882), xxix.

> sincerity until the opposite is conclusively proved; and we must not forget that conclusive proof is a much stricter requirement than a show of plausibility, and in a matter such as this only to be attained with difficulty.[72]

These Companions outdid one another in emulating his smile, his selflessness, his standing for truth, and his service of humanity. They were captivated for a lifetime by his loyalty, his clarity of thought, his balanced opinions, his gentleness in teaching, his determination, and his charismatic speech. In one of dozens of riveting narrations that have been reported from his first wave of followers, ʿAlī ibn Abī Ṭālib ﵁ says,

> When he looked at someone, he looked them in the eyes. He was the most generous-hearted of men, the most truthful of them in speech, the mildest-tempered of them and the noblest of them in lineage. Anyone who would describe him would say I never saw before or after him the like of him.[73]

These Companions were not merely good people who prayed at night and devoted their lives to God. The genius of just ʿUmar ibn al-Khaṭṭāb ﵁, for instance, has been recognized by many historians. The Columbia History of the World asserts how ʿUmar effected a superior bureaucracy than that of the juggernaut Roman Empire that preceded Muslim rule.[74] When a tribal Arab can construct a federal government with centralized power, but also the flexibility to make the peripheries of this union sustainable—and through that change the course of history—one should concede that this was at least an exceptional mind.

---

72 William Montgomery Watt, *Muhammad at Mecca* (Oxford: Clarendon Press, 1953), 52.

73 al-Tirmidhī, *Sunan al-Tirmidhī*, 6:35 #3638.

74 John A. Garraty, Peter Gay, et al., *The Columbia History of the World* (New York: Harper & Row, 1972), 264.

This is but one person who believed in the prophethood of Muhammad ﷺ, one who mimicked him with a deep admiration. Abū Bakr al-Ṣiddīq ؓ giving half his wealth for the sake of Islam, Bilāl ibn Rabāḥ ؓ refusing to recant his beliefs despite unthinkable torture, and Sumayyah bint Khayyāṭ ؓ being executed for refusing to pretend she did not believe in Muhammad ﷺ, are not trivial events. As for those who survived, they undertook the momentous task of incorporating his spirit and message into their lives, making them fully deserving of God's praise in the Qur'an: *'You are the best nation produced [as an example] for mankind. You enjoin what is right and forbid what is wrong and believe in Allah.'*[75] Being followed so ardently by this calibre of people, who experienced him before and after prophethood, and witnessed his daily behavior for decades, is a clear gauge as to how certain they were in him and his mission.

---

[75] (*Āl ʿImrān* 3: 110)

3

The Prophet's Accomplishments

Building on the *'you will know them by their fruits'* principle from the previous chapter, Muhammad's positive impact on the world was another blessed fruit harvested from his ministry. In addition to his personal actions and impeccable character, a further proof of his prophethood is found in the answer to this question: what exactly did this man accomplish? Do his achievements represent extraordinary talent and virtue, or mere hyperbolic attributions by his followers? Ibn Ḥazm (d. 1064), the Córdoban polymath, after illustrating how Muhammad ﷺ transformed the world around him in a historically unparalleled way, writes: 'The biography of Muhammad, for anyone who deeply considers it, necessitates believing him and testifying that he is certainly the Messenger of Allah. If he had no other miracle but his biography, it would have sufficed.'[1]

The Prophet Muhammad ﷺ was not just extraordinary in terms of his political reach on the world stage, but he was also a demonstrably greater influence on religiosity and spirituality than any

1 'Alī ibn Aḥmad ibn Ḥazm, *Al-Faṣl fil-Milal wal-Ahwā' wal-Niḥal* (Cairo: Maktabat al-Khānji, 1929), 2:73.

other founder of the major faiths, and on social wellbeing at large. He was unique in human history for having excelled in numerous roles simultaneously: a spiritual leader, a head of state, a general, a diplomat, a family man, and an educator. Jesus Christ was a tremendous spiritual figure, but not a general or head of state. Alexander the Great and many other iconic political leaders were not heralded for their moral virtue or spiritual motivation. On the contrary, many great kings, rulers, and emperors were ruthless, arrogant, or otherwise intoxicated by power and delusions of grandeur.

There was something different about Muhammad ﷺ—something that leaves those who discover it awestruck. It was the fact that no single aspect established his legacy, but instead a myriad of outstanding feats that converged in one person. This is what fascinated and bewildered so many over the past millennium and a half, leaving them wondering: Could such a person have existed outside of legends? Is there any other plausible explanation for this? Perhaps he really was sent by God?

John William Draper (d. 1882), an English-American historian, wrote:

> Four years after the death of Justinian, A.D. 569, was born at Mecca, in Arabia, the man who, of all men, has exercised the greatest influence upon the human race … To the declaration that there is but one God, he added, 'and Mohammed is his Prophet.' Whoever desires to know whether the event of things answered to the boldness of such an announcement, will do well to examine a map of the world in our own times. He will find the marks of something more than an imposture. To be the religious head of many empires, to guide the daily life of one-third of the human race, may perhaps justify the title of a messenger of God.[2]

---

2 John W. Draper, *A History of the Intellectual Development of Europe* (London: G. Bell and Sons, 1875), 329-330.

There is no leap of faith here. To say that that sheer luck is responsible for all these things being accomplished by any one individual can only be claimed by someone uninformed about reality or perverted by prejudice. Consider the enigma of a man who himself was illiterate, born in a backwards and feuding Arabia, isolated from the arts, philosophies, politics, warfare, and education of the surrounding empires. Consider that this very man steps forward—overnight—with a call whose profundity, impact, and permanence remain peerless. The speed at which his religion spread, the global command of his call until today, and the positive influence of this single individual were—and will remain—unparalleled in human history. Draper was certainly not the only non-Muslim historian in the West who recognized this. Samuel P. Scott (d. 1929), an American scholar and jurist, wrote:

> In any event, if the object of religion be the inculcation of morals, the diminution of evil, the promotion of human happiness, the expansion of the human intellect; if the performance of good works will avail in that great day when mankind shall be summoned to its final reckoning, it is neither irreverent nor unreasonable to admit that Mohammed was indeed an Apostle of God.[3]

As Alphonse de Lamartine (d. 1869), a French historian, skillfully put it thus:

> If greatness of purpose, smallness of means, and astounding results are the three criteria of human genius, who could dare to compare any great man in modern history with Muhammad? The most famous men created arms, laws and empires only. They founded, if anything at all, no more than material powers which often

---

3 Samuel P. Scott, *History of the Moorish Empire in Europe* (Philadelphia & London: J.B. Lippincott Company, 1904), 1:126-127.

crumbled away before their eyes. This man moved not only armies, legislations, empires, peoples and dynasties, but millions of men in one-third of the then inhabited world; and more than that, he moved the altars, the gods, the religions, the ideas, the beliefs and souls. On the basis of a Book, every letter of which has become law, he created a spiritual nationality which has blended together peoples of every tongue and of every race. He has left to us as the indelible characteristic of this Muslim nationality, the hatred of false gods and the passion for the One and immaterial God. This avenging patriotism against the profanation of Heaven formed the virtue of the followers of Muhammad: the conquest of one third of the earth to his creed was his miracle. The idea of the unity of God proclaimed amidst the exhaustion of fabulous theogonies, was in itself such a miracle that upon its utterance from his lips it destroyed all the ancient temples of idols and set on fire one third of the world ...

His life, his meditations, his heroic stance against the superstitions of his country, and his boldness in defying the furies of idolatry; his firmness in enduring them for thirteen years at Mecca, his acceptance of the role of public scorn and almost of being a victim of his fellow-countrymen: all these and, finally his incessant preaching, his wars against odds, his faith in his success and his superhuman security in misfortune, the forbearance in victory, his ambition, which was entirely devoted to one idea and in no manner striving for an empire; his endless prayers, his mystic conversations with God, his death and his triumph after death; all these attest not to an imposture but to a firm conviction which gave him the power to restore a dogma. This dogma was twofold, the unity of God and the immateriality of God; the former telling what God is, the latter telling what God is not; the one overthrowing false gods with the sword, the other starting an idea with words. Philosopher, orator, apostle, legislator, warrior, conqueror of ideas, restorer of rational dogmas, of a cult without images, the founder of twenty terrestrial empires and of one spiritual empire; that is Muhammad. As regards all the standards by which human greatness may be measured, we may well ask: is there any man greater than he?[4]

1. A Love Larger than Life

Has anyone in human history ever been as deeply loved as the Prophet Muhammad ﷺ? Many underestimate, or perhaps are unfamiliar with, the esteem and emulation he has garnered for a second millennium now. Others may realize it, then hastily assume that equally impressive shares of adoration must have been achieved by somebody else in human history. But a more critical examination tells another story.

During his life, the Prophet's Companions longed to sacrifice life and limb to defend him. When he was struck unconscious during the Battle of Uḥud, for instance, his Companions displayed extraordinary heroism as they rushed to his rescue. Abū Dujānah ؓ welcomed volleys of arrows landing in his back as he hovered over the Prophet ﷺ. Anas ibn al-Naḍr ؓ dove into the crowds until over ninety wounds were found on his martyred body. Abū Ṭalḥah ؓ shielded the Prophet ﷺ from injury with his bare chest when he found nothing else, and pleaded with him, 'Do not look, O Messenger of Allah! Let it be my neck [struck] rather than yours!' Ṭalḥah ibn 'Ubaydillāh ؓ lifted the Prophet ﷺ onto a boulder, then returned to drive back the onslaught, then returned yet again to bring the Prophet ﷺ to even safer ground.

Nusaybah bint Ka'b ؓ was a fearless woman who snatched swords away from men and charged at many physically stronger

---

4 Alphonse de Lamartine, *Histoire De La Turquie* (Paris: Librarie du Constitutionnel, 1854) 1:277-280.

warriors at Uḥud, until she fell to a saber-strike on her collarbone which was the first of many scars of valour she sustained in her life before eventually dying a martyr. By the time the dust had finally cleared, their selfless displays of love for the Prophet ﷺ were immortalized. Upon returning to the city of Madinah, a woman from the Banū Dinār tribe was told that her husband, father, and brother were all killed at Uḥud. She responded, 'But what happened to the Messenger of Allah ﷺ?' They replied, 'He is safe and well, just as you wish him to be.' She said, 'Show him to me; I must see for myself.' When she finally saw him, she said, 'Every tragedy besides losing you is insignificant, O Messenger of Allah.'[5] This single day's events, not all captured here, are but a microcosm reflecting the ethos of love and endearment that surrounded the Final Prophet of God ﷺ for the duration of his twenty-three-year ministry.

A few years after Uḥud, 'Urwah ibn Mas'ūd came as an envoy of the then enemy tribe of Quraysh, seeking to negotiate a treaty with Muhammad ﷺ. After spending three days among the Muslims, he returned to Makkah and briefed Quraysh with these observations:

> O council of Quraysh, I have visited Chosroes in his kingdom, and Caesar in his kingdom, and the Negus in his kingdom. But by God, I have never seen a king so revered among a people like Muhammad. He does not wash himself except that they rush to catch the droplets of water [falling from his body], nor does one of his hairs fall except that they take it. Whenever he speaks, they immediately lower their voices, and none stares at him directly out of reverence for him. He has offered you good terms, so accept them, for I do not see them ever deserting him. Now make your decision.[6]

---

5 Muḥammad ibn 'Umar al-Wāqidī, *Kitāb al-Maghāzī* (Beirut: Dār al-A'lamī, 1989), 1:292.

6 al-Bukhārī, *Ṣaḥīḥ al-Bukhārī*, 3:193 #2731.

Even decades after the Prophet's death, we find a Companion like 'Amr ibn al-'Āṣ ﷺ laying on his own deathbed reminiscing about his life prior to Islam, recalling how he transformed from being a militant adversary of the Prophet ﷺ to one of his greatest followers. Amidst his recollections, he says,

> Then, no one was dearer to me than the Messenger of Allah ﷺ, and none was more exalted in my eyes than him. I could not even stare at him directly out of reverence for him, and thus if I am asked to describe his features, I would not be able to describe them, for I have never eyed him fully.[7]

The Companions who outlived the Prophet ﷺ burned with similar passion and longing; an entire generation who remained incapable of hearing his name without their hearts trembling, their eyes overflowing with tears, anticipating reuniting with him in the hereafter. Bilāl ibn Rabāḥ ﷺ was a freed Ethiopian slave who was among the first handful to accept Islam at the hands of the Prophet ﷺ, tolerating unthinkable torture for defying his masters and embracing the religion of Muhammad ﷺ. He would survive to become the very first caller to prayer (mu'addin) in Muslim history. Loving Muhammad ﷺ flowed in Bilāl's veins and surviving him brought him sorrow that only a reunion could heal. Nine years later, as Bilāl ﷺ lay on his own deathbed in Damascus, he heard his wife say, 'O my grief! O my Bilāl!' To that, he retorted, 'O my joy! Tomorrow I meet my loved ones: Muhammad and his Companions!'[8]

Countless thousands have since inherited this love of the Final Prophet ﷺ en route to becoming icons of truth, justice, and contribution in world history. Among these were vanguards who

---

7 Muslim, *Ṣaḥīḥ Muslim*, 1:112 #121.

8 'Alī ibn al-Ḥasan ibn 'Asākir, *Tārīkh Madīnat Dimashq* (Beirut: Dār al-Fikr, 1995), 10:475-476.

developed profound insight into sacred truths, performed tangible and intellectual wonders, and ascended to rare heights in the footsteps of their beloved, the unlettered Prophet ﷺ. Innumerable pious sages, meticulous scholars, literary geniuses, selfless altruists, accomplished statesmen, and virtuous generals believed emulating Muhammad ﷺ was the gateway to true excellence in all endeavours and indispensable for being a torchbearer for humanity. Even today, nearly a third of this planet continues to govern their lives—in one respect or another—in ways that reflect their veneration of Muhammad ﷺ. Muslims certainly do not worship Muhammad, only God, but see his persona as their earthly pivot of faith, and his example as the paragon of virtue and thereby their conduit to God's pleasure. Dr Jonathan Brown of Georgetown University writes:

> Throughout the Muslim world, it is customary to say: 'May the peace and blessings of God be upon him', after mentioning the Prophet. As a result, during the Friday communal prayer any mention of the Prophet's name by the preacher during the sermon will elicit a collective murmur of prayers for Muhammad from the congregation. In such settings, the person of the Prophet becomes the common focus of Muslims' ritual attention. Remembering Muhammad and honouring his Sunnah act as the earthly focal point from which attention is directed upward to God.[9]

Today, Muslims' adulation of the man who connected them with their Creator has made *Muhammad* the most popular baby name in London and other regions of the U.K. in 2019, where Muslims to date only account for a small minority of the population.[10]

---

9 Jonathan Brown, *Muhammad: A Very Short Introduction* (New York: Oxford University Press, 2011), 106.

10 Office for National Statistics, 'Baby Names in England and Wales: 2019,' *ons.gov.uk*.

If one combines all the variant spellings of the name, Muhammad is likely the most popular name in the entire world.[11] Generation after generation, his devout followers continue exploring his every word, rigorously pursuing everything traceable to him, and mimicking his lifestyle down to the motions of his fingers during prayer. How many figures in human history have won such adoration, an adoration that translated into actions, for fifteen centuries and counting?

David George Hogarth (d. 1927), a British scholar and archaeologist, said:

> Serious or trivial, his daily behavior has instituted a canon which millions observe this day with conscious mimicry. No one regarded by any section of the human race as Perfect Man has ever been imitated so minutely. The conduct of the founder of Christianity has not governed the ordinary life of his followers. Moreover, no founder of a religion has been left on so solitary an eminence as the Muslim Apostle.[12]

It is fascinating that Muhammad's name foretold this phenomenon before its occurrence. *Muhammad* literally means 'the oft-praised one', and no human being has ever received greater praise and recognition. Even without the exposure opportunities of social media, without an account on Twitter or Facebook or Instagram or Whatsapp, Muhammad ﷺ has amassed 1.8 billion followers in today's world. Does it not stir amazement to consider how, 1,400 years after he passed away, there is no second that passes except that he is praised all around the world? In the Muslim call to prayer (*adhān*) which takes place every second around the world, followed by the ritual prayer itself, supplicating for

11 Paul Lagasse and Columbia University, 'Muhammad, Prophet of Islam', *The Columbia Encyclopedia* (Columbia University Press, 8th edition, 2018) via *Credo Reference*.

12 David G. Hogarth, *Arabia* (Oxford: Clarendon Press, 1922), 52.

Muhammad ﷺ and testifying to his prophethood are echoed day and night. One should marvel at just how emotionally attached people remain to Muhammad ﷺ, and how they continue to express the most passionate defense of him when he is slighted.

In fact, God Himself foretold this by saying, ‘*And We have raised for you your repute.*’[13] This verse was revealed during the early Makkan years, at a time when the Muslims were a mere handful of weak people and it was unsure what would happen to Islam, making it even more incredible to think how the verse is fulfilled now, when Muhammad ﷺ is mentioned and remembered by hundreds of millions of people all over the world. Even non-Muslim scholars of Islam, such as the German orientalist Theodore Noldeke, acknowledge the early date of this chapter from the Qur'an. He considered it to be the twelfth of its 114 chapters, and the standard Egyptian chronology of the Qur'an lists it as the eleventh.[14]

2. History's Greatest Success Story

A momentary glance at just the Prophet's life and his worldly success has commanded attention from scholars worldwide, even among those who may not recognize the great substance and truth in his teachings. As Karen Armstrong, an acclaimed author on comparative religion, puts it:

> Islam is a religion of success. Unlike Christianity, which has as its main image, in the west at least, a man dying in a devastating, disgraceful, helpless death … Mohammed was not an apparent failure. He was a dazzling success, politically as well as in spirituality, and Islam went from strength to strength to strength.[15]

---

13 (*al-Sharh* 94: 4)

14 See: Carl Ernst, *How to Read the Qur'an: A New Guide, with Select Translations* (Edinburgh University Press, 2011), 39-41.

15 Karen Armstrong, 'Transcript - Bill Moyers Interviews Karen Armstrong', *Public Broadcasting Service (PBS)*, March 1, 2002.

Michael Hart, the contemporary American historian who authored *The 100: A Ranking of the Most Influential Persons in History*, succinctly illustrates this mind-boggling success story as follows:

> My choice of Muhammad to lead the list of the world's most influential persons may surprise some readers and may be questioned by others, but he was the only man in history who was supremely successful on both the religious and secular levels. Of humble origins, Muhammad founded and promulgated one of the world's great religions and became an immensely effective political leader. Today, thirteen centuries after his death, his influence is still powerful and pervasive. The majority of the persons in this book had the advantage of being born and raised in centers of civilization, highly cultured or politically pivotal nations. Muhammad, however, was born in the year 570, in the city of Mecca, in southern Arabia, at that time a backward area of the world, far from the centers of trade, art, and learning. Orphaned at age six, he was reared in modest surroundings. Islamic tradition tells us that he was illiterate. His economic position improved when, at age twenty-five, he married a wealthy widow. Nevertheless, as he approached forty, there was little outward indication that he was a remarkable person.
>
> Most Arabs at that time were pagans, who believed in many gods. There were, however, in Mecca, a small number of Jews and Christians; it was from them no doubt that Muhammad first learned of a single, omnipotent God who ruled the entire universe. When he was forty years old, Muhammad became convinced that this one true God (Allah) was speaking to him and had chosen him to spread the true faith. For three years, Muhammad preached only to close friends and associates. Then, about 613, he began preaching in public. As he slowly gained converts, the Meccan authorities came to consider him a dangerous nuisance. In 622, fearing

> for his safety, Muhammad fled to Medina (a city some 200 miles north of Mecca), where he had been offered a position of considerable political power … When Muhammad died, in 632, he was the effective ruler of all of southern Arabia. The Bedouin tribesmen of Arabia had a reputation as fierce warriors. But their number was small; and plagued by disunity and internecine warfare, they had been no match for the larger armies of the kingdoms in the settled agricultural areas to the north. However, unified by Muhammad for the first time in history, and inspired by their fervent belief in the one true God, these small Arab armies now embarked upon one of the most astonishing series of conquests in human history.[16]

Therefore, it was also the swiftness of Islam's expansion which beckoned the wonderment of many Western historians, and Muslims who cite it as a miraculous proof for the truth of Islam's claims. And as Lamartine said earlier, it was not just the astonishing series of conquests and their striking rapidity that made Muhammad ﷺ unique, but also the meager means through which he accomplished this, the selfless relinquishing of any material gains and the retention of his transcendent purpose despite all these accomplishments, that marked his greatness. Bosworth Smith (d. 1908), a reverend schoolmaster and author, writes:

> Head of the State as well as the Church; he was Caesar and Pope in one; but he was Pope without the Pope's pretensions, and Caesar without the legions of Caesar. Without a standing army, without a bodyguard, without a palace, without a fixed revenue, if ever any man had the right to say he ruled by a right Divine, it was Mohammed;

---

16 Michael H. Hart, *The 100: A Ranking of the Most Influential Persons in History* (New York: Citadel Press/Kensington Pub, 2001), 3-10.

> for he had all the power without its instruments and without its supports.[17]

Continuning, 'By a fortune absolutely unique in history, Mohammed is a threefold founder of a nation, of an empire, and of a religion.'[18]

Many have echoed Smith's fascination with Muhammad's unique rise to power, and his enduring influence wherever his message went, irrespective of whether it had political support there. Edward Gibbon, whose writings are not void of hostility towards Muhammad ﷺ, could not help but document his admiration of Islam's resilience on the world stage. He writes:

> It is not the propagation but the permanency of his religion that deserves our wonder, the same pure and perfect impression which he engraved at Mecca and Medina is preserved after the revolutions of twelve centuries by the Indian, the African and the Turkish proselytes of the Koran.[19]

After the renowned Mahatma Gandhi (d. 1948) found himself in prison with the Prophet's biography, he was able to identify the secret behind the Prophet ﷺ overcoming insurmountable odds and reaching such stations of global success. It was the combination of political control and not allowing that political power to control him. Muslims believe that only God could have fused these two phenomena inside one man, and that He reinforced his claim to prophethood with these material and moral triumphs. In Gandhi's words:

> I wanted to know the best of the life of one who holds today an undisputed sway over the hearts of millions of

17 Bosworth Smith, *Mohammed and Mohammedanism: Lectures*, 235.

18 Ibid., 237.

19 Edward Gibbon, *The Rise and Fall of the Saracen Empire* (London, 1870), 54.

> mankind … I became more than ever convinced that it was not the sword that won a place for Islam in those days in the scheme of life. It was the rigid simplicity, the utter self-effacement of the Prophet, the scrupulous regard for pledges, his intense devotion to his friends and followers, his intrepidity, his fearlessness, his absolute trust in God and in his own mission. These and not the sword carried everything before them and surmounted every obstacle.[20]

3. Restoring the Unity of God

The Final Prophet ﷺ accomplished the rare feat of providing the world with impeccable clarity on the identity of God, His oneness, and His perfection. It was a clarity that aligned with both human nature and rationality, and thus became the hallmark of Islam. He taught a simple and intuitive theology that described to people their Creator, and the path to Him, in a way that spread like wildfire across the globe.

Islamic monotheism became the religion of Arabia in just twenty years of preaching, in stark contrast to the Roman Empire needing about three centuries to create a Christian majority. This attests to Muhammad ﷺ coming with a unique proposal, one that struck such a deep chord in humanity that it effectively stripped them of some of their most hindering tendencies—such as the blind conformity that cultures at times perpetuate, and the idolization of ancestors that has occurred in so many civilizations. Muhammad ﷺ unearthed for a vulnerable world their long-lost sanctuary; direct access to the One True God, the Most Merciful. He refused to rest until they knew that only through singling God out in devotion would they find contentment and satisfaction, and that only through Him would their moral compasses be set aright. For those who understand that only disorder

---

20 Mahatma Gandhi, *The Collected Works of Mahatma Gandhi* (New Delhi, India: Publications Division, Ministry of Information and Broadcasting, Government of India, 1960-1994), 29:133.

can exist outside an authentic God-centric lifestyle, this is the singular accomplishment of Muhammad ﷺ.

Restoring the unity of God in people's lives resulted in restoring order and meaning to life, as it did away with the notion of life being a destination-less journey. For those who struggle to see the utility of an authentic theology in our age, perhaps they should consider the emerging fascination with 'spiritual intelligence' in the turmoil-filled modern world, along with the significantly lower homicide and suicide rates in Muslim countries.[21]

Alphonse de Lamartine says on this point:

> Never has a man proposed for himself, voluntarily or involuntarily, a goal more sublime, since this goal was beyond measure: undermine the superstitions placed between the creature and the Creator, give back God to man and man to God, reinstate the rational and saintly idea of divinity in the midst of this prevailing chaos of material and disfigured gods of idolatry ... Never has a man accomplished in such short time such an immense and long-lasting revolution in the world, since less than two centuries after his prediction, Islam, preaching and armed, ruled over three Arabias and conquered to God's unity Persia, the Khorasan of Transoxania, Western India, Syria, Egypt, Abyssinia, and all the known continent of Northern Africa, many islands of the Mediterranean, Spain, and part of Gaul.[22]

Edward Gibbon adds:

> The Mahometans have uniformly withstood the temptation of reducing the object of their faith and devotion to a level with the senses and imagination of man. 'I believe

---

21 Don Soo Chon, "National Religious Affiliation and Integrated Model of Homicide and Suicide," *Homicide Studies* 21, no. 1 (February 2016); David Lester, "Suicide and Islam," *Arch Suicide Res.* 10, no. 1 (2006).

22 Alphonse de Lamartine, *Histoire De La Turquie*, 1:276-277.

> in One God and Mahomet the Apostle of God', is the simple and invariable profession of Islam. The intellectual image of the Deity has never been degraded by any visible idol; the honours of the prophet have never transgressed the measure of human virtue, and his living precepts have restrained the gratitude of his disciples within the bounds of reason and religion.[23]

This purest conceptualization of monotheism was inculcated by the Prophet Muhammad ﷺ: a purely personal relationship with God, one void of any intermediary or human interference. This strict monotheism placed all men and women on equal footing before God and with equal access to God. This helped shape the egalitarian nature of Islam, providing a social narrative in which the holiness of men was not evidenced by their material possessions or social class, but rather by their acts of piety and righteousness.

Furthermore, the theology he introduced corrected competing theologies about God, resulting in one coherent monotheistic worldview (see Chapter 4). This was the explanatory power of Islam which gave it immense appeal: its compelling ability to satisfy existential questions about God and creation. As for its spiritual appeal, that too was a driving force behind its continued imprint on the minds and hearts of people. After all, the greatest miracle of Muhammad ﷺ was the Qur'an which stands as God's verbatim address to humanity, available to all who choose to study it until the end of time.

4. Revolutionizing Human Rights

After rectifying their relationship with their Maker, mending people's relationships with one another was the natural next step. This accomplishment of the Final Prophet ﷺ was not merely

---

23 Edward Gibbon, *The Rise and Fall of the Saracen Empire*, 54.

one of advocating for virtues such as kindness, empathy, and humility in people's interpersonal exchanges, but one that also involved establishing a pragmatic system to ensure that these abstract concepts would unfold on the ground. He fraternized with all people, despite their differences, and purged their prejudices. He famously said in his Farewell Sermon:

> O people, your Lord is One and your father Adam is one. There is no distinction for an Arab over a foreigner, nor a foreigner over an Arab, and neither white skin over black skin, nor black skin over white skin, except by righteousness. Have I not delivered the message?[24]

Islam affirmed a universal human brotherhood, a brotherhood that recognized the dignity of every human being and demanded an end to every form of bigotry based on race, colour, or class. What is more, the universal brotherhood that Islam established was based on cooperation between people for the betterment of society as a whole. Humanity has suffered countless injustices due to discrimination based on lineage (ethnic patriotism), financial standing (socioeconomic elitism), or skin colour (racial supremacy). Historically, these distinctions led to more than just bitter arguments, but also endless hatred, conflict, and generations of carnage. Islam came to a people who were knee-deep in feudal tribalism and bigotry, and within two decades transformed that society into a model of social harmony in which people were liberated from the shackles of discrimination, and 'superiority' was based only on piety—which only God could judge, and all could compete for. Arnold Toynbee (d. 1975), a professor of international history at the University of London, writes in *Civilization on Trial*: 'The extinction

---

24 Ibn Ḥanbal, *Musnad Aḥmad*, 38:474 #23489; authenticated by al-Arnā'ūṭ in the comments.

> of race consciousness as between Muslims is one of the outstanding moral achievements of Islam, and in the contemporary world there is, as it happens, a crying need for the propagation of this Islamic virtue.'[25]

What the Prophet ﷺ did was more brilliant than simply eliminating bigotry and racism; he went beyond that to argue that racial and linguistic diversity should be appreciated and embraced. Allah says in the Qur'an, *'And of His signs is the creation of the heavens and the earth and the diversity of your languages and your colours. Indeed, in that are signs for those of knowledge.'*[26] The late Malik Shabazz, better known as Malcolm X, recognized this in his famous 1964 *Letter from Mecca*, in which he wrote:

> America needs to understand Islam, because this is the one religion that erases from its society the race problem. Throughout my travels in the Muslim world, I have met, talked to, and even eaten with people who in America would have been considered white—but the white attitude was removed from their minds by the religion of Islam. I have never before seen sincere and true brotherhood practiced by all colors together, irrespective of their color.[27]

It was not just racism that the Prophet ﷺ eradicated but classism as well. In an era when universal human rights norms are often applied with a double standard and weaponized for political and economic gain, there is no time like the present to appreciate the actual moral accomplishments of Muhammad ﷺ. Unlike political elites today who often settle for citing human rights verbiage, we

---

25 Arnold Toynbee, *Civilization on Trial* (New York: Oxford University Press, 1948), 205.

26 (*al-Rūm* 30: 22)

27 Malcolm X and Alex Haley, *The Autobiography of Malcolm X* (New York: Ballantine, 1992), 370.

find the Prophet Muhammad ﷺ operating at the height of his power with the universal dignity of every human being in mind. There was a pristine equity in his call, one that even validated the wealth of the wealthy and the power of the powerful, if this wealth was not the fruit of exploitation or hoarding, and if this power did not translate into domination or authoritarianism. He uplifted the downtrodden and humbled the affluent, joining them at a beautiful middle called brotherhood.

For generations after the Final Prophet ﷺ returned to God, you could find a civilization infused with justice and security for the rich, poor, Muslim, and non-Muslim alike—a lived example of what many human rights advocates aspire to today. With dictates like, 'Pay the worker his due wages before his sweat dries,'[28] the Prophet ﷺ eradicated many widely condoned financial inequities of his time. The Prophet's economic justice played an important role in improving the general standard of living in the early centuries of Islam, as prosperity is seldom reflected in the general population when financial corruption exists. We find in the *Journal of Economic History*,

> In the aftermath of the Justinian Plague, during the early centuries of Islam, real wages and per capita incomes in Iraq and Egypt rose well above the subsistence level and well above those for Roman and Byzantine Egypt in the centuries preceding the plague. This environment of high wages and high incomes contributed to and, in turn, was supported by the productivity increases associated with the Golden Age of Islam. As population levels began to recover first in Iraq and then in Egypt, real wages and per capita incomes began to come down. However, because of the period of intensive growth from

---

28 Muḥammad ibn Mājah, *Sunan Ibn Mājah* (Beirut: Dār Iḥyā' al-Turāth al-ʿArabī, 1975), 2:718 #2443; authenticated by al-Albānī in the comments.

> the eighth through the tenth centuries, productivity, incomes, and standards of living remained significantly above subsistence for long periods of time.[29]

Abū Dharr ﵁, a leading Companion of the Prophet ﷺ, could not be differentiated from his laborers as they wore identical clothing. When asked about this, he explained that the Prophet ﷺ had said:

> Your servants are your brothers whom Allah has placed under your authority. Whoever's brother is under his authority should feed him with the same food he eats, clothe him with the same clothes he wears, and not burden him beyond his ability. And if you commission them with a task, then assist him.[30]

Biographers report that another leading Companion, Abū al-Dardā' ﵁, would even say to his riding mount as it died, 'O camel, do not prosecute me before your Lord, for I never made you carry more than you could bear!' 'Urwah ibn Muhammad ﵀, the grandson of another great Companion, declared upon assuming the governorship of Yemen, 'O Yemenites! This here is my camel. If I exit your lands with anything more than it, then I am a thief.'[31]

It is well beyond the scope of this chapter to list the various human rights the Prophet Muhammad ﷺ established and the atrocious conditions he uprooted during his lifetime. Securing dignity and respect for women, and justice for non-Muslims, not to mention rights for even animals and the environment, are each a genre of unique accomplishments, many times even when contrasted with today's standards.

---

29 Şevket Pamuk and Maya Shatzmiller. 'Plagues, Wages, and Economic Change in the Islamic Middle East, 700–1500', *The Journal of Economic History* 74, no. 1 (2014): 196–229.

30 al-Bukhārī, *Ṣaḥīḥ al-Bukhārī*, 1:15 #30.

31 Ibn 'Asākir, *Tārīkh Madīnat Dimashq*, 40:290.

5. Molding a Model Generation

Over the span of just twenty-three years, the Prophet ﷺ successfully nurtured an exemplary generation whose likes humanity had never seen and will never again see. This was a conglomerate of tribes in a remote region of the world surrounded by perilous deserts, largely isolated from the ideas and events of the major civilizations of their era, and further weakened by their disunity and prevailing illiteracy. Within two decades, they somehow transformed the world forever. How could this be possible? They had become the purest servants of God in human history after the prophets, the most dutiful observers of monotheism on the planet. This not only made them the most devout worshippers but also at the forefront of contributing to humanity. At night, they would stand in prayer longing for the Divine, tears streaming down their cheeks in response to His revealed Word. By day, they would live for purposes greater than themselves, exhausting themselves in philanthropy, education, or as knights who rode to liberate humanity from tyrannical regimes. They established justice, as Isaiah had foretold (see Chapter 1), and unlocked the virtue of hundreds of thousands of ascetics, reformers, and great thinkers for centuries.

The hallmarks of Islamic civilization were justice and equality, balance and moderation, diversity, progress, and the pursuit of beauty. People traveled across the seas seeking to export these virtues to their homelands, and multitudes of experts testify that the world has never been the same since. Adam Smith (d. 1790), the eighteenth-century English economist who pioneered the West's free market system, admits:

> [T]he empire of the Caliphs seems to have been the first state under which the world enjoyed that degree of tranquility which the cultivation of the sciences requires. It was under the protection of those generous and magnificent princes, that the ancient philosophy and astronomy of the Greeks were restored and established in the East;

> that tranquillity, which their mild, just and religious government diffused over their vast empire, revived the curiosity of mankind, to inquire into the connecting principles of nature.[32]

Muslims, centuries later, look back at the Prophet's Companions as the gold standard for tolerance and magnanimity, invoking their precedent even for the rules of engagement during military conflicts. A glimpse of this precedent is narrated by Abū ʿAzīz ibn ʿUmayr ﵁, who was taken captive at the Battle of Badr as a warring idolator. He reports that the Messenger of Allah ﷺ gave clear instructions to his Companions, stating, 'Treat the captives kindly,' and so whenever his captors had lunch or dinner, they would only eat dates while giving him the bread, in compliance with the Prophet's orders.[33] As a result, well before global peace summits and in stark contrast to societies around them, Islamic history had shining examples of treating prisoners of war humanely, as well as amnesty and pardon being recognized as the restorative ideal for the human collective. John Esposito, a senior professor of religion at Georgetown University, writes:

> The Muslim army was as magnanimous in victory as it was tenacious in battle. Civilians were spared; churches and shrines were generally left untouched. The striking differences in military conduct were epitomized by the two dominant figures of the Crusades: Saladin and Richard the Lion-Hearted. The chivalrous Saladin was faithful to his word and compassionate towards noncombatants. Richard accepted the surrender of Acre then

---

32 Adam Smith, *Essays: Philosophical and Literary* (London: Ward, Lock & Co, 1880), 353.

33 Sulaymān ibn Aḥmad al-Ṭabarānī, *Al-Muʿjam al-Kabīr* (Cairo, Riyadh: Maktabat Ibn Taymīyah, Dār al-Ṣumayʿī, 1983), 22:393 #977.

> continued to massacre all its inhabitants, including women and children, despite promises to the contrary.[34]

From that model generation emerged a civilization in which virtue and chastity were the norm, and in which alcohol was never widespread. Until this very day, while the World Health Organization estimates that alcohol results in 2.5 million global deaths a year, the impact of Islam on preventing alcohol abuse in Muslim-majority nations (such as those of North Africa and Southeast Asia) is clear.[35]

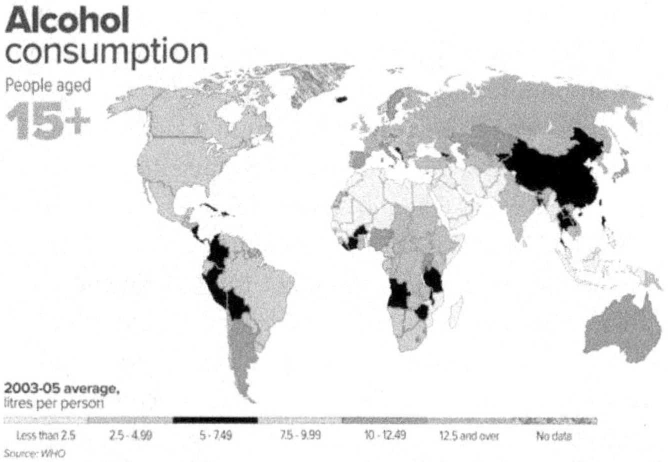

Has history ever known anyone else with the ability to tame the beast of alcoholism once it has been unleashed upon a nation? Why were Muslims able to just give it up? The Prophet ﷺ achieved that within his lifetime in a people whose glory and income were interlocked with wine. Following a divinely charted roadmap of gradualism, he was

---

34 John L. Esposito, *Islam: The Straight Path* (New York: Oxford University Press, 1988), 64.

35 'Global Status Report on Alcohol and Health 2018', *World Health Organization*, September 21, 2018.

able to witness his methodical program (see Chapter 4) culminate in wine flowing in Madinah's streets as its Muslims emptied what remained of their own wine barrels.[36] Has anyone else ever been able to ban the age-old customs of unrestricted polygyny, male-only inheritance laws, and female infanticide—let alone in such a short span of time? All the laws in today's India, for instance, designed to combat female infanticide have not eradicated the practice after more than a century of strict enforcement.[37] Has there ever been another historical parallel before or after the Prophet's era where ethnic chauvinism declined so dramatically in both theory and practice? Many of his contemporaries who were vehement Arab supremacists became people who conceded to the leadership of non-Arabs and former slaves. Sālim ﷺ, the freed slave of Abū Ḥudhayfah, would lead the senior-most Companions of the Prophet ﷺ in prayer due to his skill in reciting the Qur'an.[38] The Caliph 'Umar ibn al-Khaṭṭāb ﷺ once inquired why the Makkan governor had left Ibn Abzā ﷺ, another freed slave, of all people to preside over the religious capital of Islam during his absence. He told 'Umar that this choice was in light of Ibn Abzā's mastery of the Qur'an and its laws on estate distribution. 'Umar ﷺ expressed his approval of this justification by reporting that the Prophet ﷺ said, 'Allah elevates people in rank by virtue of this Qur'an and demotes others because of it.'[39] Mullah 'Alī al-Qārī (d. 1605) commented on this hadith:

> This phenomenon is observable in the fact that among our righteous predecessors, most of the scholars were freed slaves, and yet they were the undisputed leaders of

---

36 al-Bukhārī, *Ṣaḥīḥ al-Bukhārī*, 6:54 #4620; Muslim, *Ṣaḥīḥ Muslim*, 3:1205 #1578.

37 'Because I am a Girl: The State of the Girl Child in India 2009', *Plan India*, (2009): 6.

38 al-Bukhārī, *Ṣaḥīḥ al-Bukhārī*, 1:140 #692.

39 Muslim, *Ṣaḥīḥ Muslim*, 1:559 #817.

> the Muslim nation and its fountains of mercy while those with royal ancestry who weren't scholarly were forgotten in their spheres of ignorance.[40]

A telling account of these revolutionized norms is the well-documented encounter between ʿAṭāʾ ibn Abī Rabāh (d. 732), one of the foremost early judges of Makkah, and Sulaymān ibn ʿAbd al-Malik (d. 717), the Umayyad caliph who ruled over the largest empire known until that point in human history. ʿAṭāʾ was a freed slave who was black, blind, disabled, and had been homeless for many years of his early life. However, the dynamics of social mobility had undergone such significant changes with the advent of Islam that, within one generation, none of these social disadvantages could prevent him from enjoying prestige over Sulaymān who was, in the politico-military sense, the most powerful man alive at the time. When he approached ʿAṭāʾ in Makkah to consult him on religious matters, anxious to confirm that he was performing the hajj rites correctly, the pious judge answered without ever facing him, to assert that he was not interested in being awarded any fortune or status from the ruler. Not finding the regard and flattery he was accustomed to receiving, Sulaymān turned to his children and said, 'My sons, be relentless in your pursuit of sacred knowledge, for I will never forget our humiliation in front of that black slave.'[41]

Captured here are just some of the unique successes granted by God to the Final Prophet ﷺ. Impartial readers of history will attest that each one of these is an astonishing accomplishment on its own, and yet these and more were actualized by the generation

40 ʿAlī ibn Muḥammad Qārī al-Harawī, *Mirqāt al-Mafātīḥ: Sharḥ Mishkāt al-Maṣābīḥ* (Beirut: Dār al-Fikr, 2002), 1:288.

41 ʿAbd al-Raḥmān ibn al-Jawzī, *Ṣifat al-Ṣafwah* (Cairo: Dār al-Ḥadīth, 2000), 1:415.

molded under his care. He transformed those under his tutelage from a savage and lawless people to the best community possible. The unparalleled nature of this historical achievement serves as another sign that this could only be an act of God. As Allah says in the Qur'an, *'And [He] brought together their hearts. If you had spent all that is in the earth, you could not have brought their hearts together; but Allah brought them together. Indeed, He is Exalted in Might and Wise.'*[42]

Thereafter, Muslim civilizations in general, for almost a millennium but especially during the earlier centuries, were recognized for their distinctive balance of spirituality, morality, justice, fraternity, scientific vibrancy, and progressive thought. It was clear that Islam offered enlightened ideals which, while not always fully embraced and realized, nevertheless inspired some incredible leaps in individual and societal wellbeing.

It is understandable that the underdevelopment—in certain respects—of many Muslim countries today may detract from some people's ability to appreciate the historical greatness of Islamic civilization. However, we must be careful not to back-project that sad state today onto the terrific and exceptional 'golden ages' of the Muslim past. Certainly, if Islam is from the Divine who is perfect but its practitioners after the prophets were not, then it should not be surprising that dark painful moments exist in every epoch of human history.

However, only in the last 400–500 years did the Muslim world suffer such great and unprecedented setbacks, and only when Muslims strayed from the proper understanding and practice of Islam. But for as long as Muslims gave due respect to their religion, observing it correctly and religiously, disgraces of today's magnitude were non-existent. It is a demonstrable historical reality that Muslims thrived whenever there was greater adherence to Islam and the guidance of their Prophet ﷺ.[43] This

---

42 ' (*al-Anfāl* 8: 63)

43 See: Sayyed Abul Hasan Nadwi, *The Rise and Decline of the Muslims and Its Effect on Mankind* (UK Islamic Academy, 2003).

is unlike Europe and the Americas, for instance, whose renaissance was propelled by separating their faith from public life or dismissing it altogether.

It is for this same reason that much of the modern world is averse to the idea of merging 'church and state', because in their collective memory, religion was the very shackle that hindered progress and advancement in the past. Hence, a dominant sentiment especially in the secular West is that the revival of religion necessitates a return to backwardness and stagnation. But in our experience as Muslims, religion and spiritual strength were the driving forces that motivated the early Muslims to excel in both their worldly and otherworldly pursuits. Making that distinction will greatly assist the discerning readers of history to shed the suspicisions our current context fosters surrounding the utility of religion in general, and Islam's profound contributions to the world in particular.

People who struggle, irrespective of how many hard facts are presented, to acknowledge these achievements, are likely engaging the conversation from a paradigm in which one is unable to perceive religion as anything but a synonym for the man-made systems that have long become obsolete. This psychological baggage is predicated on an inherited civilization trauma from these belief systems and generates the stereotypes and overgeneralizations about religion that many people cannot escape today. But ultimately, those with the courage to challenge their presuppositions will continue to recognize that Muhammad ﷺ must have been a prophet of God, and that he and his teachings were responsible for many unique accomplishments and successes.

4

The Prophet's Message

The moral and intellectual greatness of the message brought by the Prophet Muhammad ﷺ—namely the Qur'an and Sunnah (his prophetic example)—testifies to its truth. As Plato famously argued in his triad of transcendental values: truth, beauty and goodness are inseparable.

In that sense, appreciating the inherent purity and beauty of the Islamic lifestyle not only attracts us to its message, but also confirms the legitimacy of its Final Prophet as a messenger from the Divine. The message can also vouch for the prophethood of Muhammad ﷺ by way of its alignment with the message of other prophets on fundamental creedal points. The Old Testament argues that the teachings of a prophet are what reveal his true identity,[1] and also warns that even if someone is able to predict the future, they are still a false prophet if they call to worshipping other gods.

A person can also marvel at the sheer volume of what has been documented of Muhammad's brief ministry from 610-632 CE. The Qur'an and Sunnah cannot be compared with the

1 See: Deuteronomy 13:1-18.

Bible, for instance, since the latter does not solely contain the teachings of Moses but rather is an aggregated historical canon whose development spanned centuries. Considering the quality of its substance and breadth of its scope, that which the Prophet ﷺ taught continues to distinguish itself as a message of exceptional depth and value. It defined people's relationships with their Maker, with those around them, even with animals and inanimate objects, and provided timeless wisdom about everything related to their individual and collective well-being.

From there, one may be drawn to consider its internal consistency; the harmony of such a comprehensive corpus that informs theology, spiritual enlightenment, individual virtue, interpersonal behavior, civil laws, and foreign policies with such intricacy that led many throughout history to find it miraculous. They saw this facet of the final message as beyond human sophistication, and more reasonably a balancing act that could only be attributable to God's perfect nature.

Finally, the profundity of the message becomes further evident when contrasted with other religious doctrines that waned in the face of criticism or simply with the passage of time. In our technological age which has facilitated the globalization of ideas and fact-checking, far more people leave Christianity than Islam in Europe and North America. Islam's growth despite its many detractors, on the other hand, continues to demonstrate its inherent veracity as well as its universality across time and place, being viable for people of very different educational, economic, and cultural backgrounds. The laws of Islam as well as its religious doctrines also continue to endure, while no society has been able to devise a comparable ever-relevant system that offers equilibrium and holistic well-being to people of all walks of life.

This chapter will highlight ten elements of this message, focusing on those more easily appreciated by people in the twenty-first century. Showcasing these dimensions should help us appreciate the message of the Final Prophet ﷺ in its totality, as they form a cumulative case in defense of his prophethood.

1. Pure Monotheism

> *Say [O Muhammad], 'This is my way; I invite to Allah with insight, I and those who follow me. And exalted is Allah; and I am not of those who associate others with Him.'*[2]

The Prophet Muhammad ﷺ never asked people to worship him. He did not even allow people to display excessive reverence to him, would always make a sharp distinction between the Divine and his own human nature, and would stop people from standing for him when he entered a room (see Chapter 2). He objected to people implicitly equating him and Allah in their statements,[3] and warned on his deathbed about the actions of past people who had turned the graves of their prophets into shrines.[4] There was no greater keystone of his message than protecting the purest understanding of monotheism in people's hearts and removing any barrier between individuals and their direct and personal connection with God.

Leo Tolstoy (d. 1910) hailed from an aristocratic Russian family and is described by some as one of the greatest novelists of all time. Many have reported his great respect for Islam, despite being a Christian, because he thought it contained valuable elements that he wanted to make accessible to a wider audience. He included the Prophet Muhammad ﷺ in a series of books entitled *The Most Remarkable Thinkers of All Times and Peoples*. In this series, Tolstoy writes about Islam:

> The essence of this faith came down to the fact that there is no deity worthy of worship except the One True Almighty God, that He is merciful and just, and will judge each person individually, according to his or her

---

2 (*Yūsuf* 12: 108)

3 'Abdullāh ibn 'Abdul-Raḥmān al-Dārimī, *Sunan al-Dārimī* (Riyadh: Dār al-Mughnī, 2000), 3:1769 #2741

4 al-Bukhārī, *Ṣaḥīḥ al-Bukhārī*, 2:102 #1390.

> faith and the balance of his or her good and bad actions which means peace for the righteous, and damnation for evildoers … He wants people to love Him as well as each other. The love for God is expressed in a prayer, compassion for others, assistance and forgiveness.[5]

If humanity's greatest existential need is to identify the one true God and develop a meaningful relationship with Him, then only the purest belief about God and His uniqueness will attract them. When demographics analysts at Pew Research Center investigated why Islam is projected to be the fastest growing religion in the world,[6] they found that 'preferring the beliefs/finding more meaning in Islam' and 'studying Islam/reading its religious texts' are in fact the two primary motivators for converting to Islam.[7] This should not be surprising. When humans see themselves as purposeful creatures, it should follow for them that there is none better than the One who fashioned and designed them to inform them of their purpose. It also follows for these people that a supremely wise, supremely merciful being would have communicated that purpose to them, and hence the undying appeal of the divine revelation model of religion, or that of heavenly inspired messengers discussed above.

From this juncture in the ancient quest to know God, we are left with either limited philosophies that fall short of answering people's most pressing questions on what makes life meaningful, or the search is narrowed to the Abrahamic faiths which agree on the oneness of God in theory but diverge thereafter. Ultimately, it is the unique emphasis of Islam on the Oneness of God and His glory that separates it from traditional Judaism which posits

---

5 Piotr Stawinski, 'Leo Tolstoy and Islam: Some Remarks on the Theme', *The Quarterly Journal of Philosophical Meditations* 2, no. 5 (Spring 2010): 18.

6 "The Changing Global Religious Landscape," *Pew Research Center*, April 5, 2017.

7 Besheer Mohamed and Elizabeth Podrebarac Sciupac, 'The Share of Americans who Leave Islam is Offset by Those who Become Muslim', *Pew Research Center*, January 26, 2018.

God as tribalist with partiality for a single bloodline, and mainstream Christianity which posits God as reductionist who accepts claims to faith in place of righteous works. As Charles Le Gai Eaton (d. 2010), the British diplomat and Islamic scholar, wrote:

> In the Muslim view, Judaism 'nationalized' monotheism, claiming it for one people alone, while in Christianity the person of Jesus as it were eclipsed the Godhead, just as the sun is eclipsed by the moon; or again: Judaism stabilized this monotheism, giving it a home and an army, but at the same time confiscated it; Christianity universalized the truth, but diluted it. Islam closed the circle and restored the purity of the faith of Abraham, giving to Moses and Jesus positions of pre-eminence in its universe and seizing upon the quintessential nature of monotheism, single-minded worship of the One, and upon the reflection of the Divine Unity in personal and social equilibrium--a balance between all contrary forces and between the different levels of human experience. Ibn Taymiyyah (d. 1328) maintained that Islam combined the Mosaic Law of Justice with the Christian Law of Grace, taking a middle way between the severity of Judaism and the mercy of Jesus; and he said that while Moses had proclaimed God's Majesty and Jesus His Goodness, Muhammad proclaimed His Perfection. In the same context, it is said that Jesus revealed what Moses had kept hidden, the secrets of the Divine Mercy and the richness of Divine Love, and that Islam finally brought everything into perspective in the light of total Truth.[8]

Though God is described in the Qur'an similarly to how He is described in the Bible in many respects, the differences are

---

8 Charles L. G. Eaton, *Islam and the Destiny of Man* (Albany: George Allen & Unwin, 1985), 44.

significant and consequential. For instance, there is no mystery surrounding God's oneness and identity in the Qur'an, as opposed to the obscurity of the trinitarian doctrine, with its convoluted nature reflected today in the fundamental disagreements between Christian denominations over the person and nature of God. Likewise, there is no exception to God's omnipotence anywhere in the Qur'an, while the Old Testament depicts God, for instance, as losing a wrestling bout with Jacob (Ya'qūb ﷺ).[9]

Only in Islam does one find a distinct focus on God who is absolute in His Oneness and perfection, transcendent in His power and justice, glorified above resembling His creation or deserting them without direction, and equally compassionate to humanity at large, addressing them all with the same message.

2. Faith in Destiny

> *No disaster strikes upon the earth or among yourselves except that it is in a register before We bring it into being. Indeed that, for Allah, is easy—in order that you not despair over what has eluded you and not exult [in pride] over what He has given you. And Allah does not like every self-deluded and boastful person.*[10]

When asked to define the fundamental belief of Islam, the Prophet Muhammad ﷺ said,

> Faith is to believe in Allah, His angels, His scriptures, His messengers, the Last Day, and to believe in destiny, the good of it and the evil of it [all being from Allah].[11]

Belief that everything is and will always be in God's hands, and that God has constructed this life with ups and downs for a

---

9 See: Genesis 32:22-30.

10 (*al-Ḥadīd* 57: 22–23)

11 Muslim, *Ṣaḥīḥ Muslim*, 1:36 #8.

wisdom only He fully knows and our finite minds cannot, are two powerful resources that make life endurable and enjoyable. The Prophet Muhammad's teachings on destiny do not just stand in contrast to the atheistic worldview that misperceives reality as random and undirected, existing solely in the grip of a merciless, relentless set of physical laws which serve no purpose and offer no reassurances. They also negate the deistic notion that God does not intervene in the world, a notion that many theists have internalized. This notion deprives people of the armor of confidence in God overseeing every atom of this universe. The Prophet ﷺ taught that donning this armor was a requirement of valid faith, by saying in one of numerous traditions about this essential truth:

> Were you to donate for God's cause an amount of gold that was equivalent to Mount Uḥud, God would not accept it from you until you believed in the Divine decree—whereby you are certain that whatever reached you would never have missed you, and that whatever missed you was never going to reach you. And were you to die believing otherwise, you would enter the Hellfire.[12]

Herbert Benson, MD, a cofounder of the Benson-Henry Institute for Mind Body Medicine, concludes near the end of his medical exploration of belief and healing, 'the data I have presented is that affirmative beliefs and hopes are very therapeutic, and that faith in God, in particular, has many positive effects on health.'[13] Similarly, Bryan Walsh, in *The Science of Happiness*, writes that 'study after study has found that religious people tend to be less depressed and less anxious than nonbelievers, better able to handle the vicissitudes of life than nonbelievers … It's as if a sense of spirituality and an active, social religious practice

---

12 Abū Dāwūd, *Sunan Abī Dāwūd*, 4:225 #4699.

13 Herbert Benson and Marg Stark, *Timeless Healing: The Power and Biology of Belief* (New York: Simon & Schuster, 1997), 211.

were an effective vaccine against the virus of unhappiness.'[14] A large, global study by Pew Research Center found that people actively involved in religious life tend to be happier.[15]

It may be claimed that these teachings of Islam on faith and deference to God are shared by other faith traditions as well. While true, this commonality can be argued as a proof for Muhammad's prophethood, not against it, since he brought a message that agrees in some respects with other scriptures that he had no knowledge of (see Chapter 7). Furthermore, the Prophet ﷺ placed distinctive emphasis on this particular topic in a way that sets it apart from the remnants of prior scriptures, in an environment replete with superstitious dogmas about fate and bad omens.

The Prophet ﷺ also taught his followers that faith in destiny coexists with human agency as an ontological reality, though not a reality that denies God's omnipotence. God granting humanity real agency is a manifestation of His perfect equity, in that it is necessary for human accountability: we are only accountable for what we freely choose to do. In teaching this doctrine, he carved a unique and powerful place in the classic free-will versus determinism debate, a place called Islam (submission). By submitting to God's creative will, one can relinquish the demoralizing burden of carrying what one cannot control in God's created universe, and by submitting to His prescriptive will, one can finally set down the burden of trying to live up to the constantly changing standards of a godless society. As Charles Taylor recognizes in his seminal work, *A Secular Age*, it is 'the call to submit to God in Islam which empowers humans in a way unavailable in any other fashion.'[16]

---

14 Bryan Walsh, 'Does Spirituality Make You Happy?' in *The Science of Happiness: New Discoveries for a More Joyful Life*, Special Time Edition (New York: Time Inc. Books, 2016), 80.

15 Conrad Hackett, Alan Cooperman, et al., "Religion's Relationship to Happiness, Civic Engagement, and Health Around the World," *Pew Research Center*, January 31, 2019.

16 Charles Taylor, *A Secular Age* (Cambridge: Harvard University Press, 2007), 818.

Without the belief that God is ultimately in control, inner peace will remain out of reach. A person would be forever haunted by the prospect of dueling cosmic forces. This would in turn destroy the integrity of a person's spirituality, because even if they worshipped God, they would still worry about other adversarial forces in the universe. But with conviction that it is ultimately God who brings events into existence, even if I may have just enough of a will to be accountable for what I can influence, contentment with life and the sweetness of faith become attainable. As the Prophet ﷺ said in an authentic tradition, 'He has tasted faith—the one who is pleased with Allah as their Lord, Islam as their religion, and Muhammad as their messenger.'[17]

Some may wonder how the therapeutic value of Muhammad's teachings can constitute a logical proof for his prophethood, when healing and happiness are merely aesthetic factors, philosophically speaking. But we cannot restrict proofs to those that can be rationalized and fail to recognize the importance of the lived experiences shared by those who imbibe these teachings. These beliefs taught by the Prophet Muhammad ﷺ afforded his followers wonderful resilience in the face of poverty, fear, and other challenges that humans everywhere encounter. This resilience and peace of mind therefore constitute yet another aspect of Islam's beauty that demonstrates its harmony with human nature.

3. The Ritual Prayer (*Ṣalāh*)

Indeed, mankind was created anxious: frantic when harm touches him and withholding when good touches him—except those who pray, those who consistently devote themselves to the prayer.[18]

---

17 Muslim, *Ṣaḥīḥ Muslim*, 1:62 #34.

18 (*al-Maʿārij* 70: 19–23)

The ritual prayer is the second pillar of Islam after the testimony of faith. Linguistically, it means a connection (*ṣilah*), and it represents a chance for people to pull themselves out of the grind of this life to reinforce their relationship with their Creator, to water the tree of their faith and to moisten their hearts, which would otherwise dry out and crack in the desert of the pursuit of worldly pleasures. For the soul, the *ṣalāh* serves the function of turning to the shade of a tree in the middle of work on a hot day. It is a chance to revive our spirituality, a reminder of our origin, our Creator, and the reason for our existence. If it is done properly and with devotion, it can be the greatest deterrent to wrongdoing and aggression.[19]

Human beings have primordially practised ritual, and in that sense, the ritual of prayer constitutes the central affirming act of human life. Its absence renders people a caricature of themselves, like a body trying to live with its heart ripped out. However, while pagans attempt to connect with the Divine through theatrical forms, and hedonists kneel for a lifetime at the crude shrine of self-indulgence, monotheists with access to confirmed prophetic teachings enjoy the real pathways disclosed by God to authentically connect with Him.

The Prophet Muhammad ﷺ taught Muslims that God enjoined them to pray five times each day in a structured format and at specific periods of time. An outsider may find this to be a cumbersome or intrusive task, but so many Muslims—upon experiencing this prayer—voluntarily choose to supplement these daily five with even more. The magnetic force of this unique devotional act should indicate its meaningfulness. Prayer is the most evident fruit of conviction, and in its depths lie its most fertile seeds. This very observation about the Muslim prayer was once expressed by the late Pope John Paul II (d. 2005), despite his theological differences with Islam:

---

19 Hatem al-Haj and Ibn Qudāmah, *'Umdat al-Fiqh Explained: A Commentary on Ibn Qudāmah's 'The Reliable Manual of Fiqh'* (Riyadh: International Islamic Publishing House, 2019), 1:129.

> The religiosity of Muslims deserves respect. It is impossible not to admire, for example, their fidelity to prayer. The image of believers in Allah who, without caring about time or place, fall to their knees and immerse themselves in prayer remains a model for all those who invoke the true God, in particular for those Christians who, having deserted their magnificent cathedrals, pray only a little or not at all.[20]

The greatest benefit of *ṣalāh* is therefore the opportunity to connect with God in this life, a connection that nurtures the soul to endure in fulfilling its purpose in life and ensures its salvation in the hereafter. However, the worldly benefits of prayer are also undeniable.

Physiologically, the Islamic ritual prayer helps stabilize our biological clocks which run genetic metabolism. We all know how traveling between time zones causes jetlag that can render us quite dysfunctional, but we may not realize that the lights we keep on at night in our rooms, or on our electronics, also work against our natural nightly release of melatonin which allows the body a rejuvenating stretch of sleep. But when the first *ṣalāh* must be offered at dawn before sunrise, and the Prophet Muhammad ﷺ discouraged needless socialization after the evening prayer,[21] the course is reversed. To better appreciate this prophetic teaching, it may help to realize that a lack of sleep does not translate into mere lethargy or underperformance the next day, but also disrupts the proper expression of genes in our body which could be linked to tissue inflammation and a reduction of the ability to fight disease and stress, which could eventually play a role in the development of obesity, diabetes, heart disease and a host of neurodegenerative disorders.[22]

---

20 Pope John Paul II and Vittorio Messori, *Crossing the Threshold of Hope* (New York: Alfred A. Knopf, 2005), 93.

21 al-Bukhārī, *Ṣaḥīḥ al-Bukhārī*, 1:118 #568.

22 Peter Russell, 'Lack of Sleep Disrupts Genes', *WebMD*, March 1st, 2013.

Psychologically, research suggests the meditative aspect of prayer enhances focus and self-control, and offsets the negative effects of daily stressful experiences.[23] In the Islamic *ṣalāh* in particular, there is an exceptional nexus between the tranquil measured motions required by the Prophet ﷺ for a valid *ṣalāh* , and the mental labor involved in recalling the elaborate segments of the Qur'an a Muslim recites in every *ṣalāh*.

Emotionally, the *ṣalāh* has notable benefits as well. The Qur'an encourages Muslims to worship together and at times links prayer to escaping the suffocating grip of sadness and social estrangement. Allah says, '*We certainly know that your chest is constrained by what they say. So glorify the praises of your Lord and be of those who prostrate.*'[24] Scientific research now illustrates how therapeutic an active religious fellowship can be for a person's emotional health, through the common purpose and social support it affords.[25] With regards to how vulnerable solitary living leaves individuals and society, the Prophet Muhammad ﷺ said in the context of the daily prayer, 'Adhere to the congregation, for the wolf eats none other than the stray sheep.'[26] The regularity of this communal ritual reduces the deep sense of alienation people naturally feel when physically separated.

Another unique facet of the Muslim style of prayer is that the Prophet ﷺ encouraged believers to 'close the gaps'[27] between them when setting their ranks for ritual prayer, and to shake hands.[28] We now know that welcome physical contact results in oxytocin being released by the body,[29] a neurotransmitter

---

23 Clay Routledge, 'Five Scientifically Supported Benefits of Prayer', *Psychology Today*, June 23rd, 2014.

24 (*al-Ḥijr* 15: 97–98)

25 Raphael Bonelli et al., "Religious and Spiritual Factors in Depression: Review and Integration of the Research," *Depression Research and Treatment* (2012).

26 Abū Dāwūd, *Sunan Abī Dāwūd*, 1:150 #547.

27 Abū Dāwūd, *Sunan Abī Dāwūd*, 1:178 #666.

28 al-Tirmidhī, *Sunan al-Tirmidhī*, 4:371 #2727.

29 "Can You Kiss and Hug Your Way to Better Health? Research Says Yes." *PennMedicine*, January 8th, 2018.

informally dubbed the 'bonding hormone' due to its association with empathy, trust and relationship-building. With the atomization of modern life, where friends are often countries apart, our social fabric has withered to the extent that London is now the 'loneliest capital in Europe', according to government records.[30] Moreover, the World Health Organization has projected that, by 2030, cardiovascular disease and major depressive disorder will be the world's most debilitating medical conditions.[31]

Considering this frightening upsurge in social isolation, depression, substance abuse,[32] and rising suicide rates,[33] the Muslim daily prayer can be a welcome antidote. Allah says, *And they used to be invited to prostration while they were [still] sound.*[34]

4. Devotional Fasting (*Ṣiyām*)

> *O you who have believed, fasting has been prescribed for you, as it was prescribed for those before you, so that you may become more mindful of Allah.*[35]

Fasting is another pillar of Islam, practised by over a billion Muslims worldwide during the lunar month of Ramadan and periodically at other times of the year. From dawn until sunset, a Muslim abstains from food, drink, and conjugal relations out of devotion to his or her Creator. This restriction of the carnal appetites feeds

30 Gillian Orr, "Britain has been voted the loneliest capital of Europe," *The Independent*, July 3rd, 2014.

31 Secretariat of the World Health Organization, "Global burden of mental disorders and the need for a comprehensive, coordinated response from health and social sectors at the country level," *World Health Organization*, December 1st, 2011.

32 'Drug Overdose Deaths', *Center for Disease Control and Prevention*, last updated March 3, 2021.

33 Sabrina Tavernise, "U.S. Suicide Rate Surges to a 30-Year High," *The New York Times*, April 22, 2016.

34 (*al-Qalam* 68: 43)

35 (*al-Baqarah* 2: 183)

one's spirituality, reinforces the religious conscience, and culti-
vates sincerity with God—for only God is always watchful of you.
It also teaches self-restraint in other spheres of life, and thus the
Prophet Muhammad ﷺ informed us, 'Whoever does not give up
foul speech while fasting, [know that] Allah has no need for this
person to give up food and drink.'[36] Of course, fasting also allows
a Muslim to experience hunger and discomfort, generating empathy for the underprivileged and downtrodden. For that reason,
the Prophet Muhammad ﷺ would outdo himself in generosity
during Ramadan,[37] and obligated his followers with a mandatory
charity (Sadaqat al-Fiṭr) at the month's end.

Both the physical and psychological health benefits gained by
fasting are quite evident. In one 2003 study at the National Institute of Aging in Baltimore, it was found that caloric restriction
extended lifespan and reduced the incidence of age-related diseases.[38] Similarly, Clive McCay of Cornell University found that
laboratory rats kept on a severely reduced-calorie diet lived almost
twice as long as expected, so long as they had the proper nutrients.[39]
Following the famous Canto and Owen Experiment, anti-aging re-
searcher Richard Weindruch, from the University of Wisconsin's
School of Medicine and Public Health, published a major paper
showcasing two rhesus monkeys of similar ages with very different
diets.[40] His research yielded a clear message: caloric restriction and
fasting reverse and slow the cellular decline associated with aging.

---

[36]   al-Bukhārī, Ṣaḥīḥ al-Bukhārī, 3:26 #1903.

[37]   Ibn 'Abbās ؓ said, 'The Prophet ﷺ was the most generous of all peo-
       ple, and he used to become [even] more generous in Ramadan when
       Gabriel met him. Gabriel used to meet him every night during Rama-
       dan to revise the Qur'an with him. Allah's Messenger ﷺ was more gen-
       erous then than the fast wind.' (al-Bukhārī, Ṣaḥīḥ al-Bukhārī, 3:26 #1902).

[38]   Joseph W. Kemnitz, 'Calorie Restriction and Aging in Nonhuman
       Primates', ILAR Journal 52, no. 1 (2011): 66–77.

[39]   Roger B. McDonald and Jon J. Ramsey, "Honouring Clive McCay
       and 75 Years of Calorie Restriction Research," The Journal of Nutrition
       140, no. 7 (July 2010): 1205–10.

[40]   David Tenenbaum, 'Monkey Caloric Restriction Study Shows Big
       Benefit; Contradicts Earlier Study', University of Wisconsin-Madison
       News, April 1, 2014.

As for the positive effects of fasting on mental health, one psychology study tracked how, while a healthy woman fasting an eighteen-hour day may report increased irritability, she may also experience an increased sense of achievement, reward, pride and control.[41] Therefore, it can be argued that the mild agitation experienced by a healthy person in their fast (the Qur'an exempts the ill from fasting) is just the challenge a person may need to develop frustration tolerance and a sense of accomplishment that fuels our happiness as purposeful beings.

It is interesting how the overall health benefits derived from intermittent fasting have only recently been investigated,[42] while only a short time ago the latest science had recommended three meals a day with snacks in between as the dietary ideal to stabilize one's metabolism and brain's glucose supply. Such theories continue to lose credibility with intermittent fasting's surging popularity and newfound benefits,[43] though it has been a consistent practice among the followers of the Prophet Muhammad ﷺ for fourteen centuries now and counting. Not only do Muslims fast daily from dawn to sundown for the month of Ramadan as an obligation and pillar of their faith but they have also been encouraged by the Prophet to observe this fast twice a week at other times of the year, or thrice a month at least.

5. Prohibiting Extramarital Relations

> *Tell [O Muhammad] the believing men to lower their gaze and guard their chastity. That is purer for them. Certainly, Allah is fully aware of whatever they do. And also tell the believing women to lower their gaze and guard their chastity.*[44]

---

41 Ellen Watkins and Lucy Serpell, 'The Psychological Effects of Short-Term Fasting in Healthy Women', *Frontiers in Nutrition*, v. 3 (2016).

42 Rafael de Cabo and Mark P. Mattson, 'Effects of Intermittent Fasting on Health, Aging, and Disease', *New England Journal of Medicine*, v. 382 no. 3 (2020): 298.

43 Kris Gunnars, '11 Myths About Fasting and Meal Frequency', *Healthline*, July 22nd, 2019.

44 (*al-Nūr* 24: 30–31)

The call to chastity in this Qur'anic chapter entitled *al-Nūr* (the Light) not only prohibited fornication and adultery but outlined a code of conduct to preempt the slippery slope leading to them. Civilizations that do not respect such codes often spiral downward to points of no return. Their licentiousness destroys their sensibilities, and they soon discover that fornication is an evil path—not just an evil end—that needs to be preempted. As Allah said, *'And do not approach unlawful sexual intercourse. Indeed, it is ever an immorality and is evil as a way.'*[45]

It may begin with extramarital relations, then making sexual orientation the central part of one's identity, followed by the acceptance of all forms of sexual expression, even pedophilia, bestiality, and necrophilia. From that vantage point, a newfound appreciation surfaces for how this verse begins: 'do not *approach* fornication', as if it were a wild blaze that will engulf those who even come close to it. Despite how common sexual freedoms have become, you will still find experts from across the ideological spectrum acknowledging the roles of abstinence and marital fidelity in preventing sexually transmitted diseases.

Another way Islam mitigates this threat is by emphasizing the family system. Fornication is not just an invitation to bodily disease but represents a selfish mentality that has no care for the families it destroys, the children that are born deprived of love and care, the millions of late-term abortions, the prison systems that we pay for collectively, and the like.[46] Islam installs safeguards against all this, chastity and social responsibility among them. Fornication even affects the elderly who die alone and dejected, for those whose parents are not married or are unknown to the child will naturally be further severed from their grandparents. As a result, the elderly find themselves abandoned in their vulnerable old age—a time that usually requires the presence of the

45 (*al-Isrā'* 17: 32)

46 See: Mohammad Elshinawy, and Tahir Khwaja, "Gender Uniqueness in Islam and the Significance of Fatherhood," *Yaqeen Institute for Islamic Research*, September 24, 2020.

extended family to shoulder the load together. The Prophet ﷺ highlighted these dangers on many occasions; for example, telling the young man who struggled with lust, 'Would you accept fornication for your mother, your sister, your daughter?'[47]

6. Prohibiting Interest-Based Lending

> *O you who have believed, fear Allah and give up what remains [due to you] of interest, if you should be believers. And if you do not, then be informed of a war [against you] from Allah and His Messenger. But if you repent, you may have your principal—[thus] you do no wrong, nor are you wronged.*[48]

Jābir ibn ʿAbdillāh ﷺ reports that the Messenger of Allah ﷺ cursed the consumer of interest, its payer, its documenter, its two witnesses, and said, 'They are all equal [in sin].'[49] Past and present, people have downplayed the danger of an interest-bearing transaction, especially when effected by mutual consent. However, the wisdom of the Divine transcends our short-sightedness and deems engaging in interest-based transactions an enormity. Nowadays, we observe firsthand how interest-based systems have destroyed nations beyond repair, with the debacle of the Nigerian and Jamaican economies being just two tragic examples[50] of what happens when such an enormous part of a nation's annual budget is apportioned to debt repayment. The villainous nature of dispensing loans for interest is clear; it appears to be an avenue for quick funds, but it often buries people and countries further in debt. It places the bulk of the risk on the debtor and little risk on

---

47 Ibn Ḥanbal, *Musnad Aḥmad*, 36:545 #22211; authenticated by al-Arnā'ūṭ in the comments and paraphrased here.

48 (*al-Baqarah* 2: 278–279)

49 Muslim, *Ṣaḥīḥ Muslim*, 3:1219 #1598.

50 See film documentary: Stefanie Black, 'Life and Debt [Motion Picture]', (USA: New Yorker Films, 2001).

the creditor who invests through lending to others. It also disparages productivity and labor, as Aristotle argued,[51] since money is what begets money here, not effort or craftsmanship. As a result, the rich steadily get richer while the poor steadily get poorer—to points of unthinkable devastation, which then become catalysts for financial meltdowns and uprisings by the underclass which have historically devoured many nations, as Plato once warned. Hence, the Prophet Muhammad ﷺ outlawed profiting in the worldly sense from loans by saying, 'Profit is contingent upon liability (the possibility of loss).'[52]

In addition to lenders being prohibited from charging interest on loans, borrowers are also prohibited from such loans. This prevents borrowers from living beyond their means, which mitigates their being exploited by lenders, and the ecological damage caused by consumerism. When you add to the perils of usury those of excessive speculation (*gharar*), which the Prophet ﷺ forbade as well,[53] you have all the ingredients of an economic crisis. The 2008 financial meltdown was a relatively recent example of this. For this reason, a global trend is emerging in Europe and elsewhere that recognizes that Islamic financial regulations offer a refreshing alternative and remedy for economic woes.[54] Highlighting a primary objective behind these regulations, Allah says about money in the Qur'an, '*so that it will not become a perpetual circulation [solely] among the rich from among you.*'[55]

Another component of this remedy is the lessening of wealth concentration through the Zakat system. It is one of Islam's five foundational pillars; an obligatory charity due on significant

---

51 Aristotle, R.F. Stalley, and Ernest Barker, *Politics: Oxford World's Classics* (Oxford: Oxford University Press, 2009), bk. 1, chap. 10, p. 29.

52 al-Tirmidhī, *Sunan al-Tirmidhī*, 2:572 #1285: authenticated by al-Tirmidhī in the comments.

53 Muslim, *Ṣaḥīḥ Muslim*, 3:1153 #1513.

54 Ismail Ozsoy, 'An Islamic Suggestion of Solution to the Financial Crises', *Procedia Economics and Finance* 38 (2016): 174–184.

55 (*al-Ḥashr* 59: 7)

amounts of capital, whereby 2.5 per cent must be redistributed annually, primarily among the poor but also to other noble causes. Of course, with the Zakat system funneling this wealth directly to those in need, the oft-cited concern of governments being overfed by taxing the rich's wealth vanishes. Also, unlike governmental taxation, the Zakat system emphasizes one's personal accountability before God; the One who cannot be deceived the way government auditors often are by creative evaders who move their assets outside of the country.

7. Prohibiting Alcohol Consumption

> *O believers! Intoxicants, gambling, idols, and divination arrows are all abominations from Satan's handiwork. So shun them so you may be successful.*[56]

Islam's straightforward, categorical rejection of alcohol consumption may be one of the easiest facets of the Prophet's message to appreciate. On one hand, that fact that it was contrary to the prevailing norms at his time among pagans, Jews, and Christians argues against the notion that his ministry was an accumulation of teachings absorbed from his surrounding environment. But in addition to its being revolutionary and original, it was incredibly wise in its framing. The Prophet Muhammad ﷺ informed people that 'whatever will intoxicate in large amounts, then even small amounts of it are unlawful.'[57] Sensible people should notice how superior this advice is to current recommendations to drink responsibly, which rely on the decision-making of those whose ability to make responsible decisions is impaired.

Some modern societies have acknowledged this failed logic and attempted to maneuver around it by requiring that a designated

---

56 (*al-Mā'idah* 5: 90)

57 Abū Dāwūd, *Sunan Abī Dāwūd*, 3:327 #3681.

driver abstain from drinking altogether to safely transport the drinkers to their homes. To illustrate the inadequacy of these measures, realize that the Harvard Alcohol Project normalized the designated driver concept by 1991 using massive networks that spanned government advocacy groups, Hollywood, professional sports leagues, major corporations, and even had public service announcements prepared by the brewing and distilling companies themselves. When the dust cleared, it turned out that this campaign was focused on the wrong target. Three decades later, a 50 per cent decline in motor vehicle crashes caused by alcohol-impairment has still not been achieved.[58]

Over 10,000 people in the United States were killed in 2016 by alcohol-impaired driving crashes, 28 per cent of all traffic deaths.[59] With nonverbal peer-pressure being a reality even for adults, along with the bother of identifying who will voluntarily remain sober while socializing with those actively drinking, this wishful thinking never had the potential to fully combat the problem. If we turn to the guidance of the Prophet ﷺ on this issue, he taught that it was not enough to prohibit people from embarking on the slippery slope of light drinking through a zero-tolerance policy on alcohol consumption. He added that insulating non-drinkers from its magnetic force is only possible through prohibiting them from sitting at a table where wine is circulated.[60] But above all, he taught that spiritual and moral refinement were the true bedrock upon which temperance and reform are built, and a person is liberated from this vice. His wife, ʿĀ'ishah ؓ, said,

> The first revelations of the Qur'an were none other than chapters from the shorter chapters (*mufaṣṣal*), which contain mention of Paradise and Hellfire. Then, once the

58 Editorial Staff, "Using a Designated Driver," *American Addiction Centers*, December 12th, 2019.

59 "Traffic Safety Facts: 2016 Data." *National Highway Traffic Safety Administration*, January 2018.

60 al-Tirmidhī, *Sunan al-Tirmidhī*, 4:410 #2801.

> people became inclined to Islam, the lawful and unlawful were revealed. If the first thing to be revealed was: 'Do not drink wine,' they would have said, 'We will never give up wine.' And if 'Do not fornicate' was revealed first, they would have said, 'We will never give up fornication.'[61]

Similarly, Alcoholics Anonymous, a world-renowned rehabilitation program with millions of beneficiaries to date, requires believing in a higher power as part of their program due to its efficacy in helping people recover from addiction.

Aside from traffic deaths, the health risks associated with alcohol consumption are vast, involving virtually every system and organ in the human body. The most severe examples of its toxicity involve brain damage and liver failure.[62] Consuming alcohol while pregnant is another epidemic, due to alcohol being so toxic to a developing fetus. Fetal alcohol syndrome remains the leading cause of preventable intellectual disability in the United States along with a variety of other clinical manifestations.[63] In addition to alcohol's direct toxicity, the detrimental consequences of the impairments it causes are found in the established correlation between alcohol consumption and reductions in workplace productivity, along with increases in HIV transmission, lethal accidents, violence, and abuse.[64] Alluding to the aggressions triggered by intoxicants, Allah cautions humanity in the Qur'an,

> *Satan only wants to stir between you animosity and hatred through intoxicants and gambling, and to avert you from the remembrance of Allah and from prayer. So will you not desist?* [65]

---

61 al-Bukhārī, *Ṣaḥīḥ al-Bukhārī*, 6:185 #4993.

62 'Global Status Report on Alcohol and Health 2014', *World Health Organization* (WHO), 2014.

63 Leo Sher, Isack Kandel, and Joav Merrick. *Alcohol-related Cognitive Disorders: Research and Clinical Perspectives* (New York: Nova Science, 2009), 5.

64 Howard B. Moss HB, 'The Impact of Alcohol on Society: A Brief Overview', *Social Work in Public Health,* 28:3-4 (2013), 175-177.

65 (*al-Mā'idah* 5: 91)

It is therefore no wonder that the Centers for Disease Control estimate that 95,000 deaths occur every year in the United States alone due to excessive alcohol consumption.[66] *The Lancet* recently published a study evaluating the burden of disease linked to alcohol, spanning 195 countries from 1990–2016. In attempting to determine the amount of alcohol consumption that would minimize its harmful effects while still reaping its minor benefits, they concluded that zero alcohol was the only nonthreatening amount.[67] In other words, the harm associated with alcohol consumption was so great that in no amount was the benefit greater than its harm. Countless medical studies reinforce the timeless message of the Prophet Muhammad ﷺ, as outlined in the Qur'an, *'They ask you [O Muhammad] about wine and gambling. Say, "In them is great sin, and yet some benefit for people. But their sin is greater than their benefit."'*[68]

Much like today, the Prophet's contemporaries would boast before Islam of how becoming drunk rendered them fearless, and consequently people of valour in battle and generosity in philanthropy. The Qur'an came to overturn this myopic thinking, by juxtaposing these advantages with the inevitable greater harms that cannot be separated from them—such as unnecessary violence and wasting of vital finances. Muhammad's ﷺ message made Islam's unique firm stance on alcohol scriptural and ever-relevant, not to be contravened by fluctuating politics or supposed benefits. Perhaps this plays a role in why minority communities, who are often disproportionately harmed by alcohol consumption, are converting to Islam in droves today.[69]

---

66 Marissa B. Esser, et al., 'Deaths and Years of Potential Life Lost From Excessive Alcohol Use: United States, 2011–2015,' *Morbidity and Mortality Weekly Report*. 69(30) (2020): 981–987.

67 GBD 2016 Alcohol Collaborators, 'Alcohol use and burden for 195 countries and territories, 1990–2016: A Systematic Analysis for the Global Burden of Disease Study 2016', *The Lancet*, 22; 392(10152) (September 2018):1015-1035.

68 (*al-Baqarah* 2: 219)

69 The Aborigines of Australia, for instance, often cite this reason as their greatest impetus for choosing Islam in such large numbers nowadays.

8. Healthy Eating and Personal Hygiene

> *O children of Adam, take your adornment at every place of prostration, and eat and drink, but be not excessive. Indeed, He likes not those who commit excess.*[70]

These divine instructions were not left unqualified. Rather, nuanced detail was provided by the Prophet Muhammad ﷺ regarding food, drink, and dress. For instance, the Qur'an forbids Muslims from eating pork unless a dire necessity compels them,[71] a prohibition which is also biblical.[72] Muslims were also discouraged (not forbidden) by the Prophet ﷺ from eating beef to avoid medical complications. In one hadith, 'I prescribe for you cows' milk, for they eat from all the herbs, and it contains a cure for every disease.' In another related report, 'And stay away from cow meat, for it is a cause of disease.'[73] The harms of excessive beef are common knowledge of late.

Not only was the kind of food addressed, but the amount as well. The Prophet ﷺ said:

> No human being fills any vessel worse than his stomach. It is sufficient for the son of Adam [to eat] a few mouthfuls, to erect his spine (i.e., sustain him). But if he must [eat more], then let one third be for food, one third for drink, and one third for air.[74]

See the documentary film: Australian Broadcasting Corporation, *Aborigines Choosing Islam*, aired November 14, 2010.

70 (*al-Aʿrāf* 7: 31)

71 (*al-Baqarah* 2: 173, *al-Māʾidah* 5: 3, *al-Anʿām* 6: 145, & *al-Naḥl* 16: 115)

72 'Also the swine is unclean for you, because it has cloven hooves, yet does not chew the cud; you shall not eat their flesh or touch their dead carcasses.' (Deuteronomy: 14:8, New King James Version)

73 Muḥammad Nāṣir al-Dīn al-Albānī and Jalāl al-Dīn al-Suyūṭī, *Ṣaḥīḥ al-Jāmiʿ al-Ṣaghīr wa Ziyādatih* (Damascus: al-Maktab al-Islāmī, 1969), 2:749–750 #4059–4061.

74 Ibn Mājah, *Sunan Ibn Mājah*, 2:1111 #3349; authenticated by al-Albānī in the comments.

Taking it a brilliant step further, Muslims were given by their Prophet ﷺ a roadmap to eating less, transitioning them from the abstract to practical applications of this guidance. Anas ibn Mālik ؓ reports that the Prophet ﷺ forbade them from drinking while standing, and [Anas added] that eating while standing was even worse.[75] This advice on eating and drinking mindfully is a proven key to avoiding the dangers of overeating and obesity.[76]

As for personal hygiene, the following words are attributed to the Prophet Muhammad ﷺ:

> Ten practices are from the natural inclinations (*fiṭrah*): trimming the mustache, letting the beard grow, brushing the teeth, rinsing the nose, clipping the nails, washing the finger joints, plucking armpit hair, shaving pubic hair, and washing oneself with water after using the lavatory.

A sub-narrator said, 'And I forgot the tenth, unless it was rinsing the mouth.'[77]

When people reflect on the wisdom of such teachings, see the effects of their application, and consider the laws of Islam from the perspective of their higher objectives, they are often stirred both intellectually and spiritually. These ten practices above, for instance, do not just testify to the Final Prophet ﷺ being centuries ahead of the most progressive civilizations of his time in hygiene, but they also indicate how kind the Most Affectionate, Lord of Might, is to His creation.

George Bernard Shaw (d. 1950), an influential Irish playwright and critic, writes:

> [T]he formulators of the superseded native religion, like Mahomet, had been enlightened enough to introduce as

75 Muslim, *Ṣaḥīḥ Muslim*, 3:1600 #2024.

76 Melinda Beck, "Putting an End to Mindless Munching," *The Wall Street Journal*, May 13th, 2008.

77 Muslim, *Ṣaḥīḥ Muslim*, 1:223 #261.

> religious duties such sanitary measures as ablution and the most careful and reverent treatment of everything cast off by the human body, even to nail clippings and hairs; and our missionaries thoughtlessly discredited this godly doctrine without supplying its place, which was promptly taken by laziness and neglect.[78]

Until Christendom's encounter with the Muslim world during the Crusades of the eleventh century, bathing was not yet customary amongst Europeans. Plagues would regularly visit their unsanitary dwellings, and they would wear grime-covered clothing until it fell off their bodies. By that time, Muslims had been washing for prayers, bathing after sexual intercourse, and for ritual devotions, and even washing their deceased—for four hundred years. As James Harpur writes about the Crusades,

> Back in Europe washing was not considered a priority, indeed it was often despised as a mark of effeminacy. But the Crusaders soon began to discover the therapeutic pleasures of the public bath—similar to a modern Turkish bath—that was a normal part of Muslim life.[79]

Islam even discouraged the consumption of raw onions, and promoted rinsing the mouth regularly and brushing the teeth frequently. As the Prophet ﷺ said, 'The toothbrush is a purification for the mouth, and a means of pleasing the Lord.'[80] Islam's Final Prophet, Muhammad ﷺ, taught that these are means of nearness to God, and of not offending people and angels who

---

78 Bernard Shaw, *The Doctor's Dilemma: Preface on Doctors* (New York: Brentano's, 1911), LXXXIV.

79 James Harpur, *The Crusades, the Two Hundred Years War: The Clash between the Cross and the Crescent in the Middle East, 1096–1291* (New York: Rosen Publishing, 2008), 44.

80 Aḥmad ibn Shu'ayb al-Nasā'ī, *Sunan al-Nasā'ī* (Aleppo: Maktab al-Maṭbū'āt al-Islāmīyah, 1986), 1:10 #5; authenticated by al-Albānī in the comments.

are bothered by bad odours. With today's advances in medical technology, most of us understand just how useful brushing one's teeth and diluting the sugar in one's mouth—for instance—can be in preventing rotting teeth and the agony that ensues from gum infection.

The Prophet Muhammad ﷺ instructed Muslims to begin their ritual ablution (*wuḍū'*), or pre-prayer wash, by thoroughly rinsing their hands. It is estimated that only 19 per cent of people across the world wash their hands after using the toilet, and the numbers on preventable diseases attributable to poor hand hygiene are more alarming in the Americas today than in the Muslim-majority Eastern Mediterranean regions.[81] Despite the amount of scientific evidence documenting the health and even life-saving benefits of this basic cleanliness practice,[82] we find that in today's modern world, where sanitary precautions in general have contributed to overall healthier populations, people are still not as hygienically motivated in this regard as Muslims have been for nearly 1,500 years.

Another component of the *wuḍū'* ritual involves rinsing the nose. Researchers are beginning to discover just how valuable this simple practice can be to our health. One study concluded that 'nasal irrigation has enormous potential in improving quality of life in a cost-efficient manner for millions of patients.'[83] Rhinologists refer to it as 'nasal irrigation' because sending small amounts of water *all the way through* is the proper way to treat and prevent sinusitis, among other things. This is precisely what the Prophet ﷺ prescribed in his statement, 'And be thorough in

81 A. Prüss-Ustün et al., 'Burden of Disease from Inadequate Water, Sanitation and Hygiene in Low and Middle-Income Settings: A Retrospective Analysis of Data from 145 Countries', *eScholarship*, University of California, 2014.

82 'Show Me the Science - Why Wash Your Hands?' *Center for Disease Control and Prevention*, last updated September 10, 2020.

83 Lance T. Tomooka, Claire Murphy, and Terence M. Davidson, 'Clinical Study and Literature Review of Nasal Irrigation', *The Laryngoscope* 110, no. 7 (2000): 1193.

irrigating the nose, unless you are fasting.'[84] In other words, the water should almost reach the throat in this nasal rinsing, hence carefulness during fasting is warranted.

The Islamic message also reinforced the notion that ritual washing is not just about outer cleanliness. The Prophet Muhammad ﷺ taught that before performing the *ṣalāh* to connect with God, this sacred engagement should begin with the *wuḍū'* even if we may be externally unsoiled. This seems to symbolize the inseparability of the physical and metaphysical realms, and that just as water originates from the heavens to cleanse our physical bodies from dirt and unpleasant odors, it too allows us to reconnect with heaven through rinsing our spirits from that which has polluted them. In the context of ritual purification, Allah concludes the discussion with an allusion to this profound dual function, saying, *'Allah loves those who are constantly repentant and loves those who purify themselves.'*[85] The Prophet ﷺ also linked the purification of the exterior and interior, helping us remember that during the ritual washing of our bodies, we are also cleansing our souls and subconscious minds from the iniquities that regularly pollute them. He said:

> No person among you brings near his ablution water, then rinses his mouth and irrigates then clears his nose, except that the sins of his face and mouth and nostrils fall therefrom. And then, he does not wash his face as Allah has instructed him, except that his face's sins fall from the tips of his beard along with the water. And then, he does not wash his arms to the elbows, except that his arms' sins fall from his fingertips along with the water. And then, he does not pass his [wet hands] over his head, except that the sins of his head are washed away through the ends of his hair along with the water. And then, he does not wash

84 al-Tirmidhī, *Sunan al-Tirmidhī,* 2:147 #788; authenticated by al-Tirmidhī in the comments.

85 (*al-Baqarah* 2: 222)

his feet to the ankles, except that his feet's sins are washed away from his toes along with the water. Then, he does not rise to prayer, wherein he praises Allah, glorifies Him, proclaims His greatness as He deserves, and pours his heart out to Allah, except that he emerges from that prayer as sin-free as the day his mother gave birth to him.[86]

9. Science and Medicine

In the first passages ever revealed to the Prophet Muhammad ﷺ, Allah said,

> *Read [O Prophet] in the name of your Lord who created. [He] created humans from a clinging substance. Read, and your Lord is the Most Generous. Who taught by the pen. [He] taught mankind what they knew not.*[87]

What may be the most overlooked teaching of the Prophet Muhammad ﷺ, and yet one of the greatest debts owed to him, is the fact that he taught the world the importance of knowledge. Liberating them from centuries of superstition, he taught his followers the necessity of investing their lives in pursuing education. Historians recognize that it was on his cue that literacy rates soared past those of contemporaneous societies, even though in the Arabia of his birth, illiteracy was the norm. In a very short span of time, the major Muslim cities such as Makkah, Madinah, Baghdad, and Cordoba (Muslim Spain) became the hubs of knowledge and scholarship. It suffices to consider that the caliphal library in Medieval Cordoba, one of its seventy libraries then, reportedly had 400,000 books while the largest library in Christian Europe probably had 400 manuscripts.[88]

---

86 Muslim, *Ṣaḥīḥ Muslim*, 1:569 #832.

87 (*al-ʿAlaq* 96: 1–5)

88 Maria Menocal, *The Ornament of the World* (Boston: Back Bay Books, 2002), 33.

He validated his followers' intellectual potential by saying, 'You know better concerning your worldly affairs.'[89] Through statements like these, the early Muslims understood that demonstrated expertise and empirical findings ought to be respected. Stemming from that paradigm, Islam instituted the liability of physicians and set intellectual standards for centuries. This was no coincidence, but rather due to the Prophet ﷺ saying, 'He who practices medicine without being known for proficiency in medicine shall be liable.'[90] Cautioned by that statement, tenth-century Baghdad (Iraq) instituted a medical licensing exam that all physicians had to take before practising medicine.[91]

In addition to pioneering this accountability, Islam also provides by it a way to counteract the enormous amount of medical misinformation circulated on the internet by non-specialists today. Now that the phenomenon of democratizing knowledge has infected our world with the inability to distinguish between reliable facts and pseudo-scientific medical claims, the Prophet Muhammad's teachings offer a safeguard against falling back into the dogmatic anti-intellectualism that characterized the world before mass literacy.

In another tradition, the Prophet ﷺ said, 'Allah has not sent down a disease except that He sent down for it a cure, regardless of who may know it and who may be ignorant of it.'[92] In other words, these cures are all discoverable, so let the

---

89 Muslim, *Ṣaḥīḥ Muslim*, 4:1836 #2363.

90 Ibn Mājah, *Sunan Ibn Mājah*, 8:52 #4830; a *ḥasan* (acceptable) chain according to al-Albānī in the comments.

91 Firas Alkhateeb, *Lost Islamic History: Reclaiming Muslim Civilisation from the Past* (London: Hurst, 2014), 72.

92 Ibn Ḥanbal, *Musnad Aḥmad*, 6:50 #3578; authenticated by al-Arnā'ūṭ in the comments. In another narration, Usāmah ibn Sharīk ؓ reports that the Bedouins said, 'O Messenger of Allah, should we seek treatments?' He said, 'Seek treatments, for Allah has not created an ailment except that He created its cure, except for one.' They said, 'O Messenger of Allah, what is it?' He said, 'Aging.' (*Sunan al-Tirmidhī*, 3:451 #2038; authenticated by al-Tirmidhī in the comments)

research renaissance begin. Muslims became so advanced in medicine that William Osler, a founder of the Medical Library Association, said the Canon (*Qānūn*) of Avicenna (*Ibn Sīna*) had remained a medical bible in Europe for a longer period than any other work.[93]

It was also the Prophet Muhammad ﷺ who introduced the concept of medical quarantine. When 'Umar ibn al-Khaṭṭāb ؓ, the Prophet's second successor, reached a place called Sargh during his travels, he was informed that there was a plague in the lands of Shām where he was heading. 'Abd al-Raḥmān ibn 'Awf ؓ, another senior Companion of the Prophet, told 'Umar that the Messenger of Allah ﷺ had said, 'When you hear about its occurrence in a land, do not enter it. And when it happens in a land, do not flee it.'[94]

On the renaissance of knowledge sparked by the guidance of Muhammad ﷺ, Yale University's Franz Rosenthal says in *Knowledge Triumphant*:

For 'ilm (knowledge) is one of those concepts that have dominated Islam and given Muslim civilization its distinctive shape and complexion. In fact, there is no other concept that has been operative as a determinant of Muslim civilization in all its aspects to the same extent as 'ilm ... There is no branch of Muslim intellectual life, of Muslim religious and political life, and of the daily life of the average Muslim that remained untouched by the all-pervasive attitude toward knowledge as something of supreme value for Muslim being. 'Ilm is Islam, even if the theologians have been hesitant to accept the technical correctness of this equation. The very fact of their

93 Evelyn B. Kelly, 'The Significance of Ibn Sina's Canon of Medicine in the Arab and Western Worlds', *Encyclopedia.com by Cengage*, updated June 13th, 2020.
94 al-Bukhārī, *Saḥīḥ al-Bukhārī*, 7:130 #5728; Muslim, *Saḥīḥ Muslim*, 4:1737 #2218.

passionate discussion of the concept attests to its fundamental importance for Islam.[95]

In *The Classical Heritage in Islam*, Rosenthal adds:

> Neither practical utilitarianism, however, which made an acquaintance with medicine, alchemy and the exact sciences appear desirable to Muslims, nor theoretical utilitarianism, which prompted them to occupy themselves with philosophical-theological questions, might have sufficed to support an extensive activity of translation, had not Muhammad's religion, from the very beginning, emphasized the role of knowledge ('ilm) as the driving force in religion and, thereby, in all human life.[96]

Robert Briffault (d. 1948), a British surgeon and social anthropologist, writes,

> The debt of our science to that of the Arabs does not consist of startling discoveries or revolutionary theories; science owes a great deal more to the Arabs; its own existence.[97]

---

95 Franz Rosenthal, *Knowledge Triumphant: The Concept of Knowledge in Medieval Islam* (Leiden: Brill, 2007), 2.

96 Franz Rosenthal, *The Classical Heritage in Islam* (London: Routledge, 2003), 5.
Rosenthal adds elsewhere that the advent of the Qur'an also stimulated historical research in a way that changed the course of history when it came to historiography. The reason, he argues, is that suddenly the actions of individuals (like prophets), the events of the past, and the circumstances of all peoples of the earth had now become matters of religious importance, in addition to the abundance of historical data in the Qur'an which Muhammad ﷺ brought that incentivized pursuing additional illustrative historical information. (See: Franz Rosenthal, *A History of Muslim Historiography* (Leiden: E.J. Brill, 1968), 28)

97 Robert Briffault, *The Making of Humanity* (London: G. Allen & Unwin Ltd, 1919), 191.

Continuing:

> Roger Bacon was no more than one of the apostles of Muslim science and method to Christian Europe; and he never wearied of declaring that knowledge of Arabic and Arabic science was for his contemporaries the only way to true knowledge ... Science is the most momentous contribution of Arab civilization to the modern world.[98]

The Prophet Muhammad ﷺ was therefore not just an orphan who adopted the world with his compassion, but an unlettered shepherd who provided an extraordinary prism that addresses every theological, ethical, or civilizational inquiry until the end of time. He propounded a message of profound substance, coupled with fine-tuned laws that remained flexible enough that the message would remain forever pertinent and never become outdated. He offered the world a definitive message, but one also versatile enough to accommodate the transformations in world dynamics that were unimaginable to the brightest minds 1,400 years ago. Such vitality reflects the impeccable equilibrium that was struck in his teachings, and somehow without any trial-and-error phase.

With that, we complete our tour of what could be described as the intellectual miracle of the Prophet Muhammad ﷺ, namely that his message was among the most compelling facets of his prophethood and the strongest indicators of its divine origins. His teachings laid the foundation for a coherent and integrated system of theology, law, and ethics that addressed all the needs of the existential human condition: physical, mental, social, and spiritual. His system endures to this day and will persist for as long as God wills, bringing enlightenment, wisdom, and comfort to millions of believers throughout history and across a diverse range of social and cultural contexts.

---

98 Ibid., 201-202.

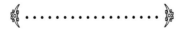

5

The Prophet's Prophecies

Some of the greatest and most convincing testimonies to the prophethood of Muhammad ﷺ are the numerous occasions on which he correctly predicted future events. Only one to whom God had granted access to the realm of the unseen could have, time and again, accurately foretold the future. This chapter will seek to capture some of these predictions—all derived from Qur'anic verses and authentic hadith—and how each one of them came to pass, just as he predicted.

Al-Qāḍī 'Iyāḍ (d. 1149) says, 'This genre of hadith are a bottomless ocean and an unending stream. They are one of his miracles which are undeniably established, transmitted to us by abundant concurrence (*tawātur*), due to their many narrators and the concordance of their meanings, all corroborating the fact that he was privy to [some of] the unseen.'[1] In this chapter, we will take a dive into this ocean, exploring some of its wonders.

1 al-Qāḍī 'Iyāḍ ibn Mūsā and Aḥmad ibn Muḥammad Shumunnī, *Al-Shifā bi-Ta'rīf Ḥuqūq al-Muṣṭafā* (Amman: Dār al-Fikr, 1988), 1:335–336.

1. The Byzantines will Rebound

From a desolate corner of the earth that had been largely unaffected by the power struggles of the world's superpowers, the Qur'an boldly foretold the most unexpected events that would transpire between Persia and Byzantium in a few short years. *'The Byzantines have been defeated. In the nearest land. But they, after their defeat, will overcome. Within three to nine years.'*[2] From 613-619, the Byzantines were decimated by the Persian Empire, losing the territories of Antioch, then Damascus, then Armenia, then their most cherished Jerusalem, then Chalcedon, and finally Egypt. In his book, *The History of the Decline and Fall of the Roman Empire*, Edward Gibbon says: 'At the time when this prediction is said to have been delivered, no prophecy could be more distant from its accomplishment, since the first twelve years of Heraclius announced the approaching dissolution of the empire.'[3]

Everyone saw Byzantium as on its deathbed. Hence, opponents of the Prophet ﷺ like Ubayy ibn Khalaf mocked this 'preposterous' foretelling in the Qur'an.[4] However, not long after, Heraclius led the Byzantine Crusade like a dagger into the heart of the Persian Empire, fulfilling the amazing prophecy six to eight years after it was made.[5]

The verses that immediately follow this prediction say, *'The decision of the matter, before and after [these events], is only with Allah. And on that Day, the believers [i.e., Muslims] will rejoice in the victory of Allah.'*[6]

Abū Ḥayyān al-Andalūsī (d. 1344) lists in *al-Baḥr al-Muḥīṭ* four reasons for this rejoicing, including that the miraculous prophecy unfolding would further validate the Muslims' belief

---

2 (*al-Rūm* 30: 2–4)

3 Edward Gibbon, *Decline and Fall of the Roman Empire: Volume the Fourth* (London: Electric Book Co, 2001), chapter XLVI, 479.

4 Ibn Kathīr, *Tafsīr al-Qur'ān al- 'Aẓīm* (Beirut: Dār al-Kutub al-'Ilmīyah, 1998), 6:270.

5 Touraj Daryaee, *Sasanian Persia: The Rise and Fall of an Empire* (London: I.B. Tauris, 2012), 33.

6 (*al-Rūm* 30: 4–5)

in his prophethood. Another reason, which involves another prophecy, is that the Muslims would then find themselves celebrating their own victory: a long-awaited triumph against the Meccan oppressors in the Battle of Badr also happened in 624.[7] It suddenly becomes quite clear why God seals this chapter of the Qur'an *(Sūrah al-Rūm)* by saying, '*So be patient. Indeed, the promise of Allah is truth. And let them not disquiet you who are not certain [in faith].*'[8]

2. The Abode of Abū Lahab

In the moments following the Prophet Muhammad's first public call to Islam, his own uncle, Abū Lahab, scoffed at and chastised him. In his defense, God immediately revealed, '*May the hands of Abū Lahab be ruined, and ruined is he. His wealth will not avail him or that which he gained. He will burn in a Fire of [blazing] flame.*'[9] It is astonishing that for the next nine years of Abū Lahab's life, despite hearing these verses being recited, his pride prevented him from taking them as an opportunity to discredit the Qur'an. Had Abū Lahab simply converted, even disingenuously, that would have brought into serious question the truth of this Revelation. Of course, He who revealed this knew Abū Lahab would never do so.

3. The Globalization of Islam

Amid the fiercest persecution and abuse that the Muslims faced in the earliest Meccan period, the Prophet Muhammad ﷺ would stand without wavering and convey to his followers God's promise of Islam spreading all over the world. Tamīm al-Dārī ؓ reports that the Messenger of Allah ﷺ said, 'This matter will certainly reach every place touched by the night and day. Allah will not leave

7 Muḥammad ibn Yūsuf Abū Ḥayyān, *Al-Baḥr al-Muḥīt fī al-Tafsīr* (Beirut: Dār al-Fikr, 1992), 8:375.

8 (*al-Rūm* 30: 60)

9 (*al-Masad* 111: 1–3)

a house of mud or even fur except that He will cause this religion to enter it, by which the honourable will be honoured, and the disgraceful will be disgraced. Allah will honour the honourable with Islam and He will disgrace the disgraceful with unbelief.'[10]

In another narration, reported by Thawbān ﷺ, 'Indeed, Allah gathered up the earth for me so that I saw its east and its west, and the dominion of my nation will indeed reach what was gathered up for me.'[11] The fact that these predictions were made at a time when Muslims were a powerless handful, and Islam was expected to be buried in its cradle, is nothing short of miraculous. At that point, presuming that the faith would even survive would be considered by most to be a pipe dream. That Islam would not just survive, but grow to thrive globally, was at that point inconceivable. We now find mosques on every inhabited continent, and even in remote places like Alaska and Hawaii. This truly complicates the argument that this hadith could have been fabricated after Islam had spread throughout the Mediterranean and Central Asia, considering it has spread so much farther since then. Millions of Muslims now reside in lands that were unknown when these prophecies were first stated, such as the Americas and Australia, and Islam is on track to becoming by 2070 the religion with the most adherents on the planet.[12]

It is no longer difficult to imagine Europe organically becoming majority Muslim in another century. Islam has already grown remarkably there, with the mayor of London currently being a Muslim, and Pew Research Center noting that Sweden could become 30 per cent Muslim by 2050.[13] In all this is a clear

10 Ibn Ḥanbal, *Musnad Aḥmad*, 28:154 #16957; authenticated by al-Arnā'ūṭ in the comments and al-Albānī in *Silsilat al-Aḥādīth al-Ṣaḥīḥah* (Riyadh: Maktabat al-Ma'ārif, 1996), 1:32 #3.

11 Muslim, *Ṣaḥīḥ Muslim*, 4:2215 #2889.

12 'The Future of World Religions: Population Growth Projections, 2010–2050', *Pew Research Center*, April 2nd, 2015.

13 'Europe's Growing Muslim Population', *Pew Research Center*, November 29, 2017.

indication of the fulfillment of the prophecy of Islam inevitably becoming a leading global religion.

4. Undeterred by Time or Distance

Regarding the night prior to the Battle of Badr, ʿUmar ibn al-Khaṭṭāb ﵁ said, 'The Prophet ﷺ showed us where those [enemies] at Badr would die. He would place his hand somewhere on the ground and say, "This is where so-and-so will die tomorrow, by God's will, and this is where so-and-so will die." I swear by the One who sent him with the Truth, none of them fell anywhere other than exactly where the Prophet's hand had touched.'[14]

Anas ibn Mālik ﵁ reported that, as the Battle of Mu'tah was taking place in Jordan, the Prophet ﷺ informed the people in Madinah of the martyrdom of Zayd ibn Ḥārithah ﵁, Jaʿfar ibn Abī Ṭālib ﵁, and ʿAbdullāh ibn Rawāḥah ﵁. Even though they were 600 miles away, the Prophet ﷺ said, 'Zayd took the flag (as commander) and was killed, then Jaʿfar took the flag and was killed, then Ibn Rawāḥah took the flag and was killed.' Anas describes that as the Prophet ﷺ was telling them this, 'his eyes were shedding tears.' He continued, 'Then the flag was taken by one of God's swords (Khālid ibn al-Walīd ﵁), and Allah made him victorious.'[15] That army eventually returned to Madinah, with eyewitness accounts that matched exactly what the Prophet ﷺ had described.

Abū Ḥumayd al-Sāʿidī ﵁ said, 'When we reached Tabūk, the Prophet ﷺ said, "There will be a strong wind tonight and so no one should stand and whoever has a camel should fasten it." We fastened our camels, and then a strong wind did in fact blow at night, and a man stood up and was consequently blown away to a mountain called Ṭayyi'.'[16]

---

14 Muslim, *Ṣaḥīḥ Muslim*, 3:1403 #1779.

15 al-Bukhārī, *Ṣaḥīḥ al-Bukhārī*, 2:72 #1246.

16 al-Bukhārī, *Ṣaḥīḥ al-Bukhārī*, 2:125 #1481.

Sahl ibn Saʿd ﷺ reports that as the Prophet ﷺ and his Companions returned to camp after a day of battle, he overheard people celebrating the valour of a man 'who vanquished every enemy that faced him; none outdid him today.' To the shock of those present, the Messenger of Allah ﷺ said, 'Rather, he will be in the Hellfire.' One man said, 'I will shadow him,' and closely followed him at every turn. Soon thereafter, this man came to the Prophet ﷺ and said, 'I testify that you are indeed the Messenger of Allah!' He said, 'Why [do you say] that?' He said, 'The people were astounded when you said this man would be in the Hellfire, so I followed him until he was badly wounded and sought to hasten his death. He placed the handle of his sword on the ground and its tip between his chest, then leaned on it and killed himself.' Explaining that this mortal sin was an indicator of prior insincerity undetected by others, the Messenger of Allah ﷺ said:

> Certainly, a man may perform the deeds of the people of Paradise, in terms of what is apparent to the people, while in reality he is among the people of the Hellfire. And a man may perform the deeds of the people of the Hellfire, in terms of what is apparent to the people, while in reality he is among the people of Paradise.[17]

5. Six in Sequence

During the Battle of Tabūk, the Prophet ﷺ said to ʿAwf ibn Mālik ﷺ:

> Count six signs before the Hour; my death, the conquest of Jerusalem, two mortal plagues that will take you [in great numbers] as the plague of sheep [depletes them], then wealth will be in such surplus that a man will be

17 al-Bukhārī, *Ṣaḥīḥ al-Bukhārī*, 4:37 #2898; Muslim, *Ṣaḥīḥ Muslim*, 1:106 #112.

> given a hundred gold coins and still be unsatisfied, then there will be a tribulation that will not leave an Arab home without entering it, then there will be a truce between you (the Muslims) and Banū al-Aṣfar (the Byzantines) which they will betray, and march against you under eighty flags, and under each flag will be twelve thousand soldiers.[18]

Jerusalem was conquered five years after his death, in the year 15H, followed by the plague of ʿAmwās in 18H which took the lives of many Companions. An unprecedented surplus of wealth was experienced during the caliphate of ʿUthmān ibn ʿAffān ﷺ, 23H, as a result of conquests on every front. As for the tribulation that would spare no Arab home, this took place following the assassination of ʿUthmān, 37H, for it resulted in much dissent and disorder. As for the truce and scourge of the Byzantines, traditional scholars seem to agree that this is a prophecy about the end-times.

6. Counting the Conquests

The Prophet Muhammad ﷺ foretold a multitude of Muslim conquests, including those of Rome, Persia, Egypt, Yemen, India, and Constantinople. None of these prophecies were described vaguely or with equivocation, but rather with an air of absolute certainty.

Al-Barā' ibn ʿĀzib ﷺ reports that while digging the trench outside Madinah to repel an approaching army, a massive boulder obstructed them that no axe would break. With time running out, and with people's fears and hunger growing, the Prophet ﷺ walked over and picked up the axe. He said, 'In God's name *(Bismillāh)*,' and hammered the boulder, reducing a chunk of it to rubble. He said, 'God is Great (*Allāhu Akbar*)! I have been given

---

18 al-Bukhārī, *Ṣaḥīḥ al-Bukhārī*, 4:101 #3176.

the keys to Shām; I can see its red palaces at this very moment.' Then he shattered another chunk and said, '*Allāhu Akbar*! I have been given the keys to Persia; I can see Madā'in's white palace.' Then he shattered the last chunk and said, '*Allāhu Akbar*! I have been given the keys to Yemen. By Allah, I can see the Gates of Ṣan'ā at this very moment from here.'[19]

Regarding Egypt, he took its conquest for granted, knowing his Lord's promise was true. Abū Dharr ﵁ narrated: The Prophet ﷺ said: 'You will certainly conquer Egypt, a land in which [a currency called] *al-qīrāṭ* is customary. When you conquer it, be gracious to its people, for they are entitled to a covenant and [the right of] family bonds. And when you see two men disputing over the place of a brick, then leave [Egypt].'[20] The Prophet ﷺ accurately spoke in the second person here, foretelling that none other than his personal Companions would conquer Egypt. Then he instructed them to honour their peace treaty with the Egyptians and reminded them that their grandmother (Hagar; the mother of Ishmael) was from this land. In this same narration, Abū Dharr ﵁ adds, 'I witnessed 'Abd al-Raḥmān ibn Shuraḥbīl ibn Ḥasanah and his brother, Rabī'ah, disputing over the place of a brick, so I departed [from Egypt].'

Regarding Constantinople, presently called Istanbul, the Prophet ﷺ said that it would become a Muslim land nearly a millennium prior to that happening. 'Abdullāh ibn 'Amr ﵁ reports that, as they were once sitting with the Messenger of Allah ﷺ and writing, he was asked, 'Which city will be liberated first; Constantinople or Rome?' He said, 'The city of Heraclius will be liberated first,'[21] meaning Constantinople. An entire 800 years later, this great feat was accomplished by the Ottoman sultan, Muhammad al-Fātiḥ.

---

19 Ibn Ḥanbal, *Musnad Aḥmad*, 30:625 #18694; a *ḥasan* (acceptable) chain according to Ibn Ḥajar al-'Asqalānī in *Fatḥ al-Bārī* (Beirut: Dār al-Ma'rifah, 1959), 7:397.

20 Muslim, *Ṣaḥīḥ Muslim*, 4:1970 #2543.

21 Ibn Ḥanbal, *Musnad Aḥmad*, 11:224-225 #6645; authenticated by al-Albānī in *al-Silsilah al-Ṣaḥīḥah*, 1:33 #4.

In another hadith: 'Constantinople will certainly be liberated, and how excellent a leader will its leader be, and how excellent an army that army will be.'[22] Some scholars hold that this second hadith may refer to a second liberation of Constantinople which was also prophesied but has not yet taken place.

7. SECURITY WILL PREVAIL

'Adī ibn Ḥātim ☙ narrates that prior to accepting Islam, 'As I was with the Prophet ☙, a man came to him complaining of poverty, and then another came to him complaining of highway robbery. He said, "O 'Adī, have you seen al-Ḥīrah (in Iraq)?" I said, "No, but I have been told about it." He said, "If you live long enough, you will see a woman travel on camel from al-Ḥīrah till she circles the Kaaba not fearing anyone but Allah." I said to myself, "Where then would the bandits of Ṭayyi' be, who have pillaged these lands?" He continued, "And if you live long enough, the treasures of Chosroes, the son of Hurmuz, will be conquered." I said, "Chosroes, the son of Hurmuz?" He confirmed, "Chosroes, the son of Hurmuz. And if you live long enough, you will see a man walking out, hand filled with gold or silver, seeking someone to accept it but he will not find anyone to accept it."'

Later in his life, 'Adī said, 'I have in fact seen a woman travel on camel from al-Ḥīrah till she circled the Kaaba while not fearing anyone but Allah, and I was among those who conquered the treasures of Chosroes, the son of Hurmuz. And if you live long enough, you will see what the Prophet ☙—Abūl Qāsim—said regarding a man walking out, hand filled.'[23] Muslim historians document that the inability to find someone eligible to accept charity took place during the reign of the 'Abbāsid caliph, 'Umar ibn 'Abd al-'Azīz (d. 720).

---

[22] Ibn Ḥanbal, *Musnad Aḥmad*, 31:287 #18957; authenticated elsewhere by al-Ḥākim and al-Dhahabī concurred, though it was deemed weak here by al-Arna'ūṭ in the comments.

[23] al-Bukhārī, *Ṣaḥīḥ al-Bukhārī*, 4:197 #3595.

8. The Last Emperors

When the Quraysh tribe embraced Islam, they feared being blocked from their trade routes to Shām and Iraq, since these territories were under Byzantine and Sassanid rule and both had rejected the call to Islam. Jābir ibn Samurah ﵁ reports the Prophet ﷺ addressing this concern by reassuring Quraysh that those empires would soon vanish from both regions. He said, 'When Chosroes dies, there will be no Chosroes after him. And when Caesar dies, there will be no Caesar after him. And I swear by the One in whose hand is Muhammad's soul, their treasures will be spent in the path of God.'[24]

Imam al-Shāfiʿī and al-Khaṭṭābī (d. 988) explained that this meant there would never be another Caesar in Greater Syria, nor any other Chosroes in Iraq (Sassanid Persia). Indeed, the final Chosroes who rose to power during the Prophet's life was Yazdegerd III (d. 651), and he indeed became the 38th and final king of the Sassanid Empire. The final Caesar during the Prophet's life was Heraclius (d. 641), and Byzantium did in fact collapse and lose Christendom's holiest site of Jerusalem during his reign. After those individuals, neither empire maintained a presence in either of the two regions.[25]

9. A Whisper in His Daughter's Ear

ʿĀ'ishah ﵂ narrates:

> As the Prophet ﷺ lay on his deathbed, with all of his wives present, his daughter Fāṭimah came forward, walking just as the Messenger of Allah ﷺ would walk. He received her, saying, 'Welcome, my dear daughter.'

---

24 al-Bukhārī, *Ṣaḥīḥ al-Bukhārī*, 4:203 #3618; Muslim, *Ṣaḥīḥ Muslim*, 4:2237 #2919.

25 Ibn Ḥajar, *Fatḥ al-Bārī*, 6:626; Muḥammad ibn ʿAbdul-Raḥmān al-Mubārakfūrī, *Tuḥfat al-Aḥwadhī bi-Sharḥ Jāmiʿ al-Tirmidhī* (Beirut: Dār al-Kutub al-ʿIlmyah, 1990), 6:383 #221.

> He then sat her down beside him and uttered a secret to her which caused Fāṭimah to weep. He then uttered another secret to her, making her laugh. I asked her what made her cry, but she said, 'I would never disclose the Messenger of Allah's secret.' I had never seen a joy and grief so closely as I saw on that day, so I said to her when she wept, 'The Messenger of Allah ﷺ privileges you with his words, and not us, and then you weep?' I asked her again what he said, but she responded, 'I would never disclose the Messenger of Allah's secret.' When he died, I asked her again, and she said he told her, 'Gabriel used to review the Qur'an with me one time each year, and he reviewed it twice with me this year. I cannot understand from this except that my time has arrived, and you will be the first of my family to catch up with me.' Fāṭimah said, 'I cried at this, and so he discreetly said to me, "Are you not pleased to be the queen of the believers [in Paradise]?' And that is what caused me to laugh."'[26]

Imam al-Nawawī (d. 1277) points out that this is actually two prophecies in one. The first is that he foretold that this sickness, and not any other illness before it, was a harbinger that his time had come, and that the young Fāṭimah—in her early twenties at that time—would die before any other member of his family.

10. The Longest Arm

'Ā'ishah ﵂ also narrates that when the Prophet Muhammad ﷺ was presented with the question, 'Which of your wives will be reunited with you first [in the hereafter]?' he responded, 'The fastest of you in catching up with me will be the one with the longest arm among you.' Due to that statement, 'Ā'ishah reports

---

26 al-Bukhārī, *Ṣaḥīḥ al-Bukhārī*, 6:10 #4433; Muslim, *Ṣaḥīḥ Muslim*, 4:1904 #2450.

that his wives used to speculate, and even measure against the wall, which wife had the longest arm. Sawdah bint Zamʿah 🕮 was the tallest of them, but when Zaynab bint Jahsh 🕮 died first, they realized 'longest arm' meant most charitable. ʿĀʾishah says, 'Zaynab had the longest arm among us, because she used to work with her hands and donate from her earnings.'[27]

11. THE MARTYRDOM OF ʿUMAR AND ʿUTHMĀN

Abū Mūsā al-Ashʿarī 🕮 said:

> I was with the Prophet 🕮 in one of the gardens in Madinah, then a man came and requested that the door be opened. The Prophet 🕮 said, 'Open it for him, and give him the glad tidings of Paradise.' I opened for him, and it turned out to be Abū Bakr, so I gave him the glad tidings of what the Prophet 🕮 had said. He praised Allah, and later another man came and requested that the door be opened. The Prophet 🕮 said, 'Open it for him, and give him the glad tidings of Paradise.' I opened for him, and it turned out to be ʿUmar, so I gave him the glad tidings of what the Prophet 🕮 had said. He praised Allah, and later another man came and requested that the door be opened. The Prophet 🕮 said, 'Open it for him, and give him the glad tidings of Paradise due to a calamity that befalls him.' It turned out to be ʿUthmān, so I informed him of what the Messenger of Allah 🕮 had said. He praised Allah, and then he said, 'Allah is sought for help.'[28]

In another narration, Anas ibn Mālik 🕮 reported that when the Prophet 🕮 ascended Mount Uhud along with Abū Bakr,

[27] al-Bukhārī, Ṣaḥīḥ al-Bukhārī, 2:110 #1420; Muslim, Ṣaḥīḥ Muslim, 4:1907 #2452.
[28] al-Bukhārī, Ṣaḥīḥ al-Bukhārī, 5:13 #3693; Muslim, Ṣaḥīḥ Muslim, 4:1867 #2403.

ʿUmar, and ʿUthmān ﷺ, the mountain shook beneath them. The Prophet ﷺ tapped it with his foot and said, 'Be firm, Uḥud, for upon you are none other than a Prophet, a *ṣiddīq*, and two martyrs.'[29] Both ʿUmar and ʿUthmān attained martyrdom by being assassinated during their respective caliphates. With ʿUthmān in particular, the Prophet ﷺ gave further details: 'O ʿUthmān, Allah—the Mighty and Majestic—may garb you in a shirt. If the hypocrites demand that you remove it, do not remove it until you meet me.'[30] It was this very accusation, that ʿUthmān was unfit to 'wear that shirt' (i.e., don the caliphate), that the mobs repeated before laying siege to and then storming his house and killing him.

12. Inevitable Infighting

Saʿd ibn Abī Waqqāṣ ﷺ narrates that the Messenger of Allah ﷺ once visited the mosque of Banū Muʿāwiyah:

> He entered, performed two units of prayer, which we prayed with him, and then he invoked his Lord for a long time. Then, he turned to us and said: 'I asked my Lord for three things; He granted me two and withheld one. I asked my Lord not to destroy my nation with a widespread famine, and He granted me that, and I asked Him that He not exterminate my nation by drowning, and He granted me that. And I asked Him that He not let their aggression be against one another, but He withheld that from me.'[31]

In another narration:

> Indeed, Allah has gathered the earth for me until I saw its east and its west, and the kingdom of my nation will

[29] al-Bukhārī, *Ṣaḥīḥ al-Bukhārī*, 5:9 #3675.
[30] al-Tirmidhī, *Sunan al-Tirmidhī*, 6:69 #3705.
[31] Muslim, *Ṣaḥīḥ Muslim*, 4:2216 #2890.

> reach whatever of it has been gathered up for me. And I have been given the two treasures; the red and white (gold and silver). And I asked my Lord that He not destroy it with a widespread famine, and that He not empower against them an external enemy that will annihilate them. My Lord said, 'O Muhammad, when I decree a matter, it cannot be repelled. I have granted you, for your nation, that I do not destroy them with a widespread famine, and that I do not empower against them an external enemy that annihilates them—even if those from every corner of the earth unite against them. However, they will ultimately kill one another, and enslave one another.' Once the sword is drawn within my nation, it will not be removed from them until the Day of Resurrection.[32]

13. Tensions Among the Prophet's Household

Abū Rāfiʿ ﷺ reported that the Prophet ﷺ said to ʿAlī ﷺ, 'There will be an issue between you and ʿĀ'ishah.' He said, 'Me, O Messenger of Allah?!' He said, 'Yes.' He said, 'Me?' He said, 'Yes.' He said, 'Then, in that case, I would be the worst person ever.' He said, 'No. But when this occurs, return her to her safe quarters.'[33] Just prior to her clash with ʿAlī, when ʿĀ'ishah ﷺ heard dogs barking near Basrah at a place called Ḥaw'ab, she said, 'Perhaps I must return home, for the Messenger of Allah ﷺ said to us (his wives), "Which one of you will be barked at by the dogs of Ḥaw'ab?"'[34] Hopeful that her presence would effect a resolution, and that this was only a prophecy and not a prohibition, ʿĀ'ishah ﷺ decided not to abort her journey.

---

32 Muslim, *Ṣaḥīḥ Muslim*, 4:2215 #2889.

33 Ibn Ḥanbal, *Musnad Aḥmad*, 45:175 #27197; a *ḥasan* (acceptable) chain according to Ibn Ḥajar in *Fatḥ al-Bārī*, 13:55.

34 Ibn Ḥibbān, *Ṣaḥīḥ Ibn Ḥibbān*, 15:126 #6732; authenticated by al-Arna'ūṭ and al-Albānī in the comments.

14. The Fate of ʿAmmār

Abū Saʿīd al-Khudrī ﵁ narrated that, as the Muslims were building the mosque in Madinah, ʿAmmār ibn Yāsir ﵁ would carry two bricks at a time while others lifted one. When the Prophet ﷺ saw him, he began wiping the dust off ʿAmmār with his hands and said, 'Woe to ʿAmmār, who will be killed by the transgressing party! He will be inviting them to Paradise, and they will be inviting him to the Fire.' To that, ʿAmmār replied, 'We seek refuge with Allah from the trials.'[35] Three decades after that prophecy, when the Battle of Ṣiffīn took place, ʿAmmār was killed by the army of Shām who transgressed against the Muslim ruler, ʿAlī ﵁, while seeking to avenge the murdered caliph, ʿUthmān ﵁. Interestingly, the army of Shām did not claim that this hadith had been fabricated, but rather argued that those who called him to fight were the 'transgressing party' ultimately responsible for his death.

This substantiates that forging hadith was unfathomable by the Companions, and thus, they did not question the authenticity of the prophecy and only differed on how to interpret it. Finally, moments before the Battle of Ṣiffīn, some milk was passed to ʿAmmār which caused him to smile. He said, 'The Prophet ﷺ told me that the last thing I would drink before dying would be some milk.'[36] Then he rose to meet the promise of his Prophet ﷺ and fought until his death.

---

35 al-Bukhārī, *Ṣaḥīḥ al-Bukhārī*, 1:97 #337. ʿAmmār ﵁ was 'invited by them to the Fire' because he rightfully believed that standing by the Muslim ruler was mandatory, and hence abandoning ʿAlī ﵁ would have been sinful rebellion. As for those who sincerely believed otherwise, the official Sunni position is that they were mistaken while pursuing the truth and therefore not sinful. Some scholars, like Ibn Baṭṭāl, held that 'they will be inviting him to the Fire' does not refer to the other army, but rather to the Khārijites to whom ʿAlī sent ʿAmmār as an ambassador and negotiator. They were also the same rebels who provoked the army of ʿAlī to eventually raise arms against them at Ṣiffīn.

36 Ibn Ḥanbal, *Musnad Aḥmad*, 31:178 #18883; authenticated by al-Arnaʾūṭ in the comments.

15. ʿAlī Suppressing the Khārijites

In another foretelling of this turbulent period, Abū Saʿīd al-Khudrī ﷺ narrates that the Prophet ﷺ said, 'A dissenting faction will splinter at a time of disunity between the Muslims, and they will be fought by the more correct of the two parties.'[37] Again, it was the army of Kūfa (led by ʿAlī ﷺ), not Shām (led by Muʿāwiyah ﷺ), who fought the Khārijite rebels at Nahrawān in 37H, making them the 'more correct' and non-transgressing party.

Regarding the roots of the Khārijites, the Prophet ﷺ was once accused by a hypocrite known as Dhul Khuwayṣirah of inequity. The Prophet ﷺ told those seeking to punish this man for his insult:

> Leave him be. He will certainly have fellows who will cause you to belittle your own prayer when compared to their prayer, and his fasting compared to their fasting. They will recite the Qur'an, but it will not pass beyond their throats [to their hearts]. They will exit the religion as an arrow passes through a game animal, whereby one would look at the arrowhead and not see any traces on it; one would look at the binding which fastens the arrowhead to the rod and not see any traces on it; one would look at the rod itself and not see any traces on it; one would look at the feathers and not see any traces on them. It would go straight through the bowels and the blood. Their sign will be a black man whose limbs will appear like a woman's breasts, or like a disfigured lump of flesh. They will emerge at a time when the people are disunited.

The narrator, Abū Saʿīd ﷺ, adds:

> I testify that I heard this hadith directly from the Messenger of Allah ﷺ, and I testify that ʿAlī ibn Abī Ṭālib ﷺ

---

37 Muslim, *Ṣaḥīḥ Muslim*, 2:745 #1064.

fought them, and that I was with him. He instructed that we search for this man. He was eventually found and brought to 'Alī, and I saw that that man appeared exactly as the Prophet 🕊 had described him.[38]

16. Repairing the Rift

Abū Bakrah al-Thaqafī 🕊 narrated that the Prophet Muhammad 🕊 brought his grandson al-Ḥasan out one day and ascended with him to the pulpit. Then, he said, 'This son of mine is a chief, and perhaps Allah will use him to reconcile between two factions of Muslims.'[39] In truth, al-Ḥasan 🕊 single-handedly mended a long and tragic split between the Muslims of Kūfa and those of Shām upon becoming caliph, by abdicating his caliphate to Mu'āwiyah ibn Abī Sufyān 🕊. In doing so, he unified two great factions of believers and allowed the progress of Islam to regain its momentum for decades. The Prophet 🕊 also foretold that, at this precise point, the Muslim nation would transition from a caliphate to a monarchy. 'The caliphate will be for thirty years, then there will be a monarchy after that.'[40]

Abū Bakr 🕊 ruled for approximately two years, then 'Umar 🕊 for ten, then 'Uthmān 🕊 for twelve, then 'Alī 🕊 for five, before al-Ḥasan within months abdicated it to Mu'āwiyah who founded the Umayyad dynasty. Ibn al-'Arabī (d. 1148) says, 'And the promise of the Truthful came to pass ... [the period of the caliphate] neither exceeded nor fell short a day, so glory be to the All-Encompassing; there is no other Lord but He.'[41]

---

[38] al-Bukhārī, Ṣaḥīḥ al-Bukhārī, 4:200 #3610; Muslim, Ṣaḥīḥ Muslim, 2:744 #1064.

[39] al-Bukhārī, Ṣaḥīḥ al-Bukhārī, 4:204 #3629.

[40] Ibn Ḥanbal, Musnad Aḥmad, 31:178 #18883; a ḥasan (acceptable) chain according to al-Arna'ūṭ in the comments.

[41] Abū Bakr Muḥammad ibn al-'Arabī, Aḥkām al-Qur'ān (Beirut: Dār al-Kutub al-'Ilmīyah, 2003), 4:152.

17. Cycling Back to Virtue is Promised

In an explicit hadith about the forms of governance the Muslim nation would experience, Ḥudhayfah ibn al-Yamān ﷺ reported that the Prophet ﷺ said:

> Prophethood will remain amongst you for as long as Allah wishes. Then Allah will remove it whenever He wishes to remove it, and there will be a caliphate upon the prophetic methodology. It will last for as long as Allah wishes it to last, then Allah will remove it whenever He wishes to remove it. Then there will be an abiding dynasty, and it will remain for as long as Allah wishes it to remain. Then Allah will remove it whenever He wishes to remove it. Then there will be forceful monarchy, and it will remain for as long as Allah wishes it to remain. Then He will remove it whenever He wishes to remove it, and then there will be a caliphate upon the prophetic methodology.[42]

18. Asmā' Sends a Tyrant Home

For confronting the tyranny of al-Ḥajjāj ibn Yūsuf, 'Abdullāh ibn al-Zubayr ﷺ was crucified in front of the Sacred House in Makkah, and his body was thrown into the graveyard of the Jews. Then al-Ḥajjāj marched to his mother's house, Asmā' bint Abī Bakr ﷺ, the Prophet's sister-in-law. He said to her, 'What do you think of what I have just done to the enemy of Allah?' referring to her son, 'Abdullāh ibn al-Zubayr. Though al-Ḥajjāj was trying to strike fear in her heart, lest a person of her position inspire more rebellion, this was a woman strengthened by a prophecy she had heard directly from the Prophet's lips. Her response was, 'I think you have destroyed his worldly life by destroying your own afterlife ... The Messenger of Allah ﷺ has

---

42 Ibn Ḥanbal, *Musnad Aḥmad*, 30:355 #18406; a *ḥasan* (acceptable) chain according to al-Arna'ūṭ in the comments.

certainly told us that emerging from Thaqīf would be a liar and a murderer. The liar we have seen, and as far as the murderer is concerned, I have no doubt that you are him.' Without saying a single word, al-Ḥajjāj rose and exited in disgrace.[43] Hadith commentators agree that the liar from Thaqīf was al-Mukhtār ibn Abī 'Ubayd, who claimed prophethood.

19. Umm Ḥarām's Date with Destiny

Umm Ḥarām bint Milḥān ﵂ heard the Messenger of Allah ﷺ say: 'The first army from my nation to ride the sea have guaranteed themselves [Paradise].' Umm Ḥarām said, 'O Messenger of Allah, will I be among them?' He said, 'You will be among them.' Later, he said, 'The first army from my nation to march in battle to the City of Caesar (Constantinople) will be forgiven.' She said, 'Will I be among them, O Messenger of Allah?' He said, 'No.'[44] During the reign of Mu'āwiyah ﵁, Umm Ḥarām rode in the first Muslim naval fleet, accompanying her husband, and died upon falling off her mount in enemy lands.[45] Imam al-Ṭabarānī and others report that the whereabouts of her gravesite on Cyprus Island were known.[46] Ibn Ḥajar said:

> This contains multiple prophecies by the Prophet ﷺ of what would take place, and it all occurred just as he said, and hence is considered among the signs of his prophethood. Of them is that his nation would remain after him, and that among them are those who would be strong, formidable, and a consequential force against the enemy, and that they would conquer territories until the army

43 Muslim, *Ṣaḥīḥ Muslim*, 4:1971 #2545.

44 al-Bukhārī, *Ṣaḥīḥ al-Bukhārī*, 4:42 #2924.

45 al-Bukhārī, *Ṣaḥīḥ al-Bukhārī*, 9:34 #7002; Muslim, *Ṣaḥīḥ Muslim*, 3:1518 #1912.

46 al-Ṭabarānī, *Al-Mu'jam al-Kabīr*, 25:130 #316; Abū Nu'aym, *Ḥilyat al-Awliyā'*, 2:62.

> rides the sea, and that Umm Ḥarām would live until that time, and that she would be with that army that rode the sea, and that she would not live to see the second military campaign [to Constantinople].[47]

20. Preempting the Questioner

Just as the Qur'an describes Jesus telling others about the secrets they concealed in the depths of their homes,[48] it was common for the Prophet Muhammad ﷺ to address the inner thoughts of those he interacted with. For instance, Wābiṣah ibn Ma'bad ؓ narrated:

> I came to the Messenger of Allah ﷺ and he said, 'You came to ask about righteousness and sin?' I said, 'Yes.' He closed his hand, tapped my chest, and said, 'Consult your heart. Consult your heart. Consult your heart. Sin is what discomforts your soul and wavers in your chest, even if the people continue to advise you otherwise.'[49]

Similarly, 'Ā'ishah ؓ, the Prophet's wife, reports that he once told her, 'You will either tell me, or the Most Subtle, the Most Acquainted, will inform me … Did you think that Allah and His Messenger would shortchange you?' She responded, 'Whatever people conceal, Allah knows … Yes, indeed.'[50] Imam al-Nawawī comments that all the manuscripts attribute 'Yes, indeed,' to 'Ā'ishah. In other words, it was not an inquiry which the Prophet ﷺ responded to in the affirmative, rather, it was as if she was agreeing with herself about the reality she had just attested to.[51]

---

47 Ibn Ḥajar, *Fatḥ al-Bārī*, 11:77.

48 (*Āl 'Imrān* 3: 49)

49 Ibn Ḥanbal, *Musnad Aḥmad*, 29:533 #18006; a *ḥasan* (acceptable) chain according to al-Nawawī in *al-Arba'īn al-Nawawiyyah*, #27.

50 Muslim, *Ṣaḥīḥ Muslim*, 2:669 #974.

51 Yaḥyā ibn Sharaf al-Nawawī, *Sharḥ Ṣaḥīḥ Muslim* (Beirut: Dār Iḥyā' al-Turāth al-'Arabī, 1972), 7:44.

21. An Unforgettable Sermon

Ḥudhayfah ibn al-Yamān ﷺ and ʿAmr ibn Akhṭab ﷺ report that the Prophet ﷺ once delivered a sermon from dawn until sunset, in which he mentioned all the major events that would take place between then and the Day of Resurrection. Ḥudhayfah says that he sometimes forgot parts of it, until he saw those events unfold before his very eyes.[52]

22. The Emergence of Selective Textualism

Miqdām ibn Maʿdīkarib ﷺ reports that the Prophet ﷺ said:

> Indeed, I have been given the Qur'an and something similar to it along with it. But soon there will be a time when a man will be reclining on his couch with a full stomach, and he will say, 'You should only adhere to this Qur'an. What you find it deeming permissible, consider it permissible, and what you find it deeming forbidden, consider it forbidden.' But indeed, whatever the Messenger of Allah forbids is like what Allah forbids.[53]

To this day, different groups of people continue to arise who attempt to delegitimize the Sunnah (prophetic tradition) in order to avoid the definitive interpretations it provides of the Qur'an.

23. A Horrific Wildfire

Abū Hurayrah ﷺ narrates that the Prophet Muhammad ﷺ said, 'The Hour will not take place until a fire emerges from the lands of Ḥijāz (central Arabia) that illuminates the necks of camels in

---

52 al-Bukhārī, *Ṣaḥīḥ al-Bukhārī*, 8:123 #6604; Muslim, *Ṣaḥīḥ Muslim*, 4:2216 #2891.

53 al-Tirmidhī, *Sunan al-Tirmidhī*, 4:335 #2664.

Basrah (Syria).'[54] As scholars such as Ibn Ḥajar, Ibn Kathīr, and al-Nawawī all confirm, this enormous fire erupted in the city of Madinah on Friday, 5th of Jumādah Thāni, 654H, and lasted for an entire month. The great historian, Abū Shāmah, experienced it firsthand and documented much of its details, including its visibility from hundreds of miles away, and how the Madinans sought refuge in the Prophet's Mosque and collectively repented from the vices they had been engaging in. Historical records seem to indicate that this was a volcanic eruption, and the lava fields around Madinah remain observable today.

24. Prosperity and Hedonism Before the End Times

Abū Hurayrah ﵁ reports that the Messenger of Allah ﷺ said, 'The Hour will not commence before wealth becomes abundant and overflowing, to the point that a man brings out the charity due on his wealth and cannot find anyone to accept it from him, and to the point that Arabia's lands will revert back to being meadows and rivers.'[55]

While acknowledging earlier manifestations of this prophecy about unprecedented affluence, current lifestyles in today's developed world illustrate that residents who live there enjoy greater luxury than 99.9 per cent of recorded human history. Even those who struggle financially own armchairs cozier than any ancient king's royal throne, climate controls on their walls and access to modes of transport that have turned an excruciating month-long journey into a few entertaining hours.

Perhaps even more intriguing is the Prophet ﷺ mentioning the agricultural transformation of Arabia in the same context as the surplus of wealth. Fourteen centuries ago, the extensive irrigation methods recently invented through modern technology

---

54 al-Bukhārī, *Ṣaḥīḥ al-Bukhārī*, 9:58 #7118; Muslim, *Ṣaḥīḥ Muslim*, 4:2227 #2902.

55 Muslim, *Ṣaḥīḥ Muslim*, 2:701 #157.

were inconceivable. We are the very first generations privileged to witness this geological phenomenon.[56] Furthermore, a related miracle here is the Prophet's awareness that Arabia once contained meadows and rivers. The petrified mud of Arabia's 'Empty Quarter' is replete with hippopotamus teeth, buffalo bones, and clam shells fossilized thousands of years ago.[57]

25. Competing in Materialism

Regarding how material prosperity will be a sign of the end times, the Prophet Muhammad ﷺ said: 'And if you see the barefoot, naked shepherds of camels competing in the construction of high-rise buildings, then this is from among the signs of the Hour.'[58] Is it not remarkable to witness the arid desert regions of the Gulf States, as impoverished as they were a century ago, develop two of the world's three tallest skyscrapers today?

In a similar hadith, the Prophet ﷺ said, 'The Hour will not commence before people boast of their mosques.' Ibn ʿAbbās ﵄, the narrator, added, 'You will ornament your mosques just as the Jews and Christians did with their temples.'[59] This intense competition will involve mistreatment of others, and thus we find parallel prophecies of hedonism and exploitation in the prophetic tradition as well.

In the hadith of al-Miswar ibn Makhramah, the Prophet ﷺ said, 'By Allah, I do not fear poverty overtaking you, but I fear that you will have abundant wealth at your disposal like the nations before you, causing you to compete in it as they competed in it, and then it destroys you as it destroyed them.'[60]

---

56 "NASA Sees Fields of Green Spring up in Saudi Arabia," *Nasa.gov*. Accessed February 2, 2021.

57 Arthur Clark and Michael Grimsdale, 'Lakes of the Rub' al-Khali', *Saudi Aramco World 40, no. 3* (May/June 1989).

58 Muslim, *Ṣaḥīḥ Muslim*, 1:36 #8.

59 Abū Dāwūd, *Sunan Abī Dāwūd*, 1:122 #448; authenticated by al-Albānī in the comments.

60 al-Bukhārī, *Ṣaḥīḥ al-Bukhārī*, 4:96 #3138; Muslim, *Ṣaḥīḥ Muslim*, 4:2273 #2961.

26. The Unavoidability of Interest (*Ribā*)

Prophet Muhammad ﷺ also foretold that interest (*ribā*), which is one of the most unethical and exploitative transactions, would become inescapable. Abū Hurayrah ؓ reports that the Messenger of Allah ﷺ said: 'A time will come over the people when they will consume *ribā*.' They asked him, 'All of them?' He said, 'Whoever does not consume it will still be reached by its dust.'[61] Whether for purchasing a property or vehicle, or simply for developing credit in today's world, interest-bearing clauses have permeated every dimension of contemporary financial dealings. There is also the sheer amount of interest in modern banking that entangles us all. For instance, the deposits in our checking accounts are loaned out by the bank to make it more money, and the bonuses we receive on credit card rewards are partly funded by the interest paid by other customers.

Government spending consistently runs at a deficit, which is in turn paid for with debts, meaning that the government services we utilize, even just driving on a highway, are thus paid for by interest. This prophecy astounds a person further when they recall that the absolute prohibition of interest already existed in medieval Christianity, and so the Prophet Muhammad ﷺ must have seen beyond this presumed safeguard against the extreme proliferation of interest in the world.

27. An Increase in Brutality and Killing

When greed causes people to see other people's wealth as violable, seeing their lives that way is simply the next step. Thus, the Prophet ﷺ said: 'Beware of oppression, for oppression will result in darknesses on the Day of Judgment. And beware of greed, for

---

[61] Ibn Ḥanbal, *Musnad Aḥmad*, 16: 258 #10410; authenticated by Aḥmad Shākir in *'Umdat al-Tafsīr 'an Ibn Kathīr* (Egypt: Dār al-Wafā', 2005), 1:332.

greed is what destroyed those before you; it drove them to spill each other's blood and violate each other's sanctity.'[62]

The past century has seen atrocities in modern warfare, cycles of genocide, abusive policing, and senseless violence at large, that are incomparable anywhere in human history and all traceable to selfish interests. Only Allah knows whether this is that prophecy manifesting, or simply a precursor to eras of even worse senseless violence which the Prophet ﷺ also foretold.

Abū Hurayrah ؓ narrates that the Messenger of Allah ﷺ said, 'By the One in whose hand is my soul, this world will not end until a day comes when the killer has no idea why he killed, nor the killed why he was killed.' It was said, 'How will that be?' He said, 'Chaos.'[63]

In another hadith, 'The Hour will not commence until knowledge is removed, earthquakes become frequent, time narrows, turmoil surfaces, and anarchy increases—namely killing, lots of killing.'[64]

As for knowledge becoming scarce, one can ask themselves what the average believer knows about their religion, and what mayhem people often have to navigate on the internet when searching for basic facts, due to personalized algorithms which confirm each of our biases, bury unwelcome truths, and subject us to targeted marketing campaigns.

As for the narrowing of time, today's ubiquity of entertainment and consumerism has time flying between the gadgets and devices that are engineered to distract. As for the carnage, again, the twentieth century has been the bloodiest in human history even without the recent and ongoing nightmares in Latin America, neocolonial Africa, the Balkans, Middle East and China; World War I alone claimed the lives of sixty-five million people and World War II another seventy-two million.

---

62 Muslim, *Ṣaḥīḥ Muslim*, 4:1996 #2578.

63 Muslim, *Ṣaḥīḥ Muslim*, 4:2231 #2908.

64 al-Bukhārī, *Ṣaḥīḥ al-Bukhārī*, 2:33 #1036; Muslim, *Ṣaḥīḥ Muslim*, 4:2057 #157.

28. THE PLUNGE INTO IMMORALITY

Abū Hurayrah 🌸 narrates that the Prophet 🌸 said that there will emerge in the future 'women who are clothed yet naked, walking with an enticing gait, with something on their heads that looks like the humps of camels, leaning to one side. They will never enter Paradise or even smell its fragrance, although its fragrance can be detected from such and such a distance.'[65]

Is it not remarkable how he not only foretold their provocative dress, but even predicted women's hairstyles? The Prophet 🌸 also stated that even Muslim communities would participate in some of these trends. 'There will be, in the end of my nation, men who ride chariots who are in reality pseudo-men; they will drop off their women, at the gates of the mosques, who are clothed and yet naked. Upon their heads will be the likes of a lean camel's hump.'[66]

While this also occurred in the past, as al-Nawawī asserts about his own premodern society, it is even less difficult now to find a Muslim man who is protective of what brand of chariot he rides and its horsepower but not protective of his women and their revealing attire in public.

'Abdullāh ibn 'Umar 🌸 narrated that the Messenger of Allah 🌸 also predicted the consequences of a hypersexualized popular culture: 'And fornication never becomes prevalent among a people to the degree that they practice it openly, except that epidemics become rampant among them which had never before existed among their ancestors.'[67] The link between sexual permissiveness and sexually transmitted diseases is not something any sensible person in our times can deny. Perhaps the unhinged pursuit of sexual gratification without liability is the reason behind this next prophecy also: 'A woman will one day be taken and

65   Muslim, Saḥīḥ Muslim, 3:1680 #2128.
66   Ibn Ḥibbān, Ṣaḥīḥ Ibn Ḥibbān, 14:64 #5753; an acceptable (ḥasan) chain according to al-Albānī in al-Silsilah al- Ṣaḥīḥah, 6:411 #2683.
67   Ibn Mājah, Sunan Ibn Mājah, 2:1332 #4019; an acceptable (ḥasan) chain according to al-Albānī in the comments.

have her abdomen cut open, then what is inside her womb will be taken and discarded, out of fear of having children.'[68] According to an extensive survey published in *Guttmacher Institute Journal*, the 'fear of dramatic life changes' is by far the most common reason for abortions today, with more than half of those surveyed citing single motherhood as the reason for that fear.[69] Another remarkable presumption in this hadith is that removing a fetus from the womb will be possible one day without much risk to the mother. This has only been possible very recently in human history and would have been extremely dangerous in the past. For this reason, a Caesarean section was usually not performed in history except on a dead or dying mother.

Finally, 'Abdullāh ibn 'Amr ﷺ narrates that the Prophet ﷺ said, 'The Hour will not commence until people mate in the streets just as donkeys mate.' I asked, 'Will that really happen?" He said, 'Yes, it most certainly will happen.'[70] Though this was stated as one of the last signs before the Day of Judgment, following major apocalyptic events, many of our modern cultures are clearly moving towards that degree of shamelessness, if not experiencing it already.

29. Muslims Becoming Easy Prey

The Prophet ﷺ also prophesied that carnal pursuits would not only infect his nation but would be the cause of their downfall and devastation. Thawbān ﷺ reports that the Prophet ﷺ said, 'The nations will soon invite one another to devour you, just as diners are invited to a dish.' It was said, 'Will it be because of our

---

68 Abū Bakr ibn Abī Shaybah, *Al-Muṣannaf* (Riyadh: Maktabat al-Rushd, 2004), 7:469 #37297; authenticated by 'Iṣām Mūsā Hādī in *Kitāb Ṣaḥīḥ Ashrāṭ al-Sā'ah* (Amman: al-Dār al-'Uthmānīyah, 2003), 83.

69 Lawrence B. Finer, et al., 'Reasons U.S. Women Have Abortions: Quantitative and Qualitative Perspectives', *Perspectives on Sexual and Reproductive Health* 37, no. 3 (2005): 110–118.

70 Ibn Ḥibbān, *Ṣaḥīḥ Ibn Ḥibbān*, 14:64 #5753; authenticated by al-Albānī in the comments.

small number on that day?' He said, 'No, rather you will be many on that day, but you will be weightless foam, like the foam on the river. And Allah will remove the fear of you from the hearts of your enemies and will cast weakness into your hearts.' Someone said, 'O Messenger of Allah, what will this weakness be?' He said, 'The love of this world, and the hatred of death.'[71]

It is incredible how one century ago, King Leopold of Belgium very famously referred to his colonial ambitions as 'this magnificent African cake,' which the European powers sliced up at will during the Berlin Conference of 1884. A person can easily find the many political cartoons of that day conceptualizing this conference in food terms, almost exactly like the hadith above had stated.

Cartoon depicting Leopold II and other emperial powers at the Berlin Conference 1884. (Artist: Francois Marechal)

---

71 Abū Dāwūd, *Sunan Abī Dāwūd*, 4:111 #4297; authenticated by al-Albāni in the comments.

This was in part due to King Leopold's metaphor, but also because the attendees were only there to formalize the divisions of Africa, fully confident that the large and resourceful continent could not hold its weight in any meaningful resistance to their ravenous greed and imperial appetite.

Reinforcing this point, Anas ibn Mālik ﷺ narrates that the Prophet ﷺ said, 'Once my nation considers five things permissible, then destruction will befall them: when cursing one another appears, when wine is drunk, silk is worn, musical instruments are played, and when men suffice themselves with men and women suffice themselves with women.'[72] Certainly, Muslims today are not insulated from the ideologies that accept same-sex acts. This is even imaginable for a practising, mosque-attending Muslim, if they allow their religiosity to be reduced to a cultural identity, as the Prophet ﷺ said in a hadith narrated by 'Abdullāh ibn 'Amr ﷺ, 'An age will surely come when people gather and pray in the mosques, while there is not a single believer amongst them.'[73]

30. The Immortality of His Nation

In a multitude of reports, the Prophet ﷺ declared, 'There will never cease to be a group from my nation victorious upon the truth, unharmed by those who will oppose them, until Allah's

---

72 Aḥmad ibn al-Ḥusayn al-Bayhaqī, *Shu'ab al-Īmān* (Riyadh: Maktabat al-Rushd lil-Nashr wal-Tawzī', 2003), 7:328 #5084; an acceptable (*ḥasan*) chain according to al-Albānī in *Ṣaḥīḥ al-Targhīb wal-Tarhīb* (Riyadh: Maktabat al-Ma'ārif, 2000), 2:608 #2386.
While these prohibitions appear absolute here, scholars have qualified them considering their cumulative read of other prophetic traditions. For instance, the prohibition of silk here is qualified by being applicable to men only, and in significant amounts, and in the absence of necessity. Similarly, scholars generally consider striking the tambourine an exception to the prohibition of musical instruments, at least on occasion, and some widen the concession further.

73 Abū Bakr ibn Abī Shaybah, *Al-Īmān* (Beirut: al-Maktab al-Islāmī, 1983), 1:40 #101; authenticated by al-Albānī in the comments.

decree comes to pass.'[74] So many religions have come and gone, and yet he boldly expressed that despite all the corruption and moral degradation, true believers in Islam will endure. Even when the adversity involved in preserving Islam will be tantamount to 'grasping onto a burning coal,'[75] Muslims will always exist who value their faith over their lives, and hence the Prophet ﷺ further described them in another hadith by saying, 'The Hour will not commence until a man passes by the grave of his brother and says, "I wish I were in his place."'[76] Ibn Baṭṭāl (d. 1057) explains that this will not be due to any suicidal ideation, but rather an anxiety that the prevalent evils and the strength of their adversaries may cost them their religion.[77]

31. Never Thought You Would Speak

Abū Saʿīd al-Khudrī reports that the Prophet ﷺ said, 'By the One in whose hand is my soul, the Hour will not commence until predators speak to people, and until the tip of a man's whip and the straps on his sandals speak to him, and his thigh informs him of what occurred with his family after he left.'[78] One can only imagine how difficult these statements were for a seventh-century desert dweller to process, but the incredible strides in electricity and electronics since then have made such possibilities mundane for most people. In TIME's *Best Inventions of 2002*, a Japanese toy-maker was showcased for creating a dog translator; a device on its collar that interprets its yelps, growls, and whines into phrases such as 'I can't stand it', 'how boring', and 'I am

---

74 al-Bukhārī, *Ṣaḥīḥ al-Bukhārī*, 4:207 #3641; Muslim, *Ṣaḥīḥ Muslim*, 3:1023 #1920.

75 al-Tirmidhī, *Sunan al-Tirmidhī*, 4:96 #2260.

76 al-Bukhārī, *Ṣaḥīḥ al-Bukhārī*, 9:58 #7115; Muslim, *Ṣaḥīḥ Muslim*, 4:2231 #157.

77 Ibn Ḥajar, *Fatḥ al-Bārī*, 13:75.

78 al-Tirmidhī, *Sunan al-Tirmidhī*, 4:46 #2181; authenticated by al-Tirmidhī in the comments.

lonely.'[79] In November of 2006, *The New York Times* published an article titled 'These Shoes Are Made for Talking,' hailing a new age of futuristic sports training.[80] In January of 2010, a security camera app was released which transformed the smart-phones on our hips and in our pockets into windows into our homes.[81] Another example is our ability to video chat with family members from afar. Perhaps these are what the Prophet ﷺ foresaw, or perhaps other phenomena that we have yet to experience.

For the sake of brevity, we will settle for this set of verified prophecies of God's Final Prophet, Muhammad ﷺ. It is noteworthy, however, that although the Prophet described so many portents of the end times, he never specified an exact date or time. Rather, he would on multiple occasions recite to people the likes of these verses from the Qur'an: '*Say, [O Muhammad], 'None in the heavens and earth knows the unseen except Allah, and they do not perceive when they will be resurrected.*'[82] Someone can argue that this too constitutes another prophecy, namely that every specific prediction about when the Final Hour will be—which countless people have made throughout history—will be mistaken. Any fair-minded person who considers the staggering number of these prophecies and reflects that we ourselves 50 years ago could never have predicted the events he predicted, must be impressed by them. Given the number and precision of these prophecies, they must be seen for what they are: overwhelmingly convincing proof of his prophethood.

---

79 'Best Inventions of 2002: Dog Translator', *Time Magazine*.

80 Matt Villano, 'These Shoes Are Made for Talking', *New York Times*, November 1st, 2006.

81 David Dahlquist, 'Security Cam App Turns iPhone into a Security Camera', *Macworld*, January 7th, 2010.

82 (*al-Naml* 27: 65)

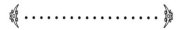

6

The Prophet's Physical Miracles

Muslims believe that the Prophet Muhammad's ministry was supported by physical miracles that were witnessed and reported by a generation of superb moral integrity. This chapter will feature some of the most authentically transmitted miracles, after assessing the utility, plausibility, and provability of miracles in the first place.

While the Qur'an is the Prophet's greatest miracle, and certainly sufficient on its own as a miracle, this does not negate that God gave him many other miraculous signs along with it.[1] In other words, conviction in the prophethood of Muhammad ﷺ is not dependent on his performance of miracles, but historically reliable reports of these miracles make their occurrence undeniable and a powerful cultivator of conviction. Of course, the believer is

1 Some have claimed that the Qur'an repeatedly denies the attribution of any miracle to the Prophet Muhammad ﷺ other than the Qur'an, but a careful reading of those passages reveals that they concerned God's refusing to grant specific miracles to a defiant people, or His censure of human beings for feeling entitled to demand a miracle from God, or for disregarding the Qur'an when nobody on earth was more equipped to recognize its miraculousness than they were.

always encouraged to pursue higher states of conviction through contemplation, seeking knowledge, and purifying their heart until they can witness the Truth through the message of Islam itself. However, we should not underestimate the fact that some people's psychospiritual makeup better orients them to traverse the 'miracles avenue' to the gates of faith. As Ibn Qayyim writes, 'The paths to guidance are diverse, as a mercy and kindness from God to His servants, due to the variation in their intellectual, mental, and spiritual insights.'[2] He then proceeded to give examples of how some are guided by recognizing the truth in the message itself, due to the purity of their own nature, such as Abū Bakr al-Ṣiddīq ﷺ, and some recognized the truth through the impeccable character of its bearer, such as Khadījah bint Khuwaylid ﷺ. A third segment of humanity was brought to faith by God through miracles, while a fourth was impressed by the triumphs and successes of the Prophet's lifetime, and a fifth group simply followed its leaders who joined the fold of Islam.

In addition to bringing some people to faith, miracles augment existing faith by instilling in those who read these stories immense love, respect, and admiration for the Prophet Muhammad ﷺ. Reflecting on God's mercy and aid to the believers grants the faithful a firm confidence in divine providence and help in times of hardship and difficulty. Reading and believing in the reality of divine omnipotence as manifested through these miracles enables a person to dream big, pushing their boundaries, and shaking off self-limiting beliefs. One recognizes that the natural order, seemingly fixed, is in fact entirely contingent on divine will.

This is the utility of miracles and why deemphasizing them to appear more rational and sophisticated is a great disservice to many sincere seekers. As for those solely interested in validating their preexisting beliefs, the Qur'an itself asserts that miracles are futile for those not willing to believe them, even if they were

---

2 Ibn Qayyim al-Jawziyyah, *Miftāḥ Dār al-Saʿādah* (Beirut: Dār al-Kutub al-ʿIlmīyah, 2002), 2:13.

to witness them with their own eyes. Allah says, *And [even] if We opened to them a gate from the heaven and they continued therein to ascend, they would say, "Our eyes have only been dazzled. Rather, we are a people affected by magic."*[3]

The Qur'an repeatedly describes this response to miracles from sceptical minds across the ages and explains why some still rejected Islam after witnessing the Prophet's miracles themselves. It demonstrates the veracity of a key epistemological perspective that the Qur'an postulates—namely, the futility of scepticism as an approach to knowledge. Even the clearest signs and miracles can be doubted if a person is willing to be sceptical of their own senses and question reality entirely. But, because our postmodern times harbour greater suspicion against religious and traditional accounts of the supernatural than any other period in human history, let us first begin with dispelling the commonly held misconceptions that miracles are either logically impossible or historically unprovable.

1. The Possibility of Miracles

For the majority of people who believe that God is the Creator of the universe and remains a willful agent in the world, God's ability to perform miracles—or to enable others to perform them—is easy to accept. After all, if God created the laws of nature, it logically follows that He is not bound by the system He designed but can also bring about occurrences outside of that system. Miracles are only problematic for atheists (who believe in no God) and deists (who posit a non-intervening God), both of whom may find

---

3 (*al-Ḥijr* 15: 14–15) To this day, when asked what proof it would take for them to reconsider their position and believe in the Divine, some prominent atheist debaters have candidly admitted that there is absolutely nothing that would change their mind. Even a miracle of the most spectacular kind would be dismissed as a hallucination. Of course, this is precisely what the Qur'an indicates: that even the greatest of miracles will not convince one who obstinately chooses to ignore every conceivable form of proof.

it refreshing to familiarize themselves with the case for Allah's existence in the Qur'an and Sunnah.[4]

While belief in miracles was standard in Christian societies, the transition to modernity signalled a shift toward a more sceptical stance. The mechanical naturalists of the Enlightenment painted a disenchanted view of nature as a closed system, describing natural laws as disconnected from God.[5] Ultimately, they had a profound aversion to any suggestion of miraculous intervention. The notion of miracles was commonly rejected because they were unscientific. Perhaps the most notable vanguards of this view were the Dutch rationalist Baruch Spinoza (d. 1677) and the Scottish empiricist David Hume (d. 1776). Both used various arguments to reject the possibility of miracles, all of which suffer from either factual errors, logical inconsistency, or irrelevance to the miracles of the Prophet Muhammad ﷺ.

In his *Theological-Political Treatise*, Spinoza argued that belief in miracles was but a remnant of the naive premodern mind, its inability to interpret natural phenomena, and not the intended meaning behind passages in the Torah. His contempt for miracles is expected, as the idea of 'supernatural intervention' was perceived to be at odds with the philosophical outlook of rationalism that dominated his era and soon produced the European Enlightenment. However, Spinoza's unbridled zeal to disprove the very possibility of miracles is contrary to his usual astuteness. For instance, he attempts to explain away every explicit biblical account of miracles as not actually miraculous. He even claimed that every supposed miracle can be seen as a misunderstood natural phenomenon.

While ignorance and superstition have certainly driven some people to prematurely classify some events as miracles, what scientific evidence suggests that staffs can be transformed into

---

4 See: Justin Parrott, 'The Case for Allah's Existence in the Qur'an and Sunnah', *Yaqeen Institute for Islamic Research*, February 27th, 2017.

5 Syed Muhammad Naquib al-Attas, *Islam and Secularism* (Lahore: Suhail Academy, 1978), 18.

snakes, people blind from birth can have their sight restored, or that the moon can be split and restored? According to Spinoza, since our knowledge of nature is incomplete, there is no way to assert that a particular event is miraculous since it may have a yet-undiscovered natural explanation. Spinoza presumed that inexplicable occurrences should simply require us to rewrite our understanding of the laws of nature. However, modern philosophy of science considers Spinoza's argument fallacious; the fundamental laws of nature are not rewritten when miracles occur. A bird being miraculously resurrected from a disassembled carcass[6] does not require us to revise our knowledge of the natural decay of corpses.

Aside from this epistemological objection to miracles, another objection Spinoza raised was quasi-theological cum ontological: 'If anyone asserted that God acts in contravention to the laws of nature, he, ipso facto, would be compelled to assert that God acted against His own nature.'[7] But this argument is entirely contingent upon accepting Spinoza's impoverished conception of God. Spinoza considered God as nothing other than nature itself (a view that limits the Divine so severely that many are convinced that Spinoza's beliefs are essentially no different from atheism). On such a view, certainly it would seem absurd for nature to contradict itself. But when God is the Supreme Master of all in existence, who says 'Be' and something comes into existence, then there is no rational objection to God intervening in His creation and delimiting the scope of some of the natural laws that He has ordained.

It is interesting that Spinoza also asserted that if miracles were true, they would imply that God created a flawed world that He had to keep repairing. Not only does this contradict his view that miracles should make us revise our understanding of natural laws, but it also constitutes a strawman argument whereby a

---

6 (*al-Baqarah* 2: 260)

7 Baruch Spinoza, *A Theological Political Treatise* (Dover Philosophical Classics: 2004), chapter VI, 83.

position no one actually holds is refuted. Believers do not claim that the purpose of miracles is to fix a flawed world. Rather, they believe that the One who created this world and the laws that govern it can also suspend them.

The weakness of Spinoza's critique was evident. It was only after Hume published his *Inquiry Concerning Human Understanding* that debates surrounding the logical and scientific possibility of miracles intensified. Not only were Hume's arguments more refined, but prevailing paradigms of the Enlightenment era such as scepticism and naturalism were conducive to a wider embrace of his views. Hume alleged that we are forced by continuous evidence of nature's uniformity to dismiss even the strongest testimony of any momentary supernatural event, since it would, by definition, violate the proven laws of nature. He further justified this by the lack of historical evidence for any one miracle, and by the multitude of the faithful who claim them in support of their conflicting doctrines.

How Islam's unique mechanism of knowledge transmission satisfies the criterion of historical evidence will be discussed shortly, but the fact that different religions offer different accounts does not justify dismissing them all. Doing so would render the very study of history useless, since sifting through conflicting reports and weighing them against one another is every historian's methodology. Even Hume himself followed this protocol when he considered nature's ongoing testimony stronger than individual accounts of miracles.

As for Hume's argument for the superiority of empirical science over historical testimony, this stems from his philosophical framework which was effectively that of an agnostic or atheist. Theists, on the other hand, perceive miracles as identical to natural phenomena, in that both originate with God. Just as the universe began by the command of God, and its laws run as ordered by God, miracles can sometimes occur in it by the will of God. The reality of miracles is ultimately an extension of the divine reality; just as God evidenced His existence and magnificence through the brilliant laws of nature, He evidenced His omnipotence and the integrity of His messengers through occasionally breaching these same laws in mind-boggling ways. Finally, the laws of nature are a mere description of the world as we experience it, not a necessary prescription for how it must function. Miracles can, therefore, simply be exceptions to the predominant natural order, contrary to it but not contradictory. That would deliver us from Hume's presumption of irreconcilability and shift our investigation from the logical possibility to the historical documentation of miracles.[8]

2. The Demonstrability of Miracles

Neither the logical possibility of an omnipotent God performing miracles, nor historical claims of their incidence, constitutes proof that miracles took place. There must be compelling evidence, and no sensible person should accept accounts of miracles without scrutiny. As is often said, 'extraordinary claims require extraordinary evidence'. However, we must discern whether we are genuinely open to evidence—albeit extraordinary—or blindly committed to our presuppositions. Consistency is an excellent litmus test; do we question whether all similar convictions we hold about life and faith meet the same stringent criteria, or has a double standard snuck in here due to prejudice or extreme scepticism?

Many people today may not realize that they are actually Humeans: dogmatic naturalists who believe no amount of historical evidence for miracles can ever suffice, and that nothing at all is provable except that which we personally experience. Consistency necessitates acknowledging that nobody actually accepts only what they themselves have experienced as evidence. Such a position would entail denying every map we have not charted ourselves and every scientific fact we have not personally established.

[8] I must acknowledge the valuable contributions of Dr. Nazir Khan, the Director of Research Strategy at Yaqeen Institute, to this subsection.

Rational and balanced people accept that testimony, its traceability, and its corroboration, are acceptable as evidence that a fact or event is certainly true or likely true.

The discipline of Hadith is an instrumental science in the Islamic intellectual tradition, invested in verifying reports about the Prophet Muhammad ﷺ, and hence central to any discussion of miracles. It is a unique and sophisticated process involving the interplay of seven sub-disciplines, all engineered to establish beyond a reasonable doubt the transmission chain for each narration. Ultimately, a tiny fraction of these transmitted narrations survives the rigorous process to be classified as authentic, but Hadith scholars did not stop there. Authentic narrations were further categorized as abundantly concurring (*mutawātir*) or solitary (*āḥād*).

Mutawātir reports are those narrated by many narrators in each layer of their transmission, making it inconceivable that they were all mistaken or had all colluded on a forgery. *Āḥād* reports—when authentic—are those transmitted reliably but without meeting the criteria of *mutawātir*, hence most Hadith scholars believe they involve preponderance (greater likelihood) as opposed to certain knowledge. However, this majority simultaneously deems *āḥād* reports worthier of being accepted than discarded, due to the reliability of their chains of transmission and the fact that all sensible people act on greater likelihood in the absence of certainty.

Miracles occurring at the hands of Prophet Muhammad ﷺ is a *mutawātir* concept, meaning the sheer multitude of reports make it uncontestable in principle, even if some specific accounts are not independently *mutawātir*. The occurrence of World War I is a simple example of a *mutawātir* concept; the concurrence of abundant testimony about it renders it inconsequential whether any particular report of it having taken place is verifiable. Rejecting a *mutawātir* concept would be tantamount to someone refusing to confirm that Mayan, Inca or Aztec civilizations existed until humans invent a time machine and travel back in time themselves. Until then, this person would be willing to entertain the possibility of all reports of these civilizations being a transhistorical conspiracy—similar to what the Flat Earth Society champions today.

Islam therefore requires a demonstrable chain of transmission before attributing a statement or action (like a miracle) to its Prophet, unlike the many other accounts of miracles in other traditions which lack a chain of transmission and are only predicated on faith. Muslim theologians often highlight this important distinction, and how it compels every honest person to not differentiate between the miracles of Prophet Moses and Jesus because of their comparable historicity (none solidly traceable to eyewitnesses), and first accept the miracles of Prophet Muhammad ﷺ since their historicity is far stronger. Ibn Qayyim says in *Ighāthat al-Lahfān*:

> If this [inconsistency] was the case with the miracles of these two messengers, alongside how long ago that was, and how fragmented their nations became in the world, and the eventual disappearance of their miracles, then what should be assumed regarding the prophethood of Muhammad and his miracles and signs when they were more recent, exceeded one thousand in number, were transmitted by the most pure and honourable individuals ever, and when this transmission was conveyed by abundant concurrence (*tawātur*) one century after another?[9]

Muhammad ﷺ would additionally be the most authoritative confirmer of the miracles of the previous prophets and the most qualified to put an end to the controversies surrounding them.

9 Ibn Qayyim al-Jawziyyah, *Ighāthat al-Lahfān* (Riyadh: Maktabat al-Maʿārif, 1975), 2:347.

3. Specific Miracles Performed by the Prophet

In addition to miracles being a *mutawātir* phenomenon of the Prophet's ministry, there are specific miracles whose *mutawātir* transmission elevates them above any possibility of fabrication. The remainder of this chapter discusses this subset, but let us first assert that requiring *mutawātir* testimony before believing anything is cynicism, not prudence. Most of acquired human knowledge comes through *āḥād* reports, such as reading something from a single source, and so this stipulation would prevent us from believing any bit of news that people circulate. It might even prevent us from believing our own eyes when we are the sole witness to an event. We generally trust our eyes, at least until we are compelled by stronger reasons to suspect them. Hence, after realizing the possibility and demonstrability of miracles in principle, even *āḥād* reports of them should not be dismissed whenever their reliability is defensible and no defects in their transmission have been identified.

In a brilliant passage in *Fatḥ al-Bārī*, Ibn Ḥajar (d. 1449) speaks on the abundance of the Prophet's miracles and says:

> This collectively confers necessary knowledge (certainty) that a great number of supernatural events occurred at his hands, in the same manner that someone can conclusively assert the generosity of Ḥātim [al-Ṭā'ī] and the courage of ʿAlī, even if the individual reports on this are only speculative due to their being reported through *āḥād* chains. However, it should be noted that many of the Prophet's miracles became well-known and widespread, were narrated by huge groups of people (*mutawātir*), and consequently conferred certainty by the scholars of transmission, biographical verification, and testimony authentication—even if those unfamiliar with these disciplines did not reach this degree of confidence

> regarding them. In fact, if someone were to claim that most of these incidents (even the non-*mutawātir*) were definitively established, this would not be far-fetched because it is undeniable how accurately these narrators usually related these accounts in every layer of transmission. Furthermore, it is not documented from the Companions [of the Prophet] or those after them a single conflicting report that challenges these accounts, and this silence necessitates approval since they are collectively above turning a blind eye to falsehood. And hypothetically, had they denied one another's reports on these miracles, this would only be due to doubting the reliability of the narrator, or accusing him of lying, poor memory, or senility. As for the content of the narration itself, nobody ever criticized it.[10]

Thus, even *āḥād* reports about miracles can be considered authentic and reliable. Despite this, the following accounts of specific miracles will be restricted to the most indisputable examples, those established by *mutawātir* transmission.

i. Splitting the Moon

> *The Hour has come near, and the moon has split [in two]. And if they see any miracle, they turn away and say, 'Passing magic.' And they denied and followed their desires—and every matter will be settled.*[11]

In an attempt to stump the Prophet ﷺ, disbelievers from the Quraysh clan demanded an undeniable sign from him, which led to God splitting the moon before their eyes. The Prophet ﷺ then

---

10 Ibn Ḥajar, *Fatḥ al-Bārī*, 6:582.

11 (*al-Qamar* 54: 1–3)

said, 'Bear witness.'[12] The baffled crowd said that Muhammad ﷺ must have cast a spell on them, but since he could not have cast a spell on everyone, they decided to ask the travelers from surrounding areas if they saw what they did. They sent riders racing out to question those beyond the city of Makkah, and they too confirmed having seen the exact same phenomenon in the night sky.[13] Ultimately, the idolaters from Quraysh chose denial and they were forced to deny their own eyes.

Numerous luminaries of Hadith have independently verified the *mutawātir*-grade reporting of this miraculous event by exploring its narrators from every layer of transmission. This was done by al-Subkī in *Sharḥ Mukhtaṣar Ibn al-Ḥājib*, Ibn Ḥajar in *al-Amālī*, al-Qurṭubī in *al-Mufhim*, Ibn Kathīr in *al-Bidāyah wal-Nihāyah*, Imam al-Munāwī in *Sharḥ Alfiyat al- 'Irāqī*, and Ibn 'Abd al-Barr (d. 1071), among others.[14]

In describing many reports of the moon splitting, Ibn Kathīr (d. 1373) brings a key aspect of this incident to our attention:

> When the moon split, it never left the sky, rather it cleaved once the Prophet gestured to it and became two pieces. It only proceeded to hover behind Mount Ḥirā', setting the mountain between itself and its counterpart, as described by Ibn Mas'ūd who reports witnessing this himself.[15]

Imam al-Khaṭṭābī (d. 988) similarly said:

> The moon splitting was a grand sign to which no other prophet's miracle could compare, for it was something

---

12 al-Bukhārī, *Ṣaḥīḥ al-Bukhārī*, 4:206 #3636.

13 Aḥmad ibn al-Ḥusayn al-Bayhaqī, *Dalā'il al-Nubuwwah* (Beirut: Dār al-Kutub al-'Ilmīyah, 1988), 2:226; Abū Ja'far al-Ṭabarī, *Jāmi' al-Bayān 'an Ta'wīl al-Qur'ān* (Beirut: Mu'assasat al-Risālah, 2000), 22:567, verse 54:1.

14 Muḥammad al-Kattānī, *Naẓm al-Mutanāthir min al-Ḥadīth al-Mutawātir* (Egypt: Dār al-Kutub al-Salafīyah, 1983), #264.

15 Ibn Kathīr, *Al-Bidāyah wal-Nihāyah*, 4:303.

> that appeared in the distant sky that was contrary to every naturally existing phenomenon which this world is comprised of. It therefore falls beyond what anyone can hope to achieve through trickery, making its proof value even more evident.[16]

Of the bizarre objections to this incident is the expectation that there should be scientifically detectable sequelae to a supernatural event, such as a gravitational disturbance or a geological trace on the moon's surface. However, this is a fallacious objection. The splitting of the moon was a miraculous phenomenon, something that transcended the natural order. It is unclear why one should expect a supernatural event to have natural effects. It is certainly within the power of an Omnipotent God to cleave asunder an astronomical object while suspending any of the expected impact.

Another objection is why people beyond the Prophet's audience did not see the moon split. This very weak objection is founded on a false presumption about historical records and the global visibility of a miracle that was intended for the Prophet's audience. Classical scholars like al-Zajjāj have offered many possible answers to satisfy this inquiry.[17] Among them is that people near Makkah did in fact confirm it and that other geographical locations were either experiencing daylight or were deeper into the night when hardly anyone would be awake and inspecting the sky. Another possibility is lack of visibility, or that a few other people saw it worldwide but assumed it to be a hallucination, or feared being accused of such, or shared it with others but were not taken seriously. People identify and report events based on context; a momentary decontextualized strange sight in the sky would be unlikely to be believed, reported or documented, let alone transmitted.

---

16 Ibn Ḥajar, *Fatḥ al-Bārī*, 7:185.

17 Ibid.

ii. The Night Journey

> *Glory be to the One Who took His servant [Muhammad] by night from the Sacred Mosque to the Farthest Mosque whose surroundings We have blessed, so that We might show him of Our signs. Indeed, He Alone is the All-Hearing, All-Seeing.*[18]

The Prophet Muhammad ﷺ was taken from Makkah to Jerusalem and back in a single night, a journey that would ordinarily take a full month for any traveler in the seventh century. When the pagans caught scent of this story being shared the following morning, they became jubilant with hopes of finally proving Muhammad ﷺ was a madman. They rushed to gather everyone around him, and to their delight, people literally fell off their seats in laughter upon hearing this ludicrous tale told by the Prophet ﷺ. Saddened by their mockery and disbelief, he proceeded to the Kaaba where he praised God and asked Him to be reshown Jerusalem. To the dismay of everyone present, the Prophet then began describing that blessed city in exquisite detail, as if he was walking through it at that very moment. People nervously turned to the Makkan traders who—unlike Muhammad ﷺ—were known to frequent Jerusalem, only to find them admitting his accuracy. Many still denied him and stormed off in frustration.

As history tends to repeat itself, the leading critics of Islam today—like the new atheists Richard Dawkins[19] and Sam Harris[20]—also love to taunt Muslims who 'reject scientific

---

18 (*al-Isrā'* 17: 1)

19 'Ridiculing belief in a winged horse is not 'bigotry,' not 'Islamophobia,' not 'racism.' It's sober, decent, gentle, scientific realism.' Richard Dawkins, *Twitter @RichardDawkins*, 2:20 am, December 27, 2015.

20 Sam Harris writes, 'Science, in the broadest sense, includes all reasonable claims to knowledge about ourselves and the world. If there were good reasons to believe that Jesus was born of a virgin, or that Muhammad flew to heaven on a winged horse, these beliefs would necessarily form part of our rational description of the universe.' ('Science must destroy religion', *samharris.org*, January 2, 2006. In this

realism' and accept that 'Muhammad flew to heaven on a winged horse'. However, this shows demonstrable ignorance about the Islamic faith, in addition to fallacious reasoning that actually undermines the scientific enterprise. With regards to their lack of familiarity with what Islamic sources actually say, it should be known that the creature called al-Burāq was emphatically not a winged horse and was never described as such by the Prophet Muhammad ﷺ.[21] Moreover, the narrations explicitly mention that al-Burāq took the Prophet to Jerusalem; the mechanism by which God raised the Prophet to Heaven is a different matter, as has been discussed in the Islamic tradition.[22]

---

essay, of course, Sam Harris merely begs the question, dismissing out of hand the notion that there could be any good reason to entertain the existence of miracles in the world, despite the overwhelming evidence of testimony to the contrary. But dismissing the evidence of testimony entails a death sentence for science, since science is grounded upon the faithful testimony of scientists regarding their accumulated experimental data, the vast majority of which could not be feasibly reproduced (See: Monya Baker, '1,500 Scientists Lift the Lid on Reproducibility,' *Nature*, 533 (2016):452–454.

21 Al-Burāq is a creature that is not from this world and has been described as a white beast that was smaller than a mule but larger than a donkey, whose stride was as far as the eye could see. When the Prophet ﷺ mounted al-Burāq, the creature shied, upon which the angel Gabriel said to al-Burāq, 'Do you behave this way with Muhammad? Verily, no one has ridden you who is more noble than him!' (*Sunan al-Tirmidhī*, 5:152 #3131). This may suggest that al-Burāq had been ridden by other riders from the home world of this creature, perhaps even indicating extra-terrestrial life-forms known only to God. (See: Yasir Qadhi, 'Night Journey & Ascension to Heavens 1', *YouTube.com*, January 2012).

22 Ibn Ḥajar notes in his commentary on the hadith that other narrations specifically mention that after the Prophet Muhammad ﷺ arrived in Jerusalem, he left al-Burāq and ascended to Heaven through the *Miʿrāj*, a portal of ascension, concerning which the Prophet ﷺ stated, 'I have never seen anything more wondrous than it.' (*Fatḥ al-Bārī*, 7:208) Al-Zarqāni and Mullah ʿAlī al-Qāri point out that the abridged version of the hadith simply mentions the ascension after mentioning the Prophet ﷺ riding al-Burāq, without mentioning that he dismounted al-Burāq in Jerusalem, which is specified in other hadith. (al-Qārī, *Mirqāt al-Mafātīḥ*, 9:3758).

As for the logical fallacy behind this argument, it is grounded only in what is known as *argumentum ad incredulum*—the argument from incredulity. They seek for people to ridicule a belief purely because it sounds unimaginable and fantastically foreign to the natural realm. Yet, it is indeed the logical consequence of belief in an omnipotent God that such miraculous matters lie entirely within His Capability. Moreover, the argument from incredulity would entail the demise of science for it is science that continually challenges our imagination of what is possible, unveiling the unfathomable world of quantum mechanics, bringing to light the possibility of multiple dimensions, and so on. To dismiss something out of hand simply based on incredulity would spell the end of the scientific enterprise which challenges us to explore the frontiers beyond what is imaginable.

Dr Hatem al-Haj, a contemporary Muslim scholar, writes:

> Al-Burāq not being described as a huge horse or something fancier stresses the point that it was not about this particular creature; it was about the will of God. Just as God said about the legions of angels He sends to support the believers, '*And Allah made it not except as [a sign of] good tidings for you and to reassure your hearts thereby. And victory is not except from Allah, the Exalted in Might, the Wise.*'[23] God created the laws of physics, and it is only rational that He is not bound by them. The inclusion of al-Burāq in the story made it more memorable. It was also meant to be familiar for the comfort and assurance of the rider, blessings and peace be upon him.[24]

In addition to the Qur'an describing this night journey, al-Kattānī (d. 1927) collected the names of forty-five different Com-

23 (*Āl 'Imrān* 3: 126)

24 Adapted from with the author's permission from his Facebook post on January 3rd, 2017.

panions who corroborated this astonishing event.[25] In one of these narrations, ʿĀʾishah 🌸 reports that even some Muslims felt this miracle was too outrageous to accept and apostatized that morning as a result. They rushed to her father, Abū Bakr 🌸, and said in protest, 'Your companion is claiming he was taken to Jerusalem last night.' Abū Bakr 🌸 asked, 'Did he say that?' They said, 'Yes.' He said, 'If he did in fact say that, then he has been truthful.' They said, 'You are willing to believe that he was carried to Jerusalem in a single night?' He said, 'Yes, for I believe him about something that is more astonishing than that: I believe that he receives messages from heaven in the blink of an eye.' ʿĀʾishah 🌸 says that it was from that day forward that Abū Bakr 🌸 was crowned with the title al-Ṣiddīq (the confirmer of truth).[26] Finally, the Qurʾan is filled with parallels of this miracle, such as God splitting time for the man who slept a hundred years without aging while his donkey decomposed,[27] and for the youth and their dog who slept for 309 years while generations were born and died outside their cave.[28]

iii. The Weeping Tree

ʿAbdullāh ibn ʿUmar 🌸 reports that the Prophet 🌼 used to deliver his sermons while standing beside the trunk of a date-palm tree. Upon the request of an Anṣārī woman, the Prophet 🌼 permitted that a small pulpit of three steps be constructed for him so that he would be more visible and project his voice further into the growing audience. When the Prophet 🌼 ascended the new pulpit on the following Friday, loud sounds of weeping emerged from this tree trunk. The Prophet 🌼 descended and went over to it and began caressing it with his hand just as someone does

---

25   al-Kattānī, *Naẓm al-Mutanāthir*, #258.
26   al-Bayhaqī, *Dalāʾil al-Nubuwwah*, 2:360; authenticated by al-Albānī in *al-Silsilah al-Ṣaḥīḥah*, 1:615 #306.
27   (*al-Baqarah* 2: 259)
28   (*al-Kahf* 18: 9–25)

to quiet a child. Anas ibn Mālik ﷺ adds, 'And the mosque shook from its whimpers.' Sahl ibn Sa'd ﷺ adds, 'Many people started weeping from hearing its crying and moaning.' Ibn 'Abbās ﷺ adds, 'He went and hugged it until it quieted, then said, "Had I not embraced it, it would have continued like this until the Day of Resurrection."' Jābir ﷺ adds, 'It was weeping over missing the Revelation that it would hear [recited] close by.'

These were only five Companions who reported this incident firsthand, though nearly twenty in total were present, according to the leading Hadith authorities. Ibn Ḥajar summarizes this investigation by saying, 'The hadith of the tree weeping and moon splitting have each been transmitted by an enormous number, one that offers sure knowledge for Hadith experts who examine their chains of transmission, not those untrained in that, and Allah knows best.'[29] Similarly, al-Munāwī reports this hadith on the tree whimpering through many authentic chains which collectively entail it being a *mutawātir* event, then states that it has been narrated from nearly twenty Companions.[30] Their corroboration led al-Bayhaqī to say that tracing the narrations of this incident to verify whether it happened or not, after an entire generation conveyed it to an entire generation, is unnecessary.[31]

iv. The Talking Stones

In the Noble Qur'an, Allah tells us that of the powerful signs He granted Prophet David (Dāwūd ﷺ) was that his melodious glorifications of God would be echoed by the towering mountains and soaring birds around the clock: *'And We certainly gave David from Us bounty. [We said], "O mountains, repeat [Our] praises with him, and the birds [as well]." And We made pliable for him iron.'*[32] With this same miracle, Allah endorsed the Prophet Muhammad ﷺ.

29 Ibn Ḥajar, *Fatḥ al-Bārī*, 6:592.
30 al-Kattānī, *Naẓm al-Mutanāthir*, #263.
31 Ibn Ḥajar, *Fatḥ al-Bārī*, 6:603.
32 (*Saba'* 34: 10)

Inanimate objects would glorify God in his hands, and even testify to his ministry as messenger and prophet. 'Abdullāh ibn Mas'ūd ﷺ said, 'We used to hear the food making *tasbīḥ* (glorifying Allah) as he ate.'[33] The dish would praise God in the presence of the Prophet ﷺ when the food was placed before him. Similarly, Abū Dharr ﷺ said:

> I was present with the Prophet ﷺ in a circle, and in his hands were pebbles, and everyone in the circle could hear their *tasbīḥ*. He then passed them to Abū Bakr, and they made *tasbīḥ* with Abū Bakr [as well]; everyone in the circle could hear their *tasbīḥ*. He then passed them back to the Prophet ﷺ and they made *tasbīḥ* in his hand again. He then passed them to 'Umar, and they made *tasbīḥ* in his hand, and everyone in the circle could hear their *tasbīḥ*. The Prophet ﷺ then passed them to 'Uthmān ibn 'Affān, and they made *tasbīḥ* in his hand. He then passed them to us, and they did not make *tasbīḥ* with any one of us.[34]

The very first miracles by which Allah prepared Muhammad ﷺ were of these types. Even before his prophethood, the stones would greet him. The Messenger of Allah ﷺ said, 'I certainly know stones in Makkah that used to greet me before I was commissioned, and I recognize them even now.'[35] And after becoming the Prophet of God, the Companions witnessed this as well. 'Alī ibn Abī Ṭālib ﷺ says, 'We were with the Messenger of Allah ﷺ in Makkah, and we did not encounter any tree or mountain but that it said, "Peace be upon you, O Messenger of Allah."'[36]

---

33 al-Bukhārī, *Ṣaḥīḥ al-Bukhārī*, 4:194 #3579.

34 Sulaymān ibn Aḥmad al-Ṭabarānī, *al-Mu'jam al-Awsaṭ* (Cairo: Dār al-Ḥaramayn, 1995) 2:59 #1244. For a variant narration, see Ibn Abī 'Āṣim, *al-Sunnah li-Ibn Abī 'Āṣim* (Beirut: al-Maktab al-Islāmī, 1980), 2:543 #1146; authenticated by al-Albānī in the comments.

35 Muslim, *Ṣaḥīḥ Muslim*, 4:1782 #2277.

36 al-Tirmidhī, *Sunan al-Tirmidhī*, 6:25 #3626; authenticated by al-Albānī in *Ṣaḥīḥ al-Targhīb wal-Tarhīb*, 2:29 #1209.

v. Increasing the Water Supply

Imam al-Nawawī says, 'These hadith on water gushing from between his fingers and increasing for him, and the food supply increasing as well, are all clear miracles performed by Allah's Messenger on many occasions and under different conditions and have collectively reached *mutawātir* status.'[37] Hadith scholars have prolific compilations on these incidents, of which is the following account from ʿAbdullāh ibn Masʿūd ﷺ:

> We used to consider miracles as Allah's Blessings, but you people consider them to be threatening. We were once with the Messenger of Allah ﷺ on a journey, and our water ran short. He said, 'Bring me the remaining water.' The people presented him a vessel containing water, in which he then placed his hands and said, 'Come get the blessed purification water, and all blessings are from Allah.' I saw the water flowing from between the fingers of Allah's Messenger ﷺ. Indeed, we used to also hear the food glorifying Allah as it was being eaten [by him].[38]

Jābir ibn ʿAbdillāh ﷺ narrated that the people became very thirsty on the Day of al-Ḥudaybiyyah.

> There was a small pot containing some water in front of the Prophet ﷺ, and he found the people rushing towards him as he finished performing his ritual ablution with it. He asked them, 'What has happened?' They said, 'We have water neither for ablution nor drinking.' So he placed his palm into that pot, and water began flowing upwards from between his fingers like springs. He said, 'All those seeking ablution, come forward; the blessing is from Allah.' Jābir ﷺ said, 'We all drank and performed

---

37 al-Nawawī, *Sharḥ Ṣaḥīḥ Muslim*, 15:38.
38 al-Bukhārī, *Ṣaḥīḥ al-Bukhārī*, 4:194 #3579.

> ablution [from that pot], and I did not care how much I drank because I knew it was blessed.'

One narrator asked Jābir ﷺ, 'How many were you?' He said, 'Even if we had been one hundred thousand, it would have been sufficient for us, but we were fifteen hundred.'[39]

Anas ibn Mālik ﷺ personally narrated several other nearly identical incidents of water pouring forth from between the Prophet's blessed fingers.[40] These reports suggest that water was emerging from the actual fingers of the Prophet ﷺ, or that it sprang through the gaps between them. Most Hadith interpreters—including al-Baghawī and al-Suyūṭī—chose the first view, and consequently deemed this feat particularly exceptional.

vi. Increasing the Food Supply

Salamah ibn al-Akwaʿ ﷺ narrates:

> We once set out on an expedition with Allah's Messenger ﷺ and faced great hardship, and decided to slaughter some of our riding animals [for food]. The Messenger of Allah ﷺ ordered us to pool our food rations, so we spread a sheet and leather where everyone's rations were collected. I stretched myself to assess how much that was, and it was only the area a small goat could sit on. We were fourteen hundred people, and we each ate to our satisfaction and then filled our bags with provisions. The Messenger of Allah ﷺ then said, 'Is there any water for performing ablution?' A man came forward with a small container that held very little water, which the Prophet ﷺ emptied into a wider basin. From that amount, all thoroughly performed their ablution. Eight individuals later came and said, 'Is there any water left

39 al-Bukhārī, *Ṣaḥīḥ al-Bukhārī*, 4:193 #3576.

40 al-Bukhārī, *Ṣaḥīḥ al-Bukhārī*, 4:192 #3572-3574.

to perform ablution?' Allah's Messenger 🌸 replied, 'The ablution water is finished.'[41]

As Imam al-Nawawī points out elsewhere:

When a Companion narrates something this incredible and cites as evidence personally attending it himself along with the other Companions, who hear his narration and claim or hear about it, and do not denounce him, that further confirms it and necessitates sure knowledge about the truth of his words.[42]

Jābir ibn 'Abdillāh 🌸 reports that his father, 'Abdullāh ibn 'Amr ibn Ḥarām 🌸, died and left behind a sizable debt. He said:

So I sought the Prophet's help with his creditors so that they would reduce his debt. He requested this from them, but they refused, so the Prophet 🌸 said to me, 'Go divide your dates according to their kinds; set the 'Ajwa dates on one side and the 'Idhq Ibn Zayd on another side. Then notify me.' I did so, then notified the Messenger of Allah 🌸. He came, sat down, then said, 'Measure for the people (creditors).' I measured out their amounts until I had repaid them all that they were owed, and my dates remained as if nothing had decreased from them.' When 'Umar ibn al-Khaṭṭāb 🌸 was informed of this miraculous surplus, he said, 'Once the Messenger of Allah 🌸 walked into the garden, I knew it would become blessed.'[43]

'Abd al-Raḥmān ibn Abī Bakr 🌸 reports:

41 Muslim, *Ṣaḥīḥ Muslim*, 3:1354 #1729.
42 al-Nawawī, *Sharḥ Ṣaḥīḥ Muslim*, 12:35.
43 al-Bukhārī, *Ṣaḥīḥal-Bukhārī*, 3:187 #2709.

> There were 130 of us with the Prophet ﷺ, and he said to us, 'Does any one of you have food with him?' One man had about a *ṣāʿ* of food, and so that was mixed. [44] Then a tall pagan man with disheveled hair came by driving some sheep. The Prophet ﷺ said to him, 'Selling or gifting?' He said, 'Selling.' He purchased a sheep from him, it was cooked, and the Prophet ﷺ ordered that the liver be roasted as well. By Allah, there was not a single person from the 130 except that the Prophet ﷺ cut for him a piece of its liver; those who were present were given, and those absent were stowed for. It was made into two dishes which they all ate from, and we had our fill, and yet the two dishes remained, and we loaded them onto a camel.[45]

Jābir ibn ʿAbdillāh ﵁ reports:

> We were digging on the Day of the Trench when a huge solid boulder hindered us. They came to the Prophet ﷺ and complained to him about this boulder, and he said, 'I am coming.' He then stood, stones tied to his stomach, as we had not tasted food in three days, and took the sledgehammer and struck the boulder until it became a dust mound. I said, 'O Messenger of Allah, would you permit me to visit my home?' I went and said to my wife, 'I saw on the Prophet ﷺ something that one cannot bear (i.e., the stones he had fastened from hunger). Do you have anything?' She said, 'I have some wheat and a small goat.' I slaughtered the small goat, ground the wheat, then placed the meat in a clay pot. Before I left, my wife said, 'Do not humiliate me in front of the Prophet ﷺ and

---

44 A *ṣāʿ* is a container which measures volume, comparable to a large salad bowl, and is equivalent to three liters.

45 Muslim, *Ṣaḥīḥ Muslim*, 3:1626 #2056.

> those with him.' I went to the Prophet ﷺ and whispered to him, 'I have a little food, so you come, O Messenger of Allah, along with a man or two.' He said, 'How much is it?' I informed him, so he said, 'That is plenty and good!' Then, he said, 'O People of the Trench! Stand [all of you]; Jābir has prepared a banquet for you. Let us go.' The Muhājirīn and Anṣār stood, and the Prophet ﷺ said to me, 'Tell her not to pull the pot, nor the bread from the oven, until I come.' When I entered upon my wife and informed her of the army behind me, she said, 'What is with you?' I said, 'I did what you said!' She said, 'Did he ask you?' I said, 'Yes.' The dough was brought out to the Prophet ﷺ, and he spat in it and prayed for blessings, then reached for the pot and did the same. Then, he tore the bread and placed it inside the pot and served ample bread and meat to each Companion. There were one thousand people and, by Allah, each of them ate until they stopped [of their own accord] and left, and our pot was still full and our bread still plenty. In the end, he said to us, 'Eat from this, or gift it, for the people [of Madinah] have been struck with hunger.'[46]

Anas ibn Mālik ﷺ reports:

> Abū Ṭalḥah said to Umm Sulaym, 'I heard the voice of Allah's Messenger ﷺ reflecting weakness, and I could recognize hunger in it. Do you have anything?' She said, 'Yes.' She pulled out several wheat loaves, wrapped them in her veil, then tucked them under my arm and wrapped me with the remaining part of the veil. She sent me to the Messenger of Allah ﷺ and, upon reaching the mosque, I found people with him. I stood beside them,

---

46 al-Bukhārī, *Ṣaḥīḥ al-Bukhārī*, 5:108 #4101-4102; Muslim, *Ṣaḥīḥ Muslim*, 3:1610 #2039.

until the Messenger of Allah ﷺ said to me, 'Did Abū Ṭalḥah send you?' I said, 'Yes.' He said, 'With food?' I said, 'Yes.' The Messenger of Allah ﷺ then said to the people, 'Let us go.' They took off, and I took off in front of them until I reached Abū Ṭalḥah and informed him. Abū Ṭalḥah said, 'O Umm Sulaym, the Messenger of Allah ﷺ has come, accompanied by many people, and we have nothing to feed them.' She said, 'Allah and His Messenger know best.' Upon arrival, the Messenger of Allah ﷺ said, 'O Umm Sulaym, what do you have?' She presented that same bread, which the Prophet ﷺ took and shredded, and then Umm Sulaym emptied her jar of shortening (butter) over it as a condiment. The Messenger of Allah ﷺ then supplicated over it for however long he wished before saying, 'Permit ten [to enter].' They were permitted entrance and ate to their fill before leaving. Then he said, 'Permit ten.' They too were permitted entrance and ate to their fill before leaving. Then he said, 'Permit ten.' Everyone ate in this fashion, until they all had their fill, and there were seventy or eighty men in total.[47]

vii. Answered Prayers

Al-Qāḍī 'Iyāḍ says, 'The Prophet's supplications being answered for those he prayed for and against is *mutawātir* in principle, known by necessity.'[48] He meant that God responded to the prayers of the Prophet ﷺ on so many occasions, and this was corroborated by testimony from so many people, that doubting it would be wholly irrational. An outnumbered and unequipped Muslim army was granted victory by God at the Battle of Badr, milk was drawn from the udders of a non-lactating goat, and rain poured

47 al-Bukhārī, *Ṣaḥīḥ al-Bukhārī*, 4:193 #3578; Muslim, *Ṣaḥīḥ Muslim*, 3:1612 #2040.

48 al-Qāḍī 'Iyāḍ, *Al-Shifā bi-Ta'rīf Ḥuqūq al-Muṣṭafā*, 1:325.

from a cloudless sky—all by virtue of the Prophet ﷺ raising his palms to the heavens, and those who spent the shortest time with him witnessed these events and many were driven to conviction by them. Anas ibn Mālik ؓ narrates:

> As the Prophet ﷺ was once delivering a Friday sermon, a man rose and said, 'O Messenger of Allah, the horses and sheep have perished! Will you not invoke Allah to bless us with rain?' The Prophet ﷺ lifted his hands and supplicated at a time when the sky was as clear as glass. Suddenly wind blew, driving together the clouds and causing heavy rain. We exited the mosque wading through the flowing water till we reached our homes. It kept raining until the following Friday, when the same man, or another man, stood up and said, 'O Messenger of Allah, the houses have almost collapsed; please ask Allah to withhold the rain!' Hearing that, the Prophet ﷺ smiled and said, 'O Allah, [let it rain] around us and not upon us.'[49] I looked to the clouds and found them separating into a crown-like formation around Madinah.[50]

Abū Hurayrah ؓ narrates that he once came to the Prophet ﷺ with tears in his eyes, which caused him to ask, 'What makes you cry, O Abū Hurayrah?' He said, 'I keep inviting my mother to Islam, but she continues to reject it. Today, I invited her again and heard from her painful words about you. Pray that Allah opens the heart of Abū Hurayrah's mother to Islam.' The Prophet ﷺ obliged and said, 'O Allah, guide the mother of Abū Hurayrah.' Abū Hurayrah ؓ narrates:

> I left hopeful due to the prayer of the Prophet ﷺ and returned home to find the door partially open and could

49 al-Bukhārī, *Ṣaḥīḥ al-Bukhārī*, 2:28 #1013.

50 al-Bukhārī, *Ṣaḥīḥ al-Bukhārī*, 4:195 #3582.

> hear water splashing inside. When my mother heard my footsteps, she said, 'Stay where you are, O Abū Hurayrah.' After putting on her clothes, she instructed me to enter. When I entered, she said, 'I testify that none is worthy of worship but Allah, and I testify that Muhammad is His servant and messenger.' I returned to the Prophet ﷺ weeping with joy, just as an hour earlier I had gone weeping in sadness, and said, 'Great news, O Messenger of Allah! Allah has answered your prayer and guided the mother of Abū Hurayrah to Islam.' He praised Allah and thanked Him, and then I said, 'O Messenger of Allah, pray that Allah make my mother and I beloved to His believing slaves, and make them beloved to us.' He obliged, and there has not since been a believing slave who hears of me, or sees me, except that he loves me.[51]

ʿAbdullāh ibn ʿAbbās ﷺ narrates:

> I once placed water for the Prophet ﷺ upon him entering the lavatory, so that he could perform his ablution. He asked, 'Who placed this?' They informed him that I had placed it, so he said, 'O Allah, grant him a deep understanding of the religion, and teach him to interpret [the Qur'an].'[52]

Shortly after the Prophet's death, even the senior-most Companions recognized that this young man had developed a unique prowess when it came to understanding the Qur'an and elucidating its nuances. Fourteen centuries later, nearly every credible Sunni work on Qur'anic commentary considers the explanations of Ibn ʿAbbās ﷺ authoritative, is filled with examples of his

51 Muslim, *Ṣaḥīḥ Muslim*, 4:1938 #2491.

52 al-Bukhārī, *Ṣaḥīḥ al-Bukhārī*, 1:41 #143; Muslim, *Ṣaḥīḥ Muslim*, 4:1927 #2477.

exegetical forte, and testifies to him being *Tarjumān al-Qur'ān* (the Master Interpreter of the Qur'an).

Anas ibn Mālik ﵁ narrates:

> The Messenger of Allah ﷺ once visited us at home when nobody was there but myself, my mother (Umm Sulaym), and her sister (Umm Ḥarām). My mother said to him, 'O Messenger of Allah, this is your little servant (Anas); invoke Allah's blessings upon him.' He supplicated that I be afforded every good, and this is what he said to conclude his supplication: 'O Allah, increase him in his wealth and progeny, and bless him in what you grant him.' By Allah, my wealth has certainly become abundant, and my children and grandchildren [combined] certainly surpass a hundred today.[53]

'Abdullāh ibn 'Umar ﵁ narrates that the Prophet ﷺ once said, 'O Allah, honour Islam through the dearest of these two men to you: through Abū Jahl or through 'Umar ibn al-Khaṭṭāb.' Ibn 'Umar ﵁ said, 'And the dearest of them turned out to be 'Umar.'[54]

Indeed, no person from the Prophet's Companions honoured Islam by advancing its public presence like 'Umar ﵁, as Ibn Mas'ūd ﵁ used to say, 'We remained powerful since the moment 'Umar embraced Islam.'[55] Even after the Prophet's death, it was the unique impact of 'Umar ﵁ in spreading the light of Islam that compelled the historian Michael Hart to showcase him in his book, *The 100: A Ranking of the Most Influential Persons in History*.

Abū 'Amrah al-Anṣāri ﵁ reports that during a battle alongside the Messenger of Allah ﷺ, the people once again suffered from great hunger, and 'Umar ﵁ said, 'O Messenger of Allah,

---

53 al-Bukhārī, *Ṣaḥīḥ al-Bukhārī*, 8:75 #6344; Muslim, *Ṣaḥīḥ Muslim*, 4:1929 #2481.

54 al-Tirmidhī, *Sunan al-Tirmidhī*, 6:58 #3681; authenticated by al-Tirmidhī in the comments.

55 al-Bukhārī, *Ṣaḥīḥ al-Bukhārī*, #5:11 #3684.

if you see it proper, you can collect what remains of our rations. We can gather them, then you can call upon Allah to bless them, for Allah the Blessed and Exalted will certainly deliver us with your supplication.' Some people brought a single handful, and nobody had more than a *ṣāʿ* of dates. The Messenger of Allah ﷺ gathered it all together, then stood and supplicated for as long as Allah willed. Then, he called the army to come forth with their containers and fill them, and there did not remain a single container in the whole army except that they filled it. The Messenger of Allah ﷺ smiled until his molars could be seen, and said, 'I testify that none is worthy of worship except Allah and that I am the Messenger of Allah. No slave meets Allah with these two statements without doubting them but that he will enter Paradise.'[56]

Ibn Taymiyyah says,

> It is known that when Allah accustoms someone to having their prayers answered, this only happens in conjunction with righteousness and religiosity. When someone claims prophethood, they are either the most pious person—in that case they are truthful—or the most wicked person—in that case they are lying. But when Allah accustoms them to answering their supplications, then it must be that they are not wicked but instead pious. Even if the claim of prophethood was accompanied by nothing but righteousness from the claimant without miracles, it would necessitate him being a genuine prophet, for such a person cannot be someone who deliberately lies, nor can he be a deluded person who assumes that he is a prophet.[57]

56 Muslim, *Ṣaḥīḥ Muslim*, 1:55 #27.

57 Taqī al-Dīn Aḥmad ibn Taymiyyah, *Al-Jawāb al- Ṣaḥīḥ li-man Baddala Dīn al-Masīḥ* (Saudi Arabia: Dār al-ʿĀṣimah, 1999), 6:297.

In summation, miracles are not the only proof of his prophethood, nor are they themselves unfounded proofs. Due to their *mutawātir* transmission, the historical proof backing them is staggering, and confer such certainty that their denial would necessitate rejecting the miracles of all other prophets and rejecting every factoid of acquired knowledge. As for the presumed logical and scientific contentions against miracles, they only stem from a faulty philosophy, such as the indefensible claims of God not existing or not being anything but nature itself. However, when such paradigms are the ethos of today's dominant culture, and when humans have such a propensity for groupthink, whether those positions are intellectually tenable becomes irrelevant. This is why God encourages reflection throughout the Qur'an, liberating us from the indoctrination that resists the patent proofs of prophethood:

> *Say [O Prophet], 'I advise you with just one thing: that you take a stand for the sake of God—individually or in pairs—then reflect. Your companion (Muhammad) surely has no traces of insanity; he is but a warner to you before the coming of a severe punishment.'*[58]

In this verse is a call to courage, as honesty and the willingness to detach oneself from the herd can sometimes come with a significant cost.

58 (*Saba'* 34: 46)

7

The Inimitable Qur'an

The inimitable nature of the Qur'an continues to be the most compelling proof that Muhammad ﷺ was in fact the Final Prophet of God. He said:

> There was no prophet except that he was granted signs that caused the people to believe in him, but what I have been uniquely granted is a revelation that Allah has inspired me with, and thus I am hopeful to have the most followers among them on the Day of Resurrection.[1]

This does not mean that the Prophet ﷺ had no other signs, just as it does not mean that the previous prophets had no revelation. Rather, the implication here is that the Qur'an would be uniquely effective in guiding people to faith over the passage of time. It should not surprise us that a permanent living miracle that can be experienced firsthand by successive generations would outperform a miraculous event witnessed by a limited group at a partic-

---

[1] al-Bukhārī, *Ṣaḥīḥ al-Bukhārī*, 9:92 #7274; Muslim, *Ṣaḥīḥ Muslim*, 1:134 #152.

ular moment in history. What does astound many is how any mere work of literature could ever qualify as otherworldly in its origins.

The Qur'an presents itself as the literal speech of God,[2] and asserts that nothing like it will ever be produced.[3] This inimitability is multidimensional, and this chapter will simply provide a taste and overview of some of these dimensions, while addressing alternative explanations posited by some critics in their attempts to deny the divine origins of the Qur'an. For a deeper exploration of this topic, readers can avail themselves the expansive genre of books dedicated entirely to it.[4]

1. A Literary Masterpiece

According to both the highest authorities of the Arabic language in early Arabia, and its foremost experts today, there is consensus on the literary uniqueness of the Qur'an. Professor Martin Zammit, the author of *A Comparative Lexical Study of Qur'anic Arabic*, says, 'Notwithstanding the literary excellence of some of the long pre-Islamic poems ... the Qur'an is definitely on a level of its own as the most eminent written manifestation of the Arabic language.'[5]

Arthur J. Arberry (d. 1969), a British scholar of Arabic literature, wrote in his popular translation of the Qur'an, 'The rhetoric and rhythm of the Koran are so characteristic, so powerful, so highly emotive, that any version whatsoever is bound in the nature of things to be but a poor copy of the glittering splendour of the original.'[6]

---

2 (*al-Tawbah* 9: 6)

3 (*al-Isrā'* 17: 88)

4 See: Gibril F. Haddad, 'Tropology and Inimitability: Ibn Ashur's Theory of Tafsir in the Ten Prolegomena to Al-Tahrir wa'l-Tanwir', *Journal of Qur'anic Studies*, 21.1 (2019): 50–111.

5 Martin R. Zammit, *A Comparative Lexical Study of Qur'anic Arabic* (Boston: Brill, 2002), 37.

6 Arthur J. Arberry, *The Koran Interpreted: A Translation* (Simon and Schuster, 1996), 24.

During the Prophet's time, Arabs were people who valued language almost as much as life itself.[7] Before Islam, they would derogatorily call non-Arabs *ʿajam* (literally: silent or speechless), implying that others were not equally alive, or were deficient, since they could not articulate with the same lucidity and emotiveness. To further illustrate the belief that language equals life, the eleventh-century poet Ibn Rashīq (d. 999) says:

> Whenever a poet emerged in an Arab tribe, other tribes would come to congratulate, feasts would be prepared, the women would play lutes as they do at weddings, and old and young men would all rejoice at the good news—for this was a shield for their honour, a defense of their lineages, and an immortalization of their triumphs. The Arabs used to congratulate each other only on the birth of a child and when a poet rose among them.[8]

Ground for such festivities was understandable, since, as Navid Kermani says:

> Old Arabic poetry is a highly complex phenomenon. The vocabulary, grammatical idiosyncrasies, and strict norms were passed down from generation to generation, and only the most gifted students fully mastered the language. A person had to study for years, sometimes even decades, under a master poet before laying claim to the title of poet.[9]

---

7 Ibn Khaldūn & Franz Rosenthal (trans.), *The Muqaddimah* (Princeton: Princeton University Press, 1967), chap. 6, sec. 58.

8 Ibn Rashīq al-Qayrawānī, *Al-ʿUmdah fī Maḥāsin al-Shiʿr wa-Ādābih* (Beirut: Dār al-Jīl, 1981), 1:65.

9 Navid Kermani, 'Poetry and Language', in *The Blackwell Companion to the Qur'an,* edited by Andrew Rippin (Hoboken: Wiley-Blackwell, 2009), 108.

Everyone else was validated by what they retained in memory of these odes and speeches that captured the history, morals, and wisdoms of this otherwise primitive desert civilization. This was the historical context within which the Qur'an was revealed. It descended amid people at the pinnacle of rhetorical expression. Virtually overnight, these same people experienced a Qur'an from Muhammad ﷺ that was pure in its Arabic, unprecedented in its eloquence, but mysteriously independent of the poetry or prose they knew and had mastered. Dr Bassam Saeh explains:

> [T]he miraculousness of the Qur'an lies in this very paradox: the paradox of its being truly Arabic, and its being, at one and the same time, a new language. This might appear to be illogical. However, the logic of miracle inheres in precisely the fact that it surpasses logic. A miracle that rests on logic ceases to be a miracle.[10]

The prideful Arabs could not explain how they collectively failed the Qur'anic challenge to produce a single chapter with merely similar literary features, according to their own biased judges, when its shortest chapter is only ten words,[11] when they were the masters of Arabic, and when Muhammad ﷺ brought over 6,000 verses of it. But that was not all. What dealt the killer blow to the Prophet's opponents in this standoff, leaving absolutely no room for further doubt, was the fact that he was unlettered to begin with. As Allah says, *'And you did not recite before it any scripture, nor did you inscribe one with your right hand. Otherwise, the falsifiers would have had [cause for] doubt.'*[12] It was an utter enigma, one that ultimately forced the Prophet's detractors to settle on the accusation of him

---

10 Bassam Saeh, *The Miraculous Language of the Qur'an: Evidence of Divine Origin* (Virginia: IIIT, 2015), 21.

11 (*al-Kawthar* 108: 1–3)

12 (*al-ʿAnkabūt* 29: 48)

being a magician,[13] unwittingly conceding that there was indeed something supernatural about this Book.

i. Muhammad or Shakespeare?

Some critics argue that while the Qur'an is a literary masterpiece, this does not mean that it is supernatural. They claim that every civilization has its unequaled works of literature, such as Shakespeare's *Sonnets* in English and Homer's *Iliad* in Greek, and the Qur'an is no different. However, this view ignores a myriad of major differences between the Prophet Muhammad ﷺ and Shakespeare:[14]

1. Unlike the Prophet Muhammad ﷺ, Shakespeare was educated in both Greek and Latin and had, alongside his mentors, access to libraries of books that he built on for his own writings.
2. Shakespeare earned a living as a professional playwright and continued refining his craft with each dramatic production, while the Prophet ﷺ was never reported to utter a single full couplet of poetry in his entire life,[15] nor was it possible for him to retract any word of the Qur'an for quality control once it was spoken to his vast Muslim and non-Muslim audiences.
3. Sonnets were known and produced for centuries before Shakespeare, while the Qur'an had a unique compositional structure that differed from every pattern of writing or speech used by Arabia's master poets.[16]

---

13 (*al-Muddaththir* 74: 24)

14 Sami Ameri, *Barāhīn al-Nubuwwah* (London: Takween Center, 2018), 222–28.

15 Muṣṭafā Ṣādiq al-Rāfiʿī, *Iʿjāz al-Qurʾān wal-Balāghah al-Nabawīyah* (Beirut: Dār al-Kutub al-ʿArabī, 1973), 308.

16 See: Gerhard Bowering, *Islamic Political Thought: An Introduction* (Princeton University Press, 2015), 186.

4. Unlike Shakespeare, whose hallmark style and vocabulary permeate all his writings, the Prophet Muhammad ﷺ brought the world a Qur'an whose style differs from the Hadith tradition—the everyday statements of Muhammad ﷺ. While this was noticed by his contemporaries, more than a dozen experiments have since been conducted to establish this objectively. Stylometry is the statistical analysis of variations in literary style to discriminate between one writer and another. It has been utilized to distinguish between the authentic and pseudonymous letters of Paul in the New Testament, and to prove that the Hadith and the Qur'an must have had two different authors. Researchers of the latter were forced to accept that it would be impossible for any human being to employ such extensive self-policing of their language for a lifetime. For instance, they found that 62 per cent of the words from *Ṣaḥīḥ al-Bukhārī*, a voluminous collection of Hadith, do not appear in the Qur'an, and 83 per cent of Qur'anic terms do not exist in Hadith.[17]
5. Shakespeare's sonnets were not uniformly eloquent, but instead had segments of distinct brilliance. In contrast, the Arabs who took great pride in their *naqd* (literary critique) tradition, a genre in which they brutally scrutinized each other's poetry to identify suboptimal word choices, never identified a single passage in the Qur'an that could be improved.[18]

---

17 Halim Sayoud, 'Author Discrimination between the Holy Qur'an and Prophet's Statements', *Literary and Linguistic Computing* 27, no. 4 (2012): 427–44.

18 When the masters of Arabic could not identify a suboptimal choice (let alone a mistake) in the Qur'an, it makes clear the absurdity of later critics who claim that the Qur'an contains grammatical errors. Not only was Arabic grammar codified over a century after the Qur'an was revealed, but the method grammarians followed in crafting the discipline involved analyzing the Qur'an itself, along with other early texts. The patterns they pinpointed became the 'grammatical principles' of

6. Shakespeare and his peers never considered his work beyond the reach of human effort; it was but the champion—to some—in an arena of worthy competitors. In fact, Professor Hugh Craig of Newcastle University ranked Shakespeare as the seventh-greatest English-speaking playwright, behind Webster, Dekker, Peele, Marlowe, Jonson, and Greene.[19] In contrast, the Qur'an shamed its deniers and challenged them at every turn to try to create anything that merely resembled it;[20] and this challenge has never been met. As Allah says:

> *And if you are in doubt about what We have sent down upon Our servant [Muhammad], then produce a sūrah the like thereof and call upon your witnesses other than Allah, if you should be truthful. But if you do not—and you will never be able to—then fear the Fire, whose fuel is men and stones, prepared for the disbelievers.*[21]

7. Shakespeare enjoyed the creative liberties of fictional storytelling. As for the Qur'an, entertainment is not its goal. It addresses theology, philosophy, history, and law—stiff technical discussions that do not ordinarily have mass appeal. The Qur'an asserted complex existential truths and taught a nuanced morality with a remarkable blend of precision and graceful elegance. It deconstructed prevalent wrongs that

Arabic, and thus whenever later linguists—irrespective of their religion—noticed an inconsistency between the Qur'an and one of these principles, they would conclude that the earlier grammarian made an oversight in observation, not that the Qur'an contained an error. Critics today reverse the process; they dismiss the Qur'an, a linguistic masterpiece heralded as the measuring stick of the language, based on a fallacious assessment.

19 Hugh Craig, 'Shakespeare's Vocabulary: Myth and Reality', *Shakespeare Quarterly* 62, no. 1 (2011): 53–74.

20 (*al-Ṭūr* 52: 33–34)

21 (*al-Baqarah* 2: 23–24)

had become normalized and revealed the hypocrisy within—all uncomfortable narratives that would not be expected to garner widespread embrace. The Qur'an also repeats its themes quite often (to inculcate and reinforce its value system), a technique that skilled authors generally try to avoid, but with such artistic variation each time that leaves its rhetorical richness unblemished.

8. Unlike the entertainment suitable for a stage in London in the seventeenth century, the Qur'an as a religious text had to resonate with the young and the old, the premodern and postmodern mind, the eastern and western personality, and the spiritually versus intellectually inclined. When analyzing the effect of the Qur'an on the vast spectrum of hearts and minds, across the globe and across generations, no other text in human history has fascinated such a wide range of people. In America today, for instance, a Qur'an recitation competition will be attended by all segments of the Muslim community. On the other hand, an English play by Shakespeare will find almost no appreciation among the common man and only attract the college-educated middle-to-upper class elite.
9. Shakespeare had decades of deliberation to decide what to include and omit from his works. Contrast this with the Prophet Muhammad ﷺ, who would convey verses from the Qur'an in response to people's unscripted inquiries. For instance, there are thirteen passages in the Qur'an that begin with *'And they ask you [O Prophet] about … Say …*[22] Furthermore, he would receive fresh Qur'anic revelations in the most stressful conditions, at times while bleeding after an attack or mourning his deceased relatives, specifically pertaining to events that had just taken place. Should not such spontaneous productions of

[22] (*al-Baqarah* 2: 189)

the Qur'an necessitate a disparity in eloquence between them and those written under serene candlelight, after the events have unfolded and the emotional turbulence has quieted?

10. Shakespeare must have written his works in a linear fashion, building from the ground up, just as any author would, and was free to decide from the onset how each drama would begin and end. The Qur'an, however, was assembled like a jig-saw puzzle over twenty-three years. The order of the Qur'an today does not reflect the chronology of its revelation, but rather the later designated location for each passage within its respective chapter. This means that the Qur'an did not just exhibit fascinating consistency in its structure,[23] despite being spoken not written, but was somehow designed with interspersed additions, of various themes and lengths, many of which addressed unpredictable external events impromptu, and yet all this never disrupted its seamless tapestry.

While it may be difficult for many people to grasp how any work of language can be miraculous, al-Bāqillānī (d. 1013) argues in his book, *Iʿjāz al-Qur'ān* (The Inimitability of the Qur'an), that it suffices to consider the reaction of the Qur'an's first audience. Instead of outperforming the unlettered man in what was their strongest suit, thereby ending his religion in its infancy by

---

23 On the thematic symmetry in Surah al-Baqarah, formally known as ring composition, Dr. Raymond Farrin says, 'Indeed this chapter exhibits marvelous justness of design. It is precisely and tightly arranged, as we have seen, according to the principles of ring composition; even the section lengths fit perfectly in the overall scheme. Moreover, the precise structure serves as a guide, pointing to key themes in the chapter. These occur, according to the logic of the pattern, at the centres of individual rings and, particularly, at the centre of the whole chapter. At the centre of the chapter, again, one finds instructions to face Mecca—this being a test of faith; identification of the Muslims as a new, middle community.' Raymond K. Farrin, *Sūrat al-Baqarah: A Structural Analysis* (Hartford, CT: Hartford Seminary, 2010), 30.

simply responding to his challenge of producing something like the Qur'an, they spent fortunes trying to smear his name and worked tirelessly to prevent a single Qur'anic verse from reaching the ears and hearts of visitors to Makkah. They disavowed their codes of chivalry and tribal honour—a massive undertaking for early Arabs—to starve his followers, torture his supporters, and ultimately wage wars against their fellow clansmen.[24] Failed by their words, they felt compelled to reach for their swords. It was not just because their greatest poets like Labīd ibn Rabīʿah were now converting to Islam and retiring from poetry, but due to them echoing in private that rivaling the Qur'an was impossible. When al-Walīd ibn al-Mughīrah—a staunch enemy of Islam until his death—was asked to critique the Qur'an, he responded:

> And what can I possibly say? There is not a single man among you who is more versed in prose or poetry than I, or in the poems of even the jinn. By God, what he says bears no resemblance to any of these things. By God, his statement which he utters has a sweetness to it, and a charm hovers over it. Its highest parts (surface meanings) are fruitful and its depths gush forth without end. It dominates and cannot be dominated, and it will certainly crush all that is beneath it.[25]

2. Knowledge of the Inaccessible Past

The Qur'an is also remarkably accurate about historical events that would have been impossible for the Prophet ﷺ to have known about. The following are some examples of the historical precision regarding ancient Egypt found in the Qur'an:

---

24 Abū Bakr Muḥammad ibn al-Ṭayyib al-Bāqillānī, *Iʿjāz al-Qur'ān* (Egypt: Dār al-Maʿārif, 1997), 1:20.

25 Muḥammad ibn ʿAbdillāh al-Ḥākim, *Al-Mustadrak ʿalā al-Ṣaḥīḥayn* (Beirut: Dār al-Kutub al-ʿIlmīyah, 1990), 2:550 #3872; authenticated by al-Ḥākim according to the criteria of *Ṣaḥīḥ al-Bukhārī.*

i. Pharaoh's Body Will Survive

While the Bible also states that the Pharaoh of Moses drowned, the Qur'an asserts that God will make an example of him for later oppressors by saving his corpse—on that same day—from being lost at sea. Allah says:

> *And We took the Israelites across the sea, and Pharaoh and his soldiers pursued them in tyranny and enmity until, when drowning overtook him, he said, 'I believe that there is no deity except that in whom the Israelites believe, and I am of the Muslims.' Now? And you had disobeyed [Him] before and were of the corrupters? So today, We will save you in [terms of] your body that you may be to those after you a sign. And indeed, many among humanity are heedless of Our signs.*[26]

Since the preservation of mummies is quite uncommon, and the fact that Muhammad ﷺ could not have known about this particular Pharaoh surviving in mummified form given the knowledge of his day, this Qur'anic assertion about the Pharoah of Moses is mindboggling. Furthermore, while the Qur'an mentions many perished nations punished by God for their rebellion, and that their accounts are a lesson for later people, Allah never stated that He would save their bodies as signs for those future generations. The sole exception in the Qur'an is that Pharaoh's corpse which happens to remain available until today in the Egyptian Museum of Cairo.

For several centuries before, and nearly 1,200 years after the Prophet Muhammad ﷺ, until the invasions of Napoleon Bonaparte, knowledge of ancient Egypt was scarce at best. It was only after the discovery of a tablet called the Rosetta Stone, in 1799, that the discipline of Egyptology was born, the hieroglyphics were deciphered, and reliable source material about this perished civilization slowly became available. Over a century

26 (*Yūnus* 10: 90–92)

later, a team of researchers was sent from France to explore these newfound tombs, among which was Dr. Maurice Bucaille, who published on this project his great work, *Mummies of the Pharaoh: Modern Medical Investigations*. Bucaille presented his findings in 1976 to the French Institute for Forensic Medicine and received multiple national awards for this groundbreaking work.

ii. The Heavens Did Not Grieve for Pharaoh

After describing their demise, the Qur'an then says about Pharaoh and his troops, *'And the heaven and earth wept not for them, nor were they reprieved.'*[27] A recently unearthed pyramid text has granted new depths to the meaning of this verse. In it, Pharaoh is described as ascending at death to claim supremacy of the heavens. The ancient hieroglyphics read, 'The sky weeps for thee; the earth trembles for thee … when thou ascendest to heaven as a star, as the morning star.'[28] In other words, the Qur'an was issuing a direct response to these specific mythological adulations, over 1,000 years before the vaults hiding them were unlocked.

iii. Joseph's King Wasn't a Pharaoh

The Qur'an identifies the ruler of Egypt as 'Pharaoh' sixty-five times, but only in the story of Moses. Not a single time is Egypt's earlier king during the time of Joseph called a Pharaoh in the Qur'an. This differs from the Old Testament which uses the title for both rulers, and even for the ruler of Egypt during the earlier time of Prophet Abraham.[29] However, it has since been established that the term Pharaoh was first coined during the reign of

---

27 (*al-Dukhān* 44: 29)

28 Samuel Alfred Browne Mercer (trans.), *The Pyramid Texts*, 1st ed. (New York: Longmans, Green, 1952), 222.

29 See: Genesis 40:7, 41:15, 41:31, 41:46, 50:7 for the era of Joseph, and 12:10-20 for the era of Abraham.

Thutmose III (d. 1436 BC), the 18th dynasty of ancient Egypt.[30] Historians have further discovered that during the era of Joseph, the 15th to 17th dynasties of Egypt were an invading force from Palestine, and hence they were called the Hyksos (literally: foreign kings). Since Pharaoh meant 'great house' or 'elite bloodline', and since the Hyksos were occupiers and not indigenous rulers, they were naturally ineligible for the honourific title—had it even existed.[31] Dr Bucaille writes:

> I must confess that when the Qur'an was first being conveyed to people, the ancient Egyptian language had vanished from the collective memory of humanity for over two centuries and remained that way until the nineteenth century. Therefore, it was impossible for us to know that the king of Egypt should be called anything other than the title mentioned in the Holy Bible. The subtle word choice of the Qur'an on this matter is thought-provoking.[32]

The historical accuracy of the Qur'an is not just confirmed by recent archaeological excavation. It astonished many early Jews and Christians as well. The fact that Muhammad ﷺ could simply speak of personalities across different cultures like Abraham, Joseph, Moses, Jesus, Dhū al-Qarnayn, and others with such detail was inexplicable. So was the fact that he could extensively illustrate scenes from the hereafter just as their earlier scriptures did, as Allah said:

> *Over it (the Hellfire) are nineteen. And We have not made the keepers of the Hellfire but angels, and We have not made their number*

---

30 'Pharaoh', *Encyclopedia Britannica Online*. Accessed February 5th, 2020.

31 Muḥammad Bayyūmī Mahrān, *Dirāsāt Tārīkhīyah fil-Qur'ān al-Karīm* (Beirut: Dār al-Nahḍah, 1988), 2:121–22.

32 Maurice Bucaille, *Moïse et Pharaon: Les Hébreux en Egypte: quelles concordances des livres saints avec l'histoire* (Paris: Pocket, 2003), 210–11. Cited in Ameri, *Barāhīn al-Nubuwwah*, 505.

except as a trial for those who disbelieve, and so that those who were given the Scripture [prior] would be certain.[33]

Some Jews in Madinah conceded that Muhammad ﷺ was in fact a true prophet, then resisted his message under the indefensible claim that it only applied to the Arabs. This was due to their inability to contest its divine origin, for they knew there was no access to any semblance of this history in the Arabic language whatsoever. As Allah says, '*That is from the news of the unseen which We reveal to you, [O Muhammad]. You knew it not, neither you nor your people, before this.*'[34]

Some of the toughest critics of the Qur'an in the past century, like William Tisdall (d. 1928), confirmed this. He writes, 'There seems to be no satisfactory proof that an Arabic version of the New Testament existed in Muhammad's time.'[35] In a similar vein, Pope Tawadrus II of Alexandria writes:

> The first Arabic translation surfaced towards the end of the eighth Gregorian century and more than one hundred years after Islam. It was done by Bishop John of Seville in Spain. It was a partial translation that did not include the entire book and was insufficiently circulated.[36]

This holds true for the Torah as well. The most authoritative academic researchers in this space largely agree that no written Arabic text of substantial length, be it scriptural or poetry, original or translated, can be traced back to the pre-Islamic period.[37]

---

33 (*al-Muddaththir* 74: 30–31)

34 (*Hūd* 11: 49)

35 William St. Tisdall, *The Original Sources of the Qur'an* (London: Society for the Promotion of Christian Knowledge, 1911), 140.

36 Pope Tawadrus II, *Miftāḥ al-'Ahd al-Jadīd* (Cairo: Batrirkiyyat al-Aqbāṭ al-Urthudux, 2013), 27.

37 See: Sidney H. Griffith, *The Bible in Arabic: The Scriptures of the 'People of the Book' in the Language of Islam* (New Jersey: Princeton University Press, 2013), 41 and 114-118.

iv. Was Muhammad Spoon-Fed Biblical History?

Some detractors of Islam argue that none of this history is remarkable, let alone miraculous. They claim Muhammad ﷺ either learned these accounts directly from the mouths of his contemporaries or that he plagiarized them from manuscripts of the Bible that have since been lost. The accusation of being spoon-fed by others existed during the Prophet's life, but it quickly disappeared, and until today most serious Qur'an critics avoid citing such a ludicrous proposition because it appears desperate. First, this would be contrary to the historically indisputable integrity of Muhammad's character. Second, the suggestions that Muhammad's knowledge of previous prophets and nations came from a Roman blacksmith in Makkah (a layman), or from an unverifiable, passing midday encounter with Baḥīrah the Monk, or to a single conversation with a dying Waraqah ibn Nawfal, are simply implausible. Sensible people realize that the bulk and veracity of what the Prophet ﷺ brought could only be attained with decades of apprenticeship that would be impossible for him to hide.

Allah says in the Qur'an, '*Say, 'If Allah had willed, I would not have recited it to you, nor would He have made it known to you, for I had remained among you a lifetime before it. Then will you not reason?'*''[38] As for the second accusation, that of plagiarism from the texts of Judeo-Christian scholars, only someone with a strong confirmation bias would consider this possibility, for two major reasons. Firstly, as established earlier, the Qur'an does not contain the many historical inaccuracies found in the Bible. Therefore, for the unique Qur'anic narrative to have been plagiarized from an earlier scripture, this would necessitate that the Prophet ﷺ somehow had access to the accurate version from the thousands of variant manuscripts. Moreover, this version would have existed only in seventh-century Arabia of all places, in a foreign language Muhammad ﷺ secretly learned, then vanished without a trace, never to be recovered again.

---

38 (*Yūnus* 10: 16)

Secondly, even if this bizarre hypothetical explanation were true, it only accounts for the source of this incredible precision and ignores the miraculous nature of the end-product. The Qur'an responds to this notion, asserting, *'And We certainly know that they say, "It is only a human being who teaches him [the Prophet]." The tongue of the one they refer to is foreign, and this Qur'an is [in] a clear Arabic language.'*[39]

3. Preserved as Promised

> *'Indeed, it is We who sent down the Qur'an and indeed, We will be its Guardian.'*[40]

The preservation and incorruptibility of the Qur'an were boldly promised therein. One should wonder how a book primarily committed to memory and documented on bones, palm leaves, and leather scraps over the span of twenty-three years could survive. People would learn some Qur'an from the Prophet ﷺ or his Companions, then travel back to their homelands and teach it to their families, friends and students, who would then relay it to others. These separate oral transmissions continued independently for centuries, across the earth.

Despite that, all 1.8 billion Muslims today somehow still recite the Qur'an exactly as it was taught to the Prophet's Companions and written in the original Uthmanic codex. Even competing denominations, such as Sunni, Shiite and Khārijite, recite the same Qur'an. And yet, a millennium and a half later, we do not find contradictions in meaning between all these oral traditions worldwide. As for the established variant readings of some verses, they only add to the beauty of the text's multi-layered meanings.[41] To accept that such consistency could be mere

39 (*al-Naḥl* 16: 103)

40 (*al-Ḥijr* 15: 9)

41 The Islamic tradition has a wealth of documented information on pre-Uthmanic readings. In a nutshell, the Prophet ﷺ had permitted

coincidence, or that global collusion on a spoken version of the Qur'an has taken place, or that a conspiracy of this magnitude was even logistically possible, is irrational.

Italian Orientalist Laura Vaglieri (d. 1989) of Naples Eastern University attests in her book, *An Interpretation of Islam*, 'We have still another proof of the divine origin of the Quran in the fact that its text has remained pure and unaltered through the centuries from the day of its delivery until today.'[42]

It is also remarkable that the Qur'an in written form today perfectly matches the original manuscripts of the Qur'an compiled by the Prophet's Companions. Even the few scribal differences reported from some of the Companions were reconciled during the reign of Islam's first four caliphs, accepted by all the Companions, and conformity with one copy won their consensus. To fully appreciate this, impartial consideration should be given to the fact that while spell-check and similar features afforded by modern technology have mitigated many lapses in our writing today, our emails and text messages still fall prey to spelling and grammatical errors. Then consider the premodern scribal tradition, rewinding to a world before the printing press and before mass literacy. It should not surprise us to have hundreds of thousands of misaligned manuscripts for the religious texts of the past—irrespective of whether this was done innocently or maliciously, and irrespective of whether originals of that text were available for cross-verification. But with the Qur'an, this was averted due to that Uthmanic codex being preserved, in addition to its mass-memorization, its strong poetic rhythm that facilitates memorization, and its daily usage in a Muslim's life, which

---

his Companions to adopt these variant readings and dialectical pronunciations in their recitation. See: Ammar Khatib and Nazir Khan, 'The Origins of the Variant Readings of the Qur'an', *Yaqeen Institute for Islamic Research*, August 23, 2019.

42 Laura Veccia Vaglieri, *An Interpretation of Islam* (Washington: American Fazl Mosque, 1957), 41.

together constitute a genius reinforcement mechanism unrivaled in history.[43]

Some people claim that the Qur'an was initially codified by a central authority, and this happened early enough to make preempting the spread of non-conforming manuscripts possible. They contend that the compilation of Abū Bakr ‎ and standardization of 'Uthmān ‎ could have purged whatever early manuscripts they arbitrarily deemed undesirable. Such a suspicion is not unexpected, given that the Bible was kept secret by government-enforced dictates and remained inaccessible to the laity until 1,500 years after Jesus Christ, following the Protestant Reformation. However, the Qur'an's unique decentralized dissemination made it impossible for anyone to later modify its content, unlike the authorized revisions of the Bible that continue being issued until the present day. Furthermore, since this transmission of the Qur'an does not solely hinge on the written records, this allows for measuring the written against the oral to ensure that the documentation and dissemination processes were scrupulous. Hence, its preservation in the hearts of those who memorized it that is what has immortalized it, as Allah says, '*Rather, the Qur'an is distinct verses [preserved] within the chests of those endowed with [sacred] knowledge, and none rejects our verses but the wrongdoers.*'[44]

Orientalist Alford T. Welch writes:

> For Muslims, the Ḳur'ān is much more than scripture or sacred literature in the usual Western sense. Its primary significance for the vast majority through the centuries has been in its oral form, the form in which it first appeared, as the 'recitation' (kur'ān) chanted by Muhammad to his followers over a period of about twenty years … The revelations were memorized by some of

---

43 See: Abu Zakariya, *The Eternal Challenge* (London: One Reason, 2015), 35–40.

44 (*al-'Ankabūt* 29: 49)

> Muhammad's followers during his lifetime, and the oral tradition that was thus established has had a continuous history ever since, in some ways independent of, and superior to, the written Ḳur'ān … Through the centuries the oral tradition of the entire Ḳur'ān has been maintained by the professional reciters, while all Muslims memorise parts of the Ḳur'ān for use in the daily prayers. Until recently, the significance of the recited Ḳur'ān has seldom been fully appreciated in the West.[45]

4. An Extraordinary Potency

Sophistication, accuracy, and preservation aside, simply hearing the Qur'an continues to have a unique and extraordinary effect on people. As al-Khaṭṭābī writes in *Bayān Iʿjāz al-Qur'ān*:

> The inimitability of the Qur'an has yet another dimension, one which people tend to overlook, and is unrecognized except by a sparse few—namely what it generates in the hearts and impresses onto the souls. Aside from the Qur'an, you do not hear of any discourse, neither poetry nor prose, that upon reaching one's ears provides such immediate pleasure and sweetness, and at other times such awe and intimidation, like the Qur'an does.[46]

He then proceeds to describe how the Qur'an has historically exhibited a unique potency for invigorating spirits with optimism and wakefulness, and uprooting the most deeply entrenched false convictions. Is there nothing remarkable, he asks, about multiple

---

45 Alford T. Welch, R. Paret, and J. D. Pearson, 'Al-Ḳur'ān', in *Encyclopedia of Islam: 2nd edition*, edited by P. Bearman, et al (Leiden: Brill, 2001).

46 Muḥammad Khalaf Allāh Aḥmad (ed.), Muḥammad Zaghlūl Sallām (ed.), and Issa J Boullata (trans.), *Three Treatises on the Iʿjāz of the Qur'ān* (Reading, UK: Garnet Publishing, 2014), 46; slightly modified to refine the translation.

murderous Arabs who each got close to the Prophet in order to assassinate him, only to be disarmed by hearing his recitation of the Qur'an, and transformed at once from enemies to allies, and from staunch disbelievers to the sincerest devotees among the faithful?

In a rigorously authenticated report, Jubayr ibn Muṭʿim ﷺ narrates that upon arriving in Madinah as a pagan idolator, to ransom his clansmen who were captured at the Battle of Badr, he found the Prophet ﷺ reciting *Sūrah al-Ṭūr* during the Maghrib prayer. He narrates:

> Once he reached the verses, '*Were they created out of nothing, or are they the creators [of themselves]? Or did they create the heavens and the earth? No, they are not certain. Or have they the repositories of your Lord, or are they the controllers [of them]?,*'[47] my heart nearly took flight.[48]

In another narration, he said, 'This was the moment that faith first settled in my heart.'[49] Similarly, Ibn ʿAbbās ﷺ narrates that one night, while the Muslims were still in hostile Makkah, the Prophet ﷺ recited in his prayer: "*Then at this statement (the Qur'an) do you wonder? And you laugh and do not weep? While you are proudly sporting? So prostrate to Allah and worship [Him].*"[50] Upon uttering these verses, Ibn ʿAbbās ﷺ says, both the believers present and several eavesdropping pagans fell into prostration along with the Prophet ﷺ.[51] Their enrapture by the recital compelled them to involuntarily comply—albeit only for a few moments until their prideful obstinacy resurfaced. Many opponents of the Prophet did eventually submit to what the Qur'an stirred within them. These were not just the adversaries who once drew their swords

47 (*al-Ṭūr* 52: 35–37)
48 al-Bukhārī, *Ṣaḥīḥ al-Bukhārī*, 6:140 #4754.
49 al-Bukhārī, *Ṣaḥīḥ al-Bukhārī*, 5:86 #4023.
50 (*al-Najm* 53: 59–62)
51 al-Bukhārī, *Ṣaḥīḥ al-Bukhārī*, 2:41 #1071.

against him, but even people whose parents had fallen in battle against the Prophet ﷺ. It is difficult to find anyone who exhibited greater enmity to Muhammad ﷺ than Abū Jahl ibn Hishām, Umayyah ibn Khalaf, and al-Walīd ibn al-Mughīrah—yet their sons ('Ikrimah, Ṣafwān, and Khālid ﷺ) embraced the Qur'an after their fathers' demise at the hands of Muslims. These are but some early examples of how the potency of the Qur'an transformed the hearts of listeners, and until now many of those who may not even understand its words find themselves unable to resist the magnetic power of its recitation.

Nasreddine Dinet (d. 1929, born Alphonse-Étienne Dinet), a French writer on Islam, said:

> The miracles wrought by earlier Prophets had been transient, so to say, and for that very reason, rapidly forgotten, while that of the Verses may be called 'The Permanent Miracle'. Its activity was unceasing. Everywhere and at all hours, each believer, by reciting the Verses, helped to realise the miracle, and in this can be found the explanation of many sudden conversions, incomprehensible for the European who knows nothing of the Qur'an, or judges it by cold and inaccurate translations.[52]

The truth of Dinet's words can be demonstrated even today, given that much of the western world is oblivious to the Qur'an and its mesmerizing charm. Search engine results in English will usually reflect that the Bible is the most read book of all time, with about four billion copies sold in the last fifty years. The second (*Quotations from Mao Tse-Tung*) and third (the *Harry Potter Series*) combined only sold 25 per cent as many copies as the Bible.[53] While this disparity between the Bible and other

52 Etienne Dinet and Sliman Ben Ibrahim, *The Life of Mohammad, the Prophet of Allah* (Paris: Paris Book Club, 1918), 3:37.

53 Jennifer Polland, 'The 10 Most Read Books in The World [Infographic]', *Business Insider*, December 27, 2012.

works seems staggering, it is eclipsed by the numbers of Muslims today who do not merely purchase or read but memorize the entire Qur'an by heart. They not only recall each of its ~600 pages, 114 chapters and 6,236 verses down to each letter and vowel sound, but in the original Arabic form, and while observing the *tajwīd* rules that govern Qur'anic pronunciation, despite Arabic usually not being their native tongue. As Allah said, *'And We have certainly facilitated the Qur'an to be remembered, so is there anyone who will remember?'*[54]

There are also countless others who are adamant about concealing their commitment of the Qur'an to memory, fearful that their motive for disclosing this achievement may involve insincerity or conceit. With regards to this aspect of the Qur'an's inimitability, that of its riveting allure, does any other book in all of human history begin to compare?

Al-Bāqillānī calls us to pause and consider the Qur'an as a standalone historical phenomenon.[55] We all witness how every society and civilization, upon becoming fond of a novel idea or artform, naturally imbibes it, competes in it, and then builds on it—or purges it when it becomes mundane. But with the Qur'an, none of this took place; it never ushered in a new genre of creative literature or spoken word. The Qur'an, unlike any other book, seems to have frozen in time the excitement of its debut and retained the fascination of its admirers forever. Never venturing beyond it, they are fulfilled by its recitation, memorization, and contemplation for an entire lifetime. In an attempt to explain this phenomenon, Ibn Taymiyyah says:

> Whoever listens carefully to the words of Allah, and the words of His Messenger with his mind and ponders over them with his heart, he will arrive through them at certain meanings, sweetness, guidance, remedy for the

54 (*al-Qamar* 54: 17)

55 al-Bāqillānī, *I'jāz al-Qur'ān*, 1:248.

> hearts, blessings, and benefits that he would never find in any other words, whether poetry or prose.[56]

Dr Muhammad Drāz (d. 1958) penned a similar explanation for the far-reaching embrace of the Qur'an and its inimitable nature in his acclaimed work, *al-Naba' al-'Aẓīm* (*The Great Tiding*). In that book, he maintained that one of the secrets behind the potency of the Qur'an is its perfect combination of persuasive arguments and emotive forces. Drāz argues that human writings never demonstrate this perfect balance of rationality and emotionality. The technical discourses of scientists and philosophers is generally devoid of emotion. Poets and writers, on the other hand, quickly swerve from reality to fantasy and feel forced to stretch facts to escape the cold truth which works against their objective.

As for the Qur'an, it fuses truth and beauty in a way that only the Almighty can. Its rhetorical depth appeals to the intellect, and its beauty appeals to emotions, but neither detracts from the other. As Drāz beautifully puts it, we all hear words that are clearly the fruit of an impressively critical mind, and others that are clearly the fruit of someone with peak emotional intelligence, but to find both fruits stemming from the same branch is truly remarkable. Only the Lord of the worlds can offer such a powerful elixir, he says, that is '*pure and salient for all those who drink it.*'[57] Only He can allot humanity '*a decisive statement*' in its accuracy,[58] and yet still one that '*causes the skins of those who fear their Lord to shiver, then their skin and hearts soften at the mention of [the mercy of] Allah.*'[59]

Al-Bayhaqī, in his famous *Dalā'il al-Nubuwwah*, quotes al-Ḥalīmī as saying, 'Whoever depends on the likes of this (Muhammad plagiarizing from Ibn al-Ḥaḍramī's slave-boys) will

---

56 Taqī al-Dīn Aḥmad ibn Taymyyah, *Iqtiḍā' al-Ṣirāṭ al-Mustaqīm fī Mukhālafat Aṣḥāb al-Jaḥīm* (Beirut: Dār 'Ālam al-Kutub, 1999), 2:270.

57 (*al-Naḥl* 16: 66)

58 (al-*Ṭāriq* 86: 13)

59 (*al-Zumar* 39: 23); Muḥammad 'Abdullāh Drāz, *Al-Naba' al-'Aẓīm* (Damascus: Dār al-Qalam, 2005), 1:148–51.

accept anything to accuse him.' He then justifies this by the fact that this charge not only ignores the inimitable language of the Qur'an but fails to explain the secret behind its potency and impact. Consider the thousands of volumes of intellectual sciences, laws, and ethics extracted from, or sparked by, this concise Qur'an. No single work—man-made or divine—has ever caused people and societies to thrive in such a holistic way.[60]

On spiritual, moral, social, and civilizational levels, it breathed new life into the world, illuminated it for centuries, and continues to do so until today. As Allah, the Mighty and Majestic, proclaims about the Qur'an:

> *And thus We have revealed to you a spirit of Our command. You did not know what the Book or [what] faith was, but We have made it a light by which We guide whom We will of Our servants. And indeed, you [O Muhammad] guide to a straight path, the path of Allah, to Whom belongs whatever is in the heavens and whatever is in the earth. Unquestionably, to Allah do all [matters] evolve.*[61]

5. Echoes of a Prophet

Muslim theologians often point out that people who simply familiarize themselves with the biography of Muhammad ﷺ quickly realize that he could not have forged the Qur'an. Only those consumed by prejudice, or critiquing from a distance, are unable to see this. For others, it is crystal-clear by simply observing his integrity, which even non-Muslim historians attest to (see Chapter 2), as well as the fact that the Qur'an consistently frames Muhammad ﷺ as its human subject and not its writer. While the following anecdotes may not be a dimension of the Qur'an's inimitability, they are included here to bring our discussion full circle. If the Prophet ﷺ was the actual author of the

60 See: Franz Rosenthal, *Knowledge Triumphant: The Concept of Knowledge in Medieval Islam* (Boston: Brill, 2007).

61 (*al-Shūrā* 42: 52–53)

Qur'an, would he have constructed it to contain the following characteristics?

1. The name of Moses appears in the Qur'an 135 times, the name of Jesus appears twenty-five times, while the name of Muhammad appears only five times. One would assume that a person would avoid citing the primary personalities of a religious tradition that he is accused of plagiarizing from, especially when experiencing regular mockery by the Jews of Madinah and facing them in warfare.
2. Mary, the Mother of Jesus, is cited by name thirty-four times in the Qur'an, while the Prophet Muhammad's own wives and daughters are not named a single time therein. Had he wanted to elevate the status of his family for political clout, for instance, one might think he would have included a tribute, or simply mentioned their names, at least once.
3. *'O Prophet, why do you prohibit [yourself from] what Allah has made lawful for you, seeking the approval of your wives? And Allah is Forgiving and Merciful.'*[62] If a community leader were to air his family disputes and charge himself with 'just trying to please his wife', especially in seventh-century Arabia, how would that be received by the masses? Yet, in this brief chapter of the Qur'an, an entire mini family drama is showcased: two wives are jealous of the third; they devise a scheme; it works; the Prophet makes a suboptimal decision; it must be rectified, and so forth.
4. *'Say, "I am not something original among the messengers, nor do I know what will be done with me or with you. I only follow that which is revealed to me."'*[63] Authors and influencers always brand their product as something special and unprecedented, not merely the replica of a prior model, while the Qur'an reminds time and

---

62 (*al-Taḥrīm* 66: 1)

63 (*al-Aḥqāf* 46: 9)

again that it does the exact opposite. While it does bring some novel revelations, its primary function was to bring humanity back to a treasure they once had.

5. *'He frowned and turned away when the blind man came to him.'*[64] Ibn Umm Maktūm ⬱, a blind man, interrupted an important meeting which displeased the Prophet ﷺ but he just frowned silently so as not to offend him. And yet, the Qur'an reveals the very thing the Prophet had tried to conceal, to be recited in prayer until the end of time. A false prophet would have chosen self-aggrandizement, but the Messenger of God ﷺ had no choice in the matter.

6. *'If not for a decree from Allah that preceded, you would have been touched for what you took by a great punishment.'*[65] Following the revelation of this verse, both the Prophet ﷺ and Abū Bakr al-Ṣiddīq ⬱ were found weeping from fear of God. This verse was censuring them for the premature ransoms they had accepted to release their captives after the Battle of Badr. If someone's boss scolded him in a private email, would they publicize it to their staff and teach it? Several such passages exist in the Qur'an, yet they never undermined the Prophet's credibility with his Companions who knew he was not threatening himself; these were not his words.

7. When Allah ordered the Prophet ﷺ to marry Zaynab ⬱ after she was divorced by Zayd ⬱ (his adopted son), he knew the hypocrites would pounce on this easy opportunity to accuse the Prophet ﷺ of being a lustful man who circumvents his own laws to marry his daughter-in-law.[66] This looming storm caused the Prophet's heart to become heavy, not from

---

64   (*'Abasa* 80: 1–2)

65   (*al-Anfāl* 8: 68)

66   Muḥammad ibn Aḥmad al-Qurṭubī, *Al-Jāmi' li-Aḥkām al-Qur'ān* (Cairo: Dār al-Kutub al-Miṣrīyah, 1964), 14:188.

guilt or shame regarding the marriage, but from the pain it would inflict through demonizing him, shaking those weak in faith, and potentially mobilizing a critical mass of Madinans to overthrow their head of state. Despite all this, Allah reveals that the Prophet Muhammad ﷺ was in fact apprehensive about taking this step and the controversy it would spark: '*And you concealed within yourself that which Allah is to disclose. And you feared the people, while Allah has more right that you fear Him.*'[67] 'Ā'ishah ؓ said, 'If the Messenger of Allah ﷺ were to conceal anything from the Qur'an, he would have concealed this verse.'[68]

8. '*Muhammad is not the father of any one of your men.*'[69] Every son of the Prophet Muhammad ﷺ died young, and thus it deeply hurt him every time the pagans called him '*abtar*,' meaning severed from having male descendants. Allah even revealed an entire chapter of the Qur'an (namely, Surah *al-Kawthar*) in response to this taunting. However, the verse above—revealed to establish that Zayd ؓ was not his biological son— indirectly captures this painful past of the Prophet's life and is recited around the clock. There are many verses of this nature, citing the slurs of his critics who called him a madman, a liar, and a sorcerer. Were Muhammad ﷺ the author of the Qur'an, one would think he would bury what hurt him, not ensure that it be never forgotten.

A person may misperceive God as being cruel to the Prophet ﷺ here, as these verses and others similar to them must have caused him pain. However, the Prophet Muhammad ﷺ never received them this way, for the Qur'an was also filled with reassurances of God's unique love and care for him, and because he understood that hardships were inseparable from the lofty rank of prophet-

---

[67]   (*al-Aḥzāb* 33: 37)
[68]   al-Bukhārī, *Ṣaḥīḥ al-Bukhārī*, 9:124 #7420.
[69]   (*al-Aḥzāb* 33: 40)

hood. Some of these difficulties were physical, like bleeding on the battlefield, which also served to prove his mortality and his courage, among other wisdoms. Others were emotional, such as some of these verses above, which served to separate him from all notions of authorship. During his life and until the end of time, this genre of verses has done just that: allowed people to realize that these can only be the echoes of an honest prophet of God. As Allah says, '*Is it not sufficient for them that We revealed to you the Book which is recited to them? Indeed, in that is a mercy and reminder for a people who believe.*'[70]

It is unbecoming of any objective person to learn about the multidimensional inimitability of the Qur'an and then say its author was a mortal. Do its mysterious linguistic form, its perfect blend of persuasive and emotive address, its precision about past and future truths, its harmonious theological and legal framework, and its gripping transformative allure all not suffice to indicate its divine origins? Is it conceivable that an unlettered man from seventh-century Arabia could spend forty years of his life preoccupied with shepherding and trade and then bring the world—overnight—a linguistic masterpiece with intricate details of lost knowledge from books that never existed in his age, and from books that would only be written more than a millennium later? Even the most educated people today, rather all of humanity as a collective, will continue to find it impossible to rival its inimitability. Hence, the Qur'an openly challenges, '*Say [O Muhammad], "If mankind and the jinn gathered in order to produce the likes of this Qur'an, they could not produce anything like it, even if they were to each other assistants."*'[71]

Just as the Almighty sent Moses with the ability to neutralize

---

70 (*al-'Ankabūt* 29: 51)

71 (*al-Isrā'* 17: 88)

the greatest sorcerers of his period and Jesus with the ability to heal in ways that the master physicians combined could never dream to match, so too did He send Muhammad ﷺ with an eternal Word that would challenge the speech of mankind until the end of time. Allah asks, '*So where then are you going? It is but a reminder to [all the] worlds. For whoever among you wishes to take the right course. And you do not wish except that Allah wishes—Lord of the worlds.*'[72]

---

72 (*al-Takwīr* 81: 26–28)

A Parting Word on the Journey of Faith

In these chapters, we have covered humanity's pressing need for prophethood, the extraordinary fruits of Muhammad's ministry in terms of his character, message, accomplishments, and legacy, and sampled a share of the events he foretold, the miracles he performed, and the Qur'an with which he shook the world. The onus now falls on the reader to rise and meet their ultimate purpose in knowing and worshipping the Lord of all the Worlds. For that end, only the leadership and luminous example of God's Final Prophet, Muhammad ﷺ, will light the way.

Abū Sufyān ibn Ḥarb ؓ was an open enemy to the Prophet Muhammad ﷺ for nearly his entire ministry. He launched more battle campaigns against him than anyone, and during the intervals between battles, he would help orchestrate uprisings in the Prophet's city of Madinah, and covert assassination attempts against him. It was only eighteen months before the Prophet's death that Abū Sufyān ؓ himself decided to accept Islam. However, it is the sequence of events on the day of his conversion that I wish to summarize here and leave my readers with, as they powerfully capture an experience many people have when engaging the proofs of prophethood.

After the tribe of Quraysh reneged on its peace treaty with Muhammad ﷺ by attacking one of his allies, the Prophet ﷺ marched to Makkah with his army to put an end to their oppression.

When they reached the outskirts of Makkah, Abū Sufyān became certain that his hometown would not be able to repel this incoming force, especially after being caught off guard by them like this. In a desperate attempt, Abū Sufyān was slipped into the Muslim camps by al-ʿAbbās ibn ʿAbdil-Muṭṭalib ﷺ, the Prophet's uncle who happened to be Abū Sufyān's lifelong friend. Just as they entered the Prophet's tent, so did his senior Companions, the latter demanding the execution of this man who had tortured many of them, killed their family members, and was a war criminal by every measure. But in a moment of supreme clemency, the Prophet ﷺ forgave him and said, 'Will you still not testify that nothing is worthy of worship except Allah?' Abū Sufyān responded, 'I am certain now that if there were any other god, he would have saved me already.' The Prophet ﷺ continued, 'Will you not testify that I am the Messenger of Allah?' Abū Sufyān said, 'As for that part, there is still some doubt inside me regarding it.' However, upon realizing that only this could redeem a criminal as notorious as himself, he professed the testimony of faith to become Muslim:

> *I testify that nothing is worthy of worship except Allah, and I bear witness that Muhammad is the Messenger of Allah.*[1]

The Prophet Muhammad ﷺ recognized that Abū Sufyān was a man of great prestige among his people (Banū Umayyah), and that this was the main reason he hesitated to concede to Muhammad's authority, as the Prophet ﷺ hailed from the rival tribe of Banū Hāshim. To help Abū Sufyān overcome his hesitation and solidify his commitment to faith, the Prophet ﷺ allowed him to return home and declared that any Makkan who entered Abū Sufyān's estate would be safe.

---

[1] Uttering this statement, while believing it, enters one into the fold of Islam. It can be stated in any language, with or without witnesses. We invite every reader to utter it now, whether that is to begin or renew their acceptance of God and Islam.

Then, he coupled that gesture with another wise directive, instructing his uncle to have Abū Sufyān ﷺ stand at the mouth of the valley at daybreak, to behold the magnitude of the Muslim forces as they marched. The next morning, Abū Sufyān ﷺ was awestruck. Each time a massive crowd in armor would pass by, he would anxiously ask al-ʿAbbās ﷺ who they were, and al-ʿAbbās ﷺ would inform him of each group's name: 'This is Ghifār … This is Juhaynah … This is Sulaym … This is Mazīnah … These are the Muhājirīn and the Anṣār.' Abū Sufyān ﷺ was beyond words, and all he could muster in response each time was, 'What business do I have fighting such a tribe? Nobody can ever contend with such people.' He then said to al-ʿAbbās ﷺ in bewilderment, 'Your nephew's kingdom has truly become a great one.' He realized then that it was no longer individuals that were becoming Muslim, but rather whole tribes and regions. He knew that some of these tribes could singlehandedly cause the extinction of Quraysh, and now—somehow—Muhammad ﷺ had united their hearts for the first time in history. As if begging his comrade to recognize the obvious, al-ʿAbbās ﷺ retorted, 'Abū Sufyān! This is no kingdom; it is prophethood.' This time the testimony must have come from his depths; Abū Sufyān ﷺ said, 'Yes, it must be.'[2]

Beautiful is the matchless mercy of the Prophet ﷺ with his greatest opponents, and the unique achievements of his brief blessed lifetime, but perhaps the story it tells about the journey of faith is what tugs at my heartstrings above all. Not everyone who has professed the truth of Islam has experienced the full sweetness of faith in their heart, and not everyone who is intellectually convinced about Islam has been able to conquer the social and emotional challenges to accepting it. The Prophet ﷺ would beseech Allah, 'and guide me, and allow guidance to be easy for me.'[3]

---

2 Ibn Hishām, *Al-Sīrah al-Nabawiyyah*, 2:402-404.

3 Ibn Ḥanbal, *Musnad Aḥmad*, 3:452 #1997; authenticated by al-Arnā'ūṭ in the comments.

This is a profound prayer, for we all subconsciously avoid accepting certain truths due to fear of their cost. It is therefore our heart being open to truth, not just our mind, that allows for objectivity and clarity of thought. Hence, Allah says, '*So whoever Allah wishes to guide, He expands their heart to welcome Islam.*'[4]

Abū Sufyān ﷺ knew full well of the Prophet's integrity, witnessed many great miracles, was forgiven, then honoured, and yet it was only when Allah inspired him with the simple statement: 'this is prophethood', that faith penetrated his worldly defenses and finally settled in his heart.

I ask Allah to grant us the sincerity that allows for conviction to settle in our hearts, to forgive this writer for all that may be inappropriate in this work of statements or intentions, and to send His finest salutations, peace, and blessings upon His Final Prophet, Muhammad ﷺ. And all praise is for Allah, Lord of the Worlds.

4 (*al-An'ām* 6: 125)

Bibliography

English Sources

The Qur'an, Saheeh International Translation and Muhsin Khan Translation.

Holy Bible, New King James Version and New American Standard Bible.

Abu Zakariya. *The Eternal Challenge.* London: One Reason, 2015.

Aḥmad, Muḥammad Khalaf Allāh (ed.), Muḥammad Zaghlūl Sallām (ed.), and Issa J. Boullata (trans.). *Three Treatises on the I'jāz of the Qur'ān.* Reading. UK: Garnet Publishing, 2014.

Alkhateeb, Firas. *Lost Islamic History: Reclaiming Muslim Civilisation from the Past.* London: Hurst, 2014.

Arberry, Arthur J. *The Koran Interpreted: A Translation.* Simon and Schuster, 1996.

Aristotle, R.F. Stalley, and Ernest Barker. *Politics: Oxford World's Classics.* Oxford: Oxford University Press, 2009.

Al-Attas, S.M. Naquib. *Islam and Secularism.* Lahore: Suhail Academy, 1978.

Attridge, Harold W, Wayne A. Meeks, and Jouette M. Bassler. *The HarperCollins Study Bible: Fully Revised and Updated.* New York, NY: HarperCollins, 2006.

Baker, Monya. "1,500 Scientists Lift the Lid on Reproducibility." *Nature.* 533 (2016): 452–454.

Bearman, P J (ed), et al. *The Encyclopedia of Islam: 2nd edition.* Leiden: Brill, 2001.

Benson, Herbert, and Marg Stark. *Timeless Healing: The Power and Biology of Belief.* New York: Simon & Schuster, 1997.

Bonelli, Raphael, et al., "Religious and Spiritual Factors in Depression: Review and Integration of the Research," *Depression Research and Treatment* (2012).

Bowering, Gerhard. *Islamic Political Thought: An Introduction.* Princeton University Press, 2015.

Briffault, Robert. *The Making of Humanity.* London: G. Allen & Unwin Ltd, 1919.

Brown, Jonathan. *Muhammad: A Very Short Introduction.* New York: Oxford University Press, 2011.

de Cabo, Rafael, and Mark P. Mattson. "Effects of Intermittent Fasting on Health, Aging, and Disease." *New England Journal of Medicine*, v. 382 no. 3 (2020).

Carlyle, Thomas, David R. Sorensen (ed.), and Brent E. Kinser (ed.). *On Heroes, Hero-Worship, and the Heroic in History.* New Haven: Yale University Press, 2013.

Chon, Don Soo. "National Religious Affiliation and Integrated Model of Homicide and Suicide." *Homicide Studies* 21, no. 1 (February 2016).

Craig, Hugh. "Shakespeare's Vocabulary: Myth and Reality." *Shakespeare Quarterly* 62, no. 1 (2011).

Daryaee, Touraj. *Sasanian Persia: The Rise and Fall of an Empire.* London: I.B. Tauris, 2012.

Descartes, René, Elizabeth S. Haldane, and G R. T. Ross. *Philosophical Works: Rendered into English.* Cambridge: University Press, 1911.

Dinet, Etienne, and Sliman Ben Ibrahim. *The Life of Mohammad, the Prophet of Allah.* Paris: Paris Book Club, 1918.

Draper, John W. *A History of the Intellectual Development of Europe.* London: G. Bell and Sons, 1875.

Eaton, Charles L. G. *Islam and the Destiny of Man.* Albany: George Allen & Unwin, 1985.

Elshinawy, Mohammad, and Tahir Khwaja. "Gender Uniqueness in Islam and the Significance of Fatherhood." *Yaqeen Institute for Islamic Research*. September 24, 2020.

Ernst, Carl. *How to Read the Qur'an: A New Guide, with Select Translations*. Edinburgh University Press, 2011.

Esposito, John L. *Islam: The Straight Path.* New York: Oxford University Press, 1988.

Esser, Marissa B., et al. "Deaths and Years of Potential Life Lost From Excessive Alcohol Use: United States, 2011–2015." *Morbidity and Mortality Weekly Report*. 69(30) (2020).

Farrin, Raymond K. *Sūrat al-Baqarah: A Structural Analysis.* Hartford, CT: Hartford Seminary, 2010.

Finer, Lawrence B., et al. "Reasons U.S. Women Have Abortions: Quantitative and Qualitative Perspectives." *Perspectives on Sexual and Reproductive Health* 37, no. 3 (2005).

Gandhi, Mahatma. *The Collected Works of Mahatma Gandhi.* New Delhi, India: Publications Division, Ministry of Information and Broadcasting, Government of India, 1960-1994.

Garraty, John A., Peter Gay, et al., *The Columbia History of the World.* New York: Harper & Row, 1972.

Gesenius, Wilhelm, and Samuel P. Tregelles. *Gesenius' Hebrew and Chaldee Lexicon to the Old Testament Scriptures*. Piscataway: Gorgias Press, 2019.

Gibbon, Edward. *Decline and Fall of the Roman Empire: Volume the Fourth.* London: Electric Book Co., 2001.

Gibbon, Edward. *Decline and Fall of the Roman Empire: Volume the Fifth.* London: Electric Book Co., 2001.

Gibbon, Edward. *The Rise and Fall of the Saracen Empire.* London, 1870.

Gibbons, Ann. "Why 536 was 'The Worst Year to be Alive.'" *Science Journal*. November 15, 2018.

Greene, Lloyd, and George Burke, "Beyond Self-Actualization." *Journal of Health and Human Services Administration.* (2007): 116-128.

Griffith, Sidney H. *The Bible in Arabic: The Scriptures of the "People of the Book" in the Language of Islam.* New Jersey: Princeton University Press, 2013.

Haddad, Gibril F. "Tropology and Inimitability: Ibn Ashur's Theory of Tafsir in the Ten Prolegomena to Al-Tahrir wa'l-Tanwir." *Journal of Qur'anic Studies*, 21.1 (2019): 50-111.

al-Haj, Hatem (trans.), and Ibn Qudāmah. *'Umdat al-Fiqh Explained: A Commentary on Ibn Qudāmah's 'The Reliable Manual of Fiqh.'* Riyadh: International Islamic Publishing House, 2019.

Hamer, Dean H. *The God Gene: How Faith Is Hardwired into Our Genes*. New York: Doubleday, 2004.

Harpur, James. *The Crusades, the Two Hundred Years War: The Clash between the Cross and the Crescent in the Middle East, 1096-1291.* New York: Rosen Publishing, 2008.

Hart, Michael H. *The 100: A Ranking of the Most Influential Persons in History.* New York: Citadel Press/Kensington Pub, 2001.

Hogarth, D. G. *Arabia.* Oxford: Clarendon Press, 1922.

Ibn Khaldūn, and Franz Rosenthal (trans.). *The Muqaddimah.* Princeton: Princeton University Press, 1967.

Irving, Washington, and Bertram R. Davis. *The Life of Mahomet.* London: G. Routledge & Co, 1850.

Kemnitz, Joseph W. "Calorie Restriction and Aging in Nonhuman Primates." *ILAR Journal* 52, no. 1 (2011).

Khan, Nazir. "Atheism and Radical Skepticism: Ibn Taymiyyah's Epistemic Critique." *Yaqeen Institute for Islamic Research*. July 7, 2020.

Khatib, Ammar, and Nazir Khan. "The Origins of the Variant Readings of the Qur'an." *Yaqeen Institute for Islamic Research.* August 23, 2019.

Lagasse, Paul, and Columbia University. *The Columbia Encyclopedia 8th ed.* New York: Columbia University Press, 2018.

de Lamartine, Alphonse. *Histoire De La Turquie.* Paris: Librarie du Constitutionnel, 1854.

Lane-Poole, Stanley. *The Speeches and Table-Talk of the Prophet Mohammad.* Macmillan & Co: London, 1882.

Lewis, Bernard. *Islam in History: Ideas, People, and Events in the Middle East.* Illinois: Open Court Publishing, 2001.

Lester, David. "Suicide and Islam." *Arch Suicide Res.* 10, no. 1 (2006).

Malcolm X, and Alex Haley. *The Autobiography of Malcolm X*. New York: Ballantine, 1992.

Margoliouth, David S. *Lectures on Arabic Historians: Delivered before the University of Calcutta 1929*. Kolkata, India: University of Calcutta, 1930.

McDonald, Roger B., and Jon J. Ramsey, "Honouring Clive McCay and 75 Years of Calorie Restriction Research." *The Journal of Nutrition* 140, no. 7 (July 2010).

McKeown, Niall. *The Invention of Ancient Slavery?* London: Bristol Classical Press, 2011.

Menocal, Maria. *The Ornament of the World.* Boston: Back Bay Books, 2002.

Mercer, Samuel Alfred Browne (trans.). *The Pyramid Texts*. New York: Longmans, Green, 1952.

Moss HB, Howard B. "The Impact of Alcohol on Society: A Brief Overview." *Social Work in Public Health,* 28:3-4 (2013).

Nadwi, Sayyed Abul Hasan. *The Rise and Decline of the Muslims and Its Effect on Mankind*. UK Islamic Academy, 2003.

O'Connor, Siobhan, David Futrelle, Laura Kubzansky, Kate Lowenstein, and Belinda Luscombe. *The Science of Happiness: New Discoveries for a More Joyful Life*. New York: Time Inc. Books, 2016.

Ozsoy, Ismail. "An Islamic Suggestion of Solution to the Financial Crises." *Procedia Economics and Finance* 38 (2016).

Paul II, John, and Vittorio Messori. *Crossing the Threshold of Hope*. New York: Alfred A. Knopf, 2005.

Pamuk, Şevket, and Maya Shatzmiller. "Plagues, Wages, and Economic Change in the Islamic Middle East, 700–1500." *The Journal of Economic History* 74, no. 1 (2014): 196–229.

Parrott, Justin. "The Case for Allah's Existence in the Qur'an and Sunnah." *Yaqeen Institute for Islamic Research*. February 27, 2017.

Rippin, Andrew (ed.). *The Blackwell Companion to the Qur'an.* Hoboken: Wiley-Blackwell, 2009.

Rosenthal, Franz. *The Classical Heritage in Islam.* London: Routledge, 2003.

Rosenthal, Franz. *A History of Muslim Historiography.* Leiden: E.J. Brill, 1968.

Rosenthal, Franz. *Knowledge Triumphant: The Concept of Knowledge in Medieval Islam.* Leiden: Brill, 2007.

Saeh, Bassam. *The Miraculous Language of the Qur'an: Evidence of Divine Origin.* Virginia: IIIT, 2015.

Sayoud, Halim. "Author Discrimination between the Holy Qur'an and Prophet's Statements," *Literary and Linguistic Computing* 27, no. 4 (2012).

Scott, Samuel P. *History of the Moorish Empire in Europe.* Philadelphia & London: J.B. Lippincott Company, 1904.

Shapiro, Marc B. *The Limits of Orthodox Theology: Maimonides' Thirteen Principles Reappraised.* Oxford: Littman Library of Jewish Civilization, 2004.

Shaw, Bernard. *The Doctor's Dilemma: With Preface on Doctors.* New York: Brentano's, 1911.

Sher, Leo, Isack Kandel, and Joav Merrick. *Alcohol-related Cognitive Disorders: Research and Clinical Perspectives.* New York: Nova Science, 2009.

Smith, Adam. *Essays: Philosophical and Literary.* London: Ward, Lock & Co, 1880.

Smith, R. Bosworth. *Mohammed and Mohammedanism.* London: Smith, Elder, and Co., 1874.

Solomon, Robert C., and Kathleen M. Higgins. *From Africa to Zen: An Invitation to World Philosophy.* Lanham, Md: Rowman & Littlefield Publishing, 2003.

Spinoza, Baruch. *A Theological Political Treatise.* Dover Philosophical Classics, 2004.

Tisdall, William St. *The Original Sources of the Qur'an.* London: Society for the Promotion of Christian Knowledge, 1911.

Stausberg, Michael, and Yuhan S.-D. Vevaina. *The Wiley Blackwell Companion to Zoroastrianism*. Chichester, West Sussex, UK: Wiley, 2015.

Stawinski, Piotr. "Leo Tolstoy and Islam: Some Remarks on the Theme." *The Quarterly Journal of Philosophical Meditations* 2, no. 5 (Spring 2010).

Taylor, Charles. *A Secular Age*. Cambridge: Harvard University Press, 2007.

Tomooka, Lance T., Claire Murphy, and Terence M. Davidson. "Clinical Study and Literature Review of Nasal Irrigation." *The Laryngoscope* 110, no. 7 (2000).

Toynbee, Arnold. *Civilization on Trial*. New York: Oxford University Press, 1948.

Vaglieri, Laura Veccia. *An Interpretation of Islam*. Washington: American Fazl Mosque, 1957.

Watkins, Ellen, and Lucy Serpell, "The Psychological Effects of Short-Term Fasting in Healthy Women," *Frontiers in Nutrition*, v. 3 (2016).

Watt, William Montgomery. *Muhammad at Mecca*. Oxford: Clarendon Press, 1953.

Zammit, Martin R. *A Comparative Lexical Study of Qur'anic Arabic*. Boston: Brill, 2002.

Arabic Sources

Abū Dāwūd, Sulaymān ibn al-Ash'ath al-Sijistānī. *Sunan Abī Dāwūd*. Sidon: al-Maktabah al-'Aṣrīyah, 1980.

Abū Ḥayyān, Muḥammad ibn Yūsuf. *Al-Baḥr al-Muḥīṭ fī al-Tafsīr.* Beirut: Dār al-Fikr, 1992.

Abū Nu'aym, Aḥmad ibn 'Abdillāh al-Iṣbahānī. *Ḥilyat al-Awliyā' wa Ṭabaqāt al-Aṣfiyā'*. Egypt: Maṭba'at al-Sa'ādah, 1974.

al-Albānī, Muḥammad Nāṣir al-Dīn, and Jalāl al-Dīn al-Suyūṭī. *Ṣaḥīḥ al-Jāmi' al-Ṣaghīr wa Ziyādatih.* Damascus: al-Maktab al-Islāmī, 1969.

al-Albānī, Muḥammad Nāṣir al-Dīn. *Ṣaḥīḥ al-Targhīb wal-Tarhīb*. Riyadh: Maktabat al-Ma'ārif, 2000.

al-Albānī, Muḥammad Nāṣir al-Dīn. *Silsilat al-Aḥādīth al-Ṣaḥīḥah.* Riyadh: Maktabat al-Ma'ārif, 1996.

Ameri, Sami. *Barāhīn al-Nubuwwah*. London: Takween Center, 2018.

al-Bāqillānī, Abū Bakr Muḥammad ibn al-Ṭayyib. *I'jāz al-Qur'ān*. Egypt: Dār al-Ma'ārif, 1997.

al-Bayhaqī, Aḥmad ibn al-Ḥusayn. *Dalā'il al-Nubuwwah*. Beirut: Dār al-Kutub al-'Ilmīyah, 1988.

al-Bayhaqī, Aḥmad ibn al-Ḥusayn. *Shu'ab al-Īmān.* Riyadh: Maktabat al-Rushd lil-Nashr wal-Tawzī', 2003.

al-Bayhaqī, Aḥmad ibn al-Ḥusayn. *Al-Sunan al-Kubrā*, Edited by Muḥammad 'Abdul-Qādir 'Aṭā. Beirut: Dār al-Kutub al-'Ilmīyah, 2003.

al-Bukhārī, Muḥammad ibn Ismā'īl. *Ṣaḥīḥ al-Bukhārī.* Edited by Zuhayr ibn Nāṣir. Beirut: Dār Ṭawq al-Najāh, 2002.

al-Dārimī, 'Abdullāh ibn 'Abdul-Raḥmān. *Sunan al-Dārimī.* Riyadh: Dār al-Mughnī, 2000.

Drāz, Muḥammad 'Abdullāh. *Al-Naba' al-'Aẓīm*. Damascus: Dār al-Qalam, 2005.

Hādī, 'Iṣām Mūsā. *Kitāb Ṣaḥīḥ Ashrāṭ al-Sā'ah.* Amman: al-Dār al-'Uthmānīyah, 2003.

al-Ḥākim, Muḥammad ibn 'Abd Allāh. *Al-Mustadrak 'alā al-Ṣaḥīḥayn*. Beirut: Dār al-Kutub al-'Ilmīyah, 1990.

Ibn Abī 'Āṣim, Aḥmad ibn 'Amr al-Ḍaḥḥāk. *Al-Sunnah li-Ibn Abī 'Āṣim*. Edited by Muḥammad Nāṣir al-Dīn Albānī. Beirut: al-Maktab al-Islāmī, 1980.

Ibn Abī Shaybah, Abū Bakr. *Al-Īmān*. Beirut: al-Maktab al-Islāmī, 1983.

Ibn Abī Shaybah, Abū Bakr. *Al-Muṣannaf.* Riyadh: Maktabat al-Rushd, 2004.

Ibn al-'Arabī, Abū Bakr Muḥammad. *Aḥkām al-Qur'ān*. Beirut: Dār al-Kutub al-'Ilmīyah, 2003.

Ibn 'Asākir, 'Alī ibn al-Ḥasan. *Tārīkh Madīnat Dimashq*. Beirut: Dār al-Fikr, 1995.

Ibn Ḥajar al-ʿAsqalāni. *Fatḥ al-Bārī*. Beirut: Dār al-Maʿrifah, 1959.

Ibn Ḥanbal, Aḥmad. *Musnad al-Imām Aḥmad ibn Ḥanbal*. Edited by Shuʿayb al-Arnā'ūṭ and ʿĀdil Murshid. Beirut: Mu'assasat al-Risālah, 2001.

Ibn Ḥazm, ʿAlī ibn Aḥmad. *Al-Faṣl fil-Milal wal-Ahwā' wal-Niḥa*. Cairo: Maktabat al-Khānji, 1929.

Ibn Ḥibbān, Muḥammad. *Ṣaḥīḥ Ibn Ḥibbān*. Beirut: Mu'assasat al-Risālah, 1993.

Ibn Hishām, ʿAbdul-Malik. *Al-Sīrah al-Nabawīyah*. Edited by Muṣṭafā Saqqā and Ibrāhīm Ibyārī. Cairo: Maktabat wa Maṭbaʿat Muṣṭafā al-Bābī al-Ḥalabī, 1955.

Ibn al-Jawzī, ʿAbdul-Raḥmān. *Ṣifat al-Ṣafwah*. Cairo: Dār al-Ḥadīth, 2000.

Ibn Kathīr, Ismāʿīl. *Al-Bidāyah wal-Nihāyah*. Edited by ʿAbdullāh ibn ʿAbd al-Muḥsin Turkī. Cairo: Dār Hajr, 1997.

Ibn Kathīr, Ismāʿīl. *Tafsīr al-Qur'ān al-ʿAẓīm*. Beirut: Dār al-Kutub al-ʿIlmīyah, 1998.

Ibn Mājah, Muḥammad. *Sunan Ibn Mājah*. Edited by Muḥammad Fu'ād ʿAbdul-Bāqī. Beirut: Dār Iḥyā' al-Turāth al-ʿArabī, 1975.

Ibn Qayyim al-Jawzīyah. *Ighāthat al-Lahfān*. Riyadh: Maktabat al-Maʿārif, 1975.

Ibn Qayyim al-Jawzīyah. *Madārij al-Sālikīn Bayna Manāzil Iyyāka Na'budu wa Iyyāka Nasta'īn*. Beirut: Dār al-Kutub al-ʿArabī, 1996.

Ibn Qayyim al-Jawziyyah. *Miftāḥ Dār al-Saʿādah*. Beirut: Dār al-Kutub al-ʿIlmīyah, 2002.

Ibn Saʿd, Muḥammad. *Al-Ṭabaqāt al-Kubrā*, Edited by Iḥsān ʿAbbās. Beirut: Dār Ṣādir, 1968.

Ibn Taymiyyah, Taqī al-Dīn Aḥmad. *Iqtiḍā' al-Ṣirāṭ al-Mustaqīm fī Mukhālafat Aṣ'ḥāb al-Jaḥīm*. Beirut: Dār ʿĀlam al-Kutub, 1999.

Ibn Taymiyyah, Taqī al-Dīn Aḥmad. *Al-Jawāb al-Ṣaḥīḥ li-man Baddala Dīn al-Masīḥ*. Saudi Arabia: Dār al-ʿĀṣimah, 1999.

Ibn Taymiyyah, Taqī al-Dīn Aḥmad. *Sharḥ al-ʿAqīdah al-Aṣfahānīyah*. Riyadh: Maktabat al-Rushd, 2001.

al-Kattāni, Muḥammad. *Naẓm al-Mutanāthir min al-Ḥadīth al-Mutawātir*. Egypt: Dār al-Kutub al-Salafīyah, 1983.

Mahrān, Muḥammad Bayyūmī. *Dirāsāt Tārīkhīyah fil-Qur'ān al-Karīm*. Beirut: Dār al-Nahḍah, 1988.

al-Mubārakfūrī, Muḥammad ʿAbdul-Raḥmān. *Tuḥfat al-Aḥwadhī bi-Sharḥ Jāmiʿ al-Tirmidhī*. Beirut: Dār al-Kutub al-ʿIlmīyah, 1990.

al-Mubārakfūrī, Ṣafī al-Raḥmān. *Al-Raḥīq al-Makhtūm*. Cairo: Dār al-Wafā', 1987.

Muslim ibn al-Ḥajjāj al-Qushayrī. *Ṣaḥīḥ Muslim*. Edited by Muḥammad Fu'ād ʿAbdul-Bāqī. Beirut: Dār Iḥyā' al-Kutub al-ʿArabīyah, 1955.

al-Nasā'ī, Aḥmad ibn Shuʿayb. *Sunan al-Nasā'ī*. Edited by ʿAbdul-Fattāḥ Abū Ghuddah. Aleppo: Maktab al-Maṭbūʿāt al-Islāmīyah, 1986.

al-Nawawī, Yaḥyā ibn Sharaf. *Sharḥ al-Nawawī ʿalā Ṣaḥīḥ Muslim*. Beirut: Dār Iḥyā' al-Turāth al-ʿArabī, 1972.

al-Qāḍi ʿIyāḍ ibn Mūsā and Aḥmad ibn Muḥammad Shumunnī. *Al-Shifā bi-Taʿrīf Ḥuqūq al-Muṣṭafā*. Amman: Dār al-Fikr, 1988.

Qārī al-Harawī, ʿAlī ibn Sulṭān Muḥammad. *Mirqāt al-Mafātīḥ: Sharḥ Mishkāt al-Maṣābīḥ*. Beirut: Dār al-Fikr, 2002.

al-Qayrawānī, Ibn Rashīq. *Al-ʿUmdah fī Maḥāsin al-Shiʿr wa-Ādābih*. Beirut: Dār al-Jīl, 1981.

al-Qurṭubī, Muḥammad ibn Aḥmad. *Al-Jāmiʿ li-Aḥkām al-Qur'ān*. Cairo: Dār al-Kutub al-Miṣrīyah, 1964.

al-Rāfiʿī, Muṣṭafā Ṣādiq. *Iʿjāz al-Qur'ān wal-Balāghah al-Nabawīyah*. Beirut: Dār al-Kutub al-ʿArabī, 1973.

al-Rāzī, Fakhr al-Dīn. *Manāqib al-Imām al-Shāfiʿī, al-Kitāb al-Musammā Irshād al-Ṭālibīn ilā al-Manhaj al-Qawīm*. Beirut: Dār al-Kutub al-ʿIlmīyah, 2015.

Shākir, Aḥmad. *ʿUmdat al-Tafsīr ʿan Ibn Kathīr*. Egypt: Dār al-Wafā', 2005.

al-Ṭabarānī, Sulaymān ibn Aḥmad. *Al-Muʿjam al-Awsaṭ*. Edited by Ṭāriq ibn ʿAwaḍ Allāh Ibn Muḥammad. Cairo: Dār al-Ḥaramayn, 1995.

al-Ṭabarānī, Sulaymān ibn Aḥmad. *Al-Muʿjam al-Kabīr*. Cairo, Riyadh: Maktabat Ibn Taymīyah, Dār al-Ṣumayʿī, 1983.
al-Ṭabarī, Abū Jaʿfar. *Jāmiʿ al-Bayān ʿan Taʾwīl al-Qurʾān*. Beirut: Muʾassasat al-Risālah, 2000.
Tawadrus II. *Miftāḥ al-ʿAhd al-Jadīd*. Cairo: Batrirkiyyat al-Aqbāṭ al-Urthudux, 2013.
al-Tirmidhī, Muḥammad ibn ʿĪsā. *Sunan al-Tirmidhī*. Edited by Bashshār ʿAwwād Maʿrūf. Beirut: Dār al-Gharb al-Islāmī, 1998.
al-Wāqidī, Muḥammad ibn ʿUmar. *Kitāb al-Maghāzī*. Beirut: Dār al-Aʿlamī, 1989.

Index

P

Q

CPSIA information can be obtained
at www.ICGtesting.com
Printed in the USA
JSHW051335130323
38869JS00005B/114

9 781847 742070